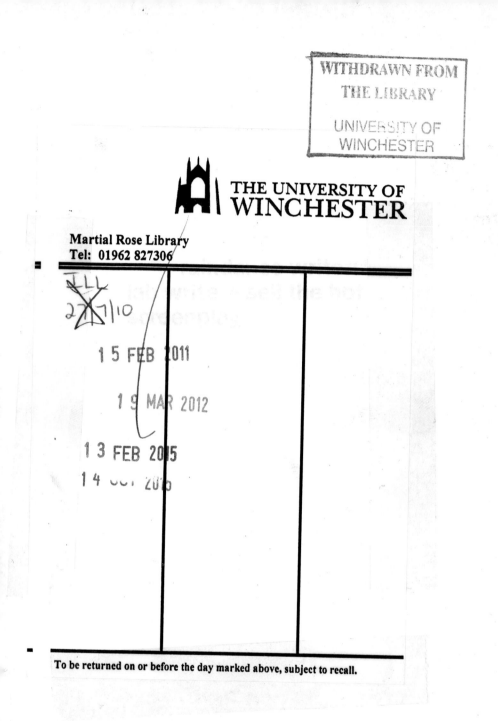

THE UNIVERSITY OF WINCHESTER

Martial Rose Library
Tel: 01962 827306

ILL
27/7/10

1 5 FEB 2011

1 9 MAR 2012

1 3 FEB 2015

1 4 ОСТ 2015

To be returned on or before the day marked above, subject to recall.

D0278385

To a master of storytelling
silenced too soon

Merlin Russell Grove
1929–1962

raindance writers' lab write + sell the hot screenplay

ELLIOT GROVE

ELSEVIER

AMSTERDAM • BOSTON • HEIDELBERG • LONDON • NEW YORK • OXFORD
PARIS • SAN DIEGO • SAN FRANCISO • SINGAPORE • SYDNEY • TOKYO
Focal Press is an imprint of Elsevier

Focal Press

Focal Press is an imprint of Elsevier
Linacre House, Jordan Hill, Oxford OX2 8DP, UK
30 Corporate Drive, Suite 400, Burlington, MA 01803, USA

First published 2009

British Library Cataloguing in Publication Data
A catalogue record for this book is available from the British Library

Library of Congress Cataloging-in-Publication Data
A catalog record for this book is available from the Library of Congress

ISBN: 978-0-240-52079-7

For information on all Focal Press publications
visit our website at www.focalpress.com

Printed and bound in Great Britain by MPG Books Ltd, Bodmin, Cornwall

09 10 11 12 12 11 10 9 8 7 6 5 4 3 2 1

Design and cover illustration by Dominic Thackray

Working together to grow
libraries in developing countries

www.elsevier.com | www.bookaid.org | www.sabre.org

ELSEVIER   BOOK AID
             International   Sabre Foundation

Contents

Exclusive Online Resources   vii
Acknowledgements   viii
Preface   ix
About the Author   x

1 Introduction   1
What is a Hot Script?

2 Seven Elements of Your Script   5

3 Getting Your Ideas on to Paper   15
Getting Started – Creating a Workable Blueprint for Your Movie – Three Reasons You Won't Write Your Screenplay

4 Tale Assembly   25
Story Structure Paradigms: Three-Act Story Structure – Beginning – The Middle – Endings – Other Structure Ideas – Planning Your Structure – Finding the Ending

5 Characters   51
Creating Characters – Tools for Creating Character Development – Relationships of the Hero – Stage of the Relationship – Conflict – The Staging – Symbols, Symbolism and Metaphor – Setting the Social Stage – Using the Social Stage – Social Metaphors

6 Scene Writing   85
The Basic Rules – The Eighteen Tricks and Traps of Successful Description – Exercise for Writing Descriptive Passages

7 Dialogue   101
Dialogue Tracks – The Fifteen Tricks and Traps of Dialogue – Writer's Block – Dialogue Diagnostic Tool

8 Writing for Short Films   113
Short Story Writing Tools – Writing for the Internet – Story Design in the Short Fiction Film

9 The Writer's Blueprint 127
The Writer's Lab: A Recap – The Seven Steps to a Successful Screenplay

10 Marketing Your Script 137
Preparation – Building the Pedigree for Your Screenplay

11 10 000 Monkeys – Copyright 145
Protecting Your Screenplay

12 The Movie Game 155
The Second Ring – The Outer Ring – Playing Piece – The Onanist's Rash

13 The Power File 173
Adding to the Power File – Packaging Your Screenplay – Other Ways to Add to Your Power File

14 Pitching 185
The Structure of a Pitch Meeting – Three Golden Rules of Salesmanship – Pitching Tools – Tips for Pitching

15 Eight-Line Letter 195
Elements of an Eight-Line Letter – What Happens to Your Letter?

16 The Deal 201
Outright Purchase – Option Deal – Step Deal – Writing a Treatment – Reality Check: Negotiating the Sale of Your Script – More Reality Checks

17 The Life of a Screenwriter 217
Understanding Genre – The Screenwriter and Creativity – Alpha State – Getting an Agent – The Four Routes to Getting an Agent – Researching the Marketplace – Map of the Film Industry

18 Script Format and Style Guide 229
Basic Principles – The Screenplay

19 Troubleshooting Guide 241

20 Three Golden Rules 245
Rule Number One: Quantity, Not Quality – Rule Number Two: Discipline – Rule Number Three: Reject Rejection

Glossary 251

Index 259

Exclusive Online Resources

This book contains access to an exclusive website containing:
– PDFs of all diagrams
– Audio interviews
– Writing exercises including film clips
– Database of useful writers research websites
– Updated production company databases
– Useful articles

How to use the resources

Log onto www.booksite.focalpress.com/Grove/RaindanceWritersLab2e.

All the files are PDFs. To access the files you will have to have either Adobe Acrobat reader 4.0 or higher.

To access the MP3/MPEG-1 audio and video clips and interviews you will need to have a media player installed on your computer. There are many players available. For Windows, we recommend Windows Media Player. Apple users can use Quicktime.

For information on all Focal Press publications visit our website at www.focalpress.com

Raindance Feedback

Your comments are important to us. If you read and enjoyed this book, Raindance offers you the chance to participate in spreading the word.

Simply type your review into any website, like Amazon or Barnes and Noble, and when the review appears we will send you a copy of the Raindance Film Festival Shorts DVD. We compile a DVD every year of the best shorts from the festival, so we'll send you the most recent edition. We normally sell these for £15 ($30).

How to claim your free DVD

To prove you have written a review that has been published on the internet, or in print, send a link to the page where your review appears or a cutting to info@raindance.co.uk or to Raindance, 81 Berwick Street, London W1F 8TW, UK along with your street address and we will send you your free gift. We will not use your details for any other purpose.

Acknowledgements

I CONSIDER MYSELF fortunate to be working in the film industry in the 21st century. Working, as I do at the Raindance Film Festival I am blessed to meet people from all walks of life – people so incredibly talented and gifted that one is constantly humbled.

This book is the product of working at Raindance since 1992, and meeting and working with hundreds of people. Three people stand out – my editor at Focal Press, Elinor Actipus, whose energy, wisdom and patience helped me write, edit and complete this second edition, Dominic Thackray, graphic designer and therapist, and my life partner Suzanne Ballantyne, whose love and support has nurtured me throughout.

I also thank the staff of Raindance, past and present, whose suggestions and advice enrich this book, in particular Damjan Bogdanovic, Jamie Greco, Oli Harbottle, Deena Manley James Merchant, Jesse Vile, Will Pearce, Joe Pearshouse, and Xavier Rashid. My thanks and respect go to Dean Goldberg and Will Stevenson who bear the financial and legal responsibilities of Raindance. To Philippa Juul for sub-editing, to Richard Raskin for his insightful article and to Michele Cronin and all at Focal Press.

I especially thank the many interns who have passed through Raindance – interns who have stuffed envelopes, copy-typed manuscripts, run packages and above all, been so positive – thank you. Raindance is run on intern power.

Finally, to all the students I have met over the years, thank you for your questions and patience while I struggled to find the best answers. Without you, this book would have been impossible.

Lastly, the film business is tough, bruising and fiercely competitive. To all the talented writers, directors, producers and actors who have crossed my path and offered friendship, assistance, feedback and inspiration over the years, I thank you for your wisdom and shared experiences that have made this book possible.

Preface to the Second Edition

THE CHANGES BROUGHT on by the technological advances in digital filmmaking and digital distribution since 2005 have been revolutionary. With these huge changes have come new challenges and opportunities, unprecedented in movie history. What, if any, impact do these changes have on storytelling? I believe that storytelling has never changed, although in the new digital world, the type of stories that sell has certainly changed. For example, shorts now sell, because they can easily be distributed and delivered on mobile IPTV channels like Raindance.tv. Demand has outstripped supply for episodic stories where each segment can be viewed in a few minutes, rather than television's half hour. Called webisodes or mobisodes, these mini soap operas are a challenging and much pilloried form. Successful writers will need to master such forms.

Many questions are unanswered at the time of writing. What is the impact of mobile telephony distribution, especially in the Third World? How do traditional film stories sit on the new distribution platforms?

The demand for good scripts has never been stronger. Everyone, it seems, wants into the film business. Terrestrial television stations are desperate for hot new scripts to combat the threat of IPTV, and IPTV platforms are forever scouring for content. They have the distribution power – the hardware, if you like but you as a writer have the software.

The trick, I believe, is combining a sensible marketing plan with a solid creative writing plan.

A student of mine called into my office last week proudly displaying a file folder with an enormous database containing the contact details of each and every film producer in the world. He was determined to deliver his script to the hundred most likely buyers and if no one rose to the bait, go through the next hundred, until, as he said every last film company in the world has my script. Of course I tried to explain the difference between getting your film delivered and having it read, but to no avail.

This book is about writing the best story possible in screenplay style and getting it read and sold.

This is what I mean by a hot script.

Elliot Grove
London, September 2008

About the Author

MESMERIZED BY THE moving image from a young age, but unable to watch TV or films until his early teens due to the constraints of his Amish background, Canadian-born Elliot Grove followed up formal art school training with a series of jobs behind the scenes in the film industry.

Working as a scenic artist on 68 feature films and over 700 commercials in his native Toronto, he developed a distaste for the wasted resources on set and union red tape that prevented filmmaker wannabe's like himself from getting their own features off the ground.

Elliot moved to London in the late 1980s and in 1993, when the British Film Industry was drowning in self-pity, launched the Raindance Film Festival, devoted to independent filmmaking and its emerging talent.

Initially, Raindance catered mainly to American Independents who understood that the combination of a positive mental attitude and a pioneering spirit provides the essential foundation upon which to produce and distribute films successfully. Happily, that attitude has now filtered through to the UK and independent filmmaking has become a global phenomenon.

He lectures on screenwriting and filmmaking throughout the UK and Europe, and in 1992 set up the training division of Raindance which now offers nearly two dozen evening and weekend masterclasses on writing, directing, producing and marketing a feature film. Making films is expensive, so Raindance works on the assumption that course participants do not have Hollywood-scale amounts of money to throw around.

Elliot founded the prestigious British Independent Film Awards in 1998, and www.raindance.tv in 2007. In 2008 he was awarded an Honorary Doctorate by the Open University for his contribution to education.

His second book, Raindance Producer's Lab – Lo-To-No Budget Filmmaking was published by Focal Press in July 2004. His first novel based on his experiences on the Ogaden Desert as a child is currently scheduled for publishing.

His production company operates under the Raindance banner and is currently developing a slate of ten features. In 2005 he produced The Living and the Dead which premiered at the Rotterdam Film Fesitval.

Elliot firmly believes that success in the moviemaking business is a simple matter of demystifying the process of breaking into the film industry and allowing individual talent to prosper.

1 Introduction

I DIDN'T GO to film school. I went to art school. I started out in movies working as a scenic artist. It was after I had done this job as a crewmember on nearly seventy features and countless hundreds of commercials that I began to work on screenplays. I have no formal training in movies.

I come from a small Protestant community just outside Toronto. My forebears forsook modern changes: everything from electricity to zippers. You might know them as Amish. As a child I was told that the Devil lived in the cinema. One day while waiting for a farm repair at the blacksmith, I saw the cinema on the high street. I had noticed the cinema before, but ignored it, because of what my family had taught me. But on that hot spring day it beckoned to me. I paid my ninety-nine cents and went in to see what the Devil looked like. I was totally unprepared for what I saw.

The interior of the cinema was a bit like church: rows of seats facing the front. Everything seemed very ordinary – until they suddenly switched off all the lights! You have to understand that at this point in my life I had no understanding or knowledge of what the cinema was – I had simply been told to keep away. I could just as easily have been on the moon. The movie started playing – it was Lassie Comes Home – and I was transported far away from my seat in that cinema on a dusty high street in a small farmers' town in Southern Ontario. Not only was I asking myself 'How did they do that?' but I believed then, as I do now, that cinema contains a special form of magic for which there is no explanation. My next encounter with the Devil was The Sound of Music a couple weeks later, followed by hundreds if not thousands of movies since. But I will never forget that first experience.

As my childhood until then had been devoid of movies or television, my personal cinema history only started when I was sixteen, which meant that I had missed a great many of the classic films of American and European cinema. I still make a point of watching the great black and white classics of yesteryear – classics I missed as a youth. As a compensation perhaps for my lack of early experience of classical cinema, I have inherited a strong oral story-telling tradition through the Bible and community stories I was told as a child. Story after story told to me, as if I could be cajoled into righteousness. I can remember hardly being able to sleep at night because Daniel was in that hole in the ground surrounded by hungry lions and he was going to get hurt!

The farming and gardening stories that were recounted each night at family dinner enthralled me. We sat at a table that could easily consist of twenty people: children, relatives and travelling farmhands.

I was also encouraged to learn all of the Greek myths, not because of the religious tone of my upbringing, but because my mother thought I should broaden my education.

In addition, at one point in my childhood I was fortunate enough to spend time in Somalia – a nation with a long and proud oral storytelling history.

Much later, I read many of the Chinese books on spirituality and warfare and noted that those stories stirred in me the same primal emotions as the stories from my childhood.

And very much later, after I had started Raindance, I had an epiphany about writers and the film industry, when I realized that the ancient writers of the Bible, had foreseen the difficulties of the film industry and of screenwriters, and had included a few words of wisdom, which would foretell the entire writing process.

I discovered this by accident: It was a cold, wet and windy day in London when two envelopes arrived in the mail: the first, a letter from my bank saying they were pretty unhappy with the state of my overdraft, and if I didn't go there immediately to discuss repayments, they were going to cancel my account; the second was from my mother in Canada, writing to tell me that a favourite Aunt had died. Had she called me, I would have scraped together the airfare and gone home for the funeral. But because of the communication gap, the letter arrived with me on the actual day of the funeral. Now, walking up to a telling off by my bank manager, I was trying to reconcile the way I was brought up, my current occupation, and the recent loss of my favourite Aunt. All of a sudden it hit me, like a freak wind from the east: Those ancient prophets had foretold the film industry and the problems of writers after all: 'In the Beginning was the Word, and nothing but the Word, and the Word was God'! And indeed, all screenplays start with a script.

I base my knowledge of script writing on two things:

Firstly, my love and experience in oral storytelling, the positive product of a strict upbringing. Secondly, I consider that everything formal I learned about screenplay I have learned from reading scripts, and from working with screenwriters during my time at the Raindance Film Festival. I have worked with hundreds of writers since 1991, and read over 2500 scripts – an average of one per day since the beginning of 1992.

My screenwriting training began as a script reader. I started reading scripts for free and wrote up a five-page critique on dialogue, characterization, plot, structure and writing style. I realized after reading and critiquing about a dozen scripts that these writers were making, in my humble opinion, the same mistakes and falling into common pitfalls. Much of the time I could take the template of the previous script critique and where it said 'Characterization', for example, I could write exactly what I had written for the script before, but change the character names. After a while I could read a script and write a five-page critique in under an hour.

If nothing else, this book will show you the common errors of first time screenwriters and how to avoid them. Of course, I hope to show you much more as well, and to give you the most advanced tools for screenwriting currently available.

The first half of this book contains the prevailing theories contained in all those other expensive screenwriting books and seminars. I have tried to compress them into a few short chapters. By showing you all those so-called rules, I will try to give you a simple new paradigm that will enable you to plan your script and your career for the new demands of screenwriting and filmmaking in the digital age. Lastly, and throughout this book, I want you to remember that there are no rules. Rules are only the attempts by others to explain patterns they have identified, or, to explain a fancy paradigm illustrated with examples that prove their 'rules' and verify their theories. By showing you the theorems and the facts, you should be able to see how to transcend these rules and develop your own unique and highly personal writing style.

I have a few observations I would like to share with you in the hope that you find them useful. It's important to me that you remember that I am not an expert, and that everyone, including you, is an intuitive storyteller. Just let the story out. I will have succeeded if you find this useful.

What I am proposing in this book is a system that you can use in order to get that great story out of your head and onto paper. Once the story is on paper, you can then work on structuring it into a screenplay. Cinema is a very different medium from the stage play or the novel and, if I have learned anything over my journey, it is the importance of a system of approach to realizing your vision. Without a plan of attack, the chances are that your story will come out meandering and confused, which could mean that you become frustrated and give up writing altogether.

It then follows that the entire movie making process is one of originating ideas, finding the right words to express the idea on paper, making sure those words are in the right order, and then transferring these words to the screen. No movie ever starts without words. This process is what distinguishes the movie industry from, say, the property business, where deals might start with measurements, financial calculation and an artist's impression of the finished project.

Screenwriters can be certain that they have this biblical ordination, this biblical recognition, which separates them from us mere mortals. You need all the help you can get in the fiercely competitive film business.

What is a Hot Script?

A screenplay those elusive script buyers are offering to buy. The more buyers chasing the script, the hotter it is, and by association, the hotter you are. Finding a script good enough to buy is every film producer's nightmare. The common complaint of producers I meet in London and abroad is not how to get the money. Getting the money for a film is a series of telephone calls, and is relatively simple once you have the right screenplay. The common complaint of producers is the dearth of quality material in the market place. Write a quality script and producers and agent will send the limos.

Hint You never get paid to write a script. You only get paid when you sell it.

Consider this story about Andrew Macdonald and the making of the British feature film, Shallow Grave: The year I started Raindance, Andrew was working as a runner in Edinburgh, and knew he wanted to produce. He found a wannabe writer, a medical doctor by the name of John Hodge, and paid him a thousand pounds to create a treatment. It was delivered to him in longhand on the back of NHS prescription forms. Over the next nine months, he and Hodge worked together until the script was completed. He then teamed up with the then-television director, Danny Boyle. The problem Andrew had was convincing movie people in the UK that Danny Boyle could direct a feature, a difficult and seemingly impossible task despite his stellar television work. That year he discovered that David Aukin, the then head of Film Four – the UK film outfit owned by Channel 4, was giving a talk at the Edinburgh Film Festival. He dug deeper and found out that Aukin was flying up to Edinburgh in the morning, and catching the last flight back to London. He found out the name of the limo company in charge of getting Aukin back to the airport, and paid the driver a fiver to give the script to Aukin on the way to the airport. Which he did. It's a one-hour flight back to London. Put yourself in Aukin's shoes: wouldn't you read the script? At the time it was the first script of its genre in the UK for many years. The deal was done a few days later and the careers of Boyle, Hodge and Macdonald were launched.

The most glamorous route into the world of the filmmaker is as a director. The quickest way in is with a script. And the hotter the better.

Summary

1. There is no right way to write a script – there is only your way.

2. Never forget that you are an intuitive storyteller.

3. Writing a hot script is the quickest way to establish yourself in the film industry.

Let's make sure we are singing from the same sheet, and agree some basic definitions.

2   Seven Elements of Your Script

IN ORDER TO clarify some common terms and principles, allow me to take a few pages of your time to define some areas where there could otherwise be confusion. If you are new to screenwriting, these few pages will be of interest because of the film industry information. If you are a seasoned industry insider, I hope these definitions and descriptions will shed a different light on what you already know.

1. Entertainment

There are the rules of screenwriting and the tools of screenwriting, and you should remember the difference. Rules are made to be broken. But first you need to learn the rules, so that you know what you are breaking. A tool exists to make your work easier. If a tool I mention in this book works for you, great. If not, discard it and find another.

The only product of the film business is entertainment. By 'entertainment' I do not mean solely diversion. There are many examples of films which seek only to divert: films which unnecessarily exploit sex and violence, but which make no attempt to use any of the other tools at the disposal of the screenwriter and filmmaker such as setting, action, characterization, plot, structure and dialogue.

Entertainment comes from the Latin root of the word meaning 'to intertwine'. This is the task of the screenwriter: to take all the elements available to a screenwriter and weave them together into an entertaining story. In a well-crafted screenplay, the weft should be tight and invisible. Setting, action, characterization, plot, structure and dialogue should be seamlessly combined. A writer who has learned how to do this is mastering the craft of screenwriting. An exercise: list three films that you feel were created solely to divert.

```
┌─────────────────────────────────────────────────────┐
│                                                     │
│                                                     │
│                                                     │
└─────────────────────────────────────────────────────┘
```

List three films you feel come close to weaving these elements together.

```
┌─────────────────────────────────────────────────────┐
│                                                     │
│                                                     │
│                                                     │
└─────────────────────────────────────────────────────┘
```

Can you find any common elements that link the films in each area?

There is no science to this approach but, if you deconstruct a story, you may discover techniques that you can use (or avoid) in your own work.

2. Commerce

Orson Welles said 'A poet needs a pen, a painter needs a brush, but a filmmaker needs a whole army'.

Like it or not, that is the film business and it is a complex business at that. Writers tend to be drawn by the making of the film – the technicians, the actors, the scoring, the cinematography, costume design and the props. But these are the actions of the film industry (read car industry, aerospace industry). The actual creation and making of the film is the role of the film industry and not of the writer.

Writers who forget the business side of the industry do so at their peril. The bankers and financiers, the marketing and public relations people, the owners and employees of the cinemas, the accountants with their complex procedures, the tax lawyers, the copyright and royalty collect-ors: these are a few of the silent faces who are employed by the business side of the film industry.

Add in the more glamorous roles of the actors, the directors, the editors, make-up artists, scenic artists, lighting and sound specialists and you really do have an army of people involved in the making of a film.

Each area is really a sub-industry and the people in each sub-industry tend to distrust, and sometimes even hate the people in other sub-industries. But money and collaboration govern the entire movie business. Therefore a writer who includes camera directions in a screenplay, or is too specific with stage directions, is precluding the possibility of collaboration with the cameraman and the actors – two very important categories of creatives. The trick is to write a screenplay that inspires each and every category of person likely to be involved in the making of the movie. A successful writer learns how to do this, and to incorporate everyone's creativity into the movie. Thus a finished screenplay should be considered the blueprint for a movie, or the suggestion for a movie, and not a carefully bound package of precisely typed paper that represents the death of a few trees! Writers who ignore this, or fail to research and educate themselves about the intricacies of the movie business, will hinder their chances of success.

Writers must learn as much as possible about the industry.

As a writer, you are inevitably going to spend long hours writing alone, and the commercial and collaborative aspects of the film business can be easy to forget. Also remember that, as a writer, you are basically setting up your very own business where you manufacture products (scripts and treatments) and for which the cost of manufacture (paper, some ink and some envelopes) is minuscule compared to the possible sale price of a script!

Hint Read the trade papers. Read the film magazines. Read the trashy weeklies. Scour these various publications for hard news and juicy gossip that will arm you with knowledge.

A writer friend of mine once boasted to a dinner table of light industrialists that he had started a business with a 10 000 per cent mark up. The table went dead – the usual mark-up is sixty to eighty per cent – and finally, one of the more arrogant businessmen asked him what his business was. My friend replied 'I'm writing a screenplay'.

Oddly enough, many astute businessmen recognize the financial limitations of their own businesses, even though they look financially secure and wealthy beyond belief. I have met several highly successful businessmen who know to a cent how much their business will earn this year and the next. Whereas most businesses crank out a profit at a predictable rate, affected only by basic economic factors such as employment and interest rate rises, in the movie business it is not uncommon for an individual to turn from pauper to multi-millionaire overnight. Writing a well-crafted and commercially viable screenplay could catapult you straight into the movie business at the very highest level. But before you order the Rolls Royce catalogue, remember the following: You will never get paid for writing a script. You only get paid if you sell it. And only a hot script sells.

The bottom line in the film industry is the movie. If you have that one idea that no one else has, but which someone thinks is a money-maker, the movie business will send the limos. Only a well-crafted commercially viable script counts.

3. Contrivance

There is nothing more contrived than the film business. Everything about the industry, from the way we view the images on a screen, to the way that films are created by groups of technicians, shows the movie business to be the most contrived of any art form in the world. As screenwriters, we must learn to fill the void of the screen with images and voices that follow the contrivance in the cinemas.

Remember too, that as children we all looked forward to the bedtime stories that our parents told us. Now that we are adults, we still love a good story and go to the cinema to get one. The fact that filmmakers use a series of contrivances to bring us the story is something that we expect and accept.

For example, it is common knowledge that films are shot out of sequence. Suppose the script calls for the first scene to be in her bedroom downtown, getting dressed, and the second scene with her at the airport flying into the arms of her lover whom she hasn't seen in two days. We all know that the director doesn't film the first scene, yell 'Cut', and drag everyone to the airport for the second scene, and so on. We know that films are shot out of sequence for matters of economy. Yet we accept this when we sit in front of a screen and watch a movie.

When I go to the cinema I hope for one of two things — that the story I see will change my life forever, or that I don't fall asleep.

4. Peeping Tom

Human beings are fixated by what happens to others: Walk down any street and notice the crowd gathered around the accident victim, or feel your head turn when you see the shadow of a naked body against a bedroom curtain.

Let's face it — we love to gape.

For screenwriters, the challenge is to create a world that people want to stare at, and to make the screen characters, dialogue, setting and action so compelling that they cannot wrench themselves away from the screen until the very last frame, the very last words in the script.

5. Maximize, in minimal circumstances

Creative economy is a bit of a challenge. To achieve this, a screenwriter has to maximize everything that he or she has at his or her disposal. Remember too that, as a screenwriter, you are denied many of the literary tools available to other writers. Alliteration, simile and metaphor are devices best left to poets, lyricists or novelists.

Also, a screenwriter can only write what can be shown on the screen. Therefore, you can't say 'It's very cold' because how do you show cold? You could say 'Hail bounces off the windscreen'.

But I refer not only to the creative tools. As a writer you need to maximize your own personal life, to be able to take the energy and patience to explain to those with whom you share your life that what you are doing is very important to you. Know when to pull back and when to involve them. This is also a big challenge.

Earning their keep

Each word must earn its keep on the page. Thus a description like: 'a late Victorian sixteen-room country house overgrown with perennials' could better be stated as 'run-down mansion'.

One of the worst things about writing is sneaking into your workspace and turning on the computer. Something about the click of the switch, or the chime the machine makes when you switch it on creates a black hole of energy. Energy that sucks in all sorts of things — the telephone rings, a pet (if you have one) needs attention, or worst of all, if you share your life with someone else, a human being tries to help you. It usually goes like this — 'Honey, I'm going to write now for forty-five minutes.' Fifteen minutes later, the love of your life walks in behind you and starts massaging your neck and cooing words like 'You look really tired' or 'You really

RAINDANCE WRITERS' LAB: WRITE AND SELL THE HOT SCREENPLA

should do something about those bags under your eyes' and, before you know it, you have stopped writing and gone to bed!

Handling your personal life so that your family and friends know that while you are writing you must not and cannot be disturbed, takes a special skill. You have to learn how to do this too, if you want to write the hot script.

6. Hollywood, love it or leave it?

First of all, let me explain that by 'Hollywood' I mean the professional film and television community centred in Los Angeles – yes, Hollywood is the major centre of film production. But by 'Hollywood' I also mean the centre of film production in other major cities – New York, Toronto, Hamburg, Vancouver, Barcelona and London.

In these cities, and others, professional film production companies also churn out movie after movie, although perhaps not on the same scale as in Los Angeles. These film production companies vary in size from mini-majors like FilmFour, Canal Plus, Pathe or Kinoveldt to small companies producing a picture or two directly for TV or the home DVD market.

I myself love Hollywood films!

This always gets me into trouble. Running the Raindance Film Festival, which is noted for its cutting-edge independent films, my acquaintances ask me 'But how could you possibly like Hollywood? Most Hollywood films suck!'

True. But so do most ballets, most novels, most operas, most paintings, most poems, most symphonies and most rock songs.

By saying that I love Hollywood films, I mean that I love seeing vast expanses of scenery, sparkling special effects, snappy and crisp dialogue, gorgeous costumes and settings, ambitious and grand camera movements – all the characteristics of most Hollywood films. And when Hollywood succeeds and tells a story that compels the viewer, that elicits emotion in the audience, that brings a lump to the throat, or a gasp of laughter, Hollywood is fantastic! It also follows that one of the best ways to write for the screen is to study Hollywood movies.

Hint Go and see as many Hollywood films as you can.

Some acquaintances of mine who are attempting to make a career in the film industry belabour the Hollywood point and insist that they are tired or bored with Hollywood films.

To them, and to you, if you find yourself sharing this sentiment, I respectfully suggest that you are in the wrong profession. If you say you are fed up with glitz, with glamour, and fatigued by sparkle, then I really think you are in the wrong business!

If you do fall into this category, then view this book merely as a means of increasing your understanding of the movie business, and use it as

Producers agree that the main reason so many sub-standard screenplays are shot is because of the negotiating logistics foisted on producers and on screenwriters by the system of 'pay or play'.

The only way to secure major talent is to book them for a specific production time slot and agree to pay them, whether or not the project actually starts shooting at that time.

So, if the screenplay needs to be rewritten or revised at the risk of delaying the agreed start date, producers would rather push unfinished screenplays into production than accept the accompanying onerous financial penalties. They reason being that at least then they will have a finished film which they can use to try and recoup their money.

something that will enhance your enjoyment of the films you choose to see, but please don't pretend to be a part of it. You are just setting yourself up for disappointment.

By 'Hollywood' I also refer to the time-honoured tradition of passing each script through a series of filters. The Hollywood filtering system is not without fault. Hollywood produces many poor scripts. The reason for this is more to do with the politics of the movie business than anything else and specifically the pay-or-play deals that dominate the business.

The Hollywood system spends hundreds of millions of dollars each and every year on developing screenplays, and in the process, creates opportunities for writers to write and to get paid.

Since 1999, a whole new breed of film company has leapt out of nowhere. Their remit is to produce moving pictures for the Internet, mobile telephones and handheld devices. I also refer to those companies which are producing work for these new platforms as 'Hollywood'. Yet another Hollywood medium demanding film script after script after script.

In summary, the films produced by Hollywood companies are created for the sole purpose of earning money for the producers and investors who have financed the production budget (and supplied the writer with his cheque).

7. Audience

The biggest mistake a writer can make at the outset of writing a screenplay is fantasising about his or her screenplay as a finished movie playing at hundreds or thousands of cinemas around the world. To write with this goal in mind is demonstrating a fundamental lack of knowledge about the different role of the filmmaker and the screenwriter.

A filmmaker makes a film to play to an audience in a cinema or in front of a TV. That is their goal: to elicit emotion from an audience in a cinema.

The goal of a screenwriter is entirely different. A screenwriter's audience is just one person – a reader. And the screenwriter's goal is to elicit emotion from that one person. Usually in the film industry, the reader is late fifties/early sixties and over-weight with a tight silk shirt tucked into a pair of expensive slacks, secured by an enormous crocodile skin belt. The reader's body is adorned with gold rings and bracelets. Very often, this reader has absolutely no training in film, but they are reading your script, and they have the one thing you want – a chequebook. If you succeed in eliciting emotion in this unattractive creature, chances are very much better that you will get a cheque. If you fail to do so, you won't.

Because the role of the audience is so important, let's take a closer look at the status of the observer.

After I finished high school, I went to art school in Toronto and, in order to keep my mother happy, I enrolled at the local university for a series of classes including an English literature class. I dropped out after three classes, because the lecturers were so dry. But on the first two nights

I had the most brilliant lectures by the Canadian philosopher, Marshal Macluan. Here is his version of the importance of an audience, and the role of the writer:

Suppose that I am a DJ and my job is to attend the radio station and choose music for my show which airs every morning from 3am – 4am. Hardly a favourable time but, in addition to my cheque, the other benefit is that I can choose any music I like without any outside interference. Many would consider this an ideal job, albeit with unsociable hours.

figure 2.1
Audience Chart A

The model looks like this:

DJ   RADIO   LISTENER

SOURCE → MEDIUM → AUDIENCE

Suppose one evening as I am about to leave for work, the radio producer calls and says that there is conclusive proof that this evening during my show, absolutely no one will be listening. Is there any point in my attending to play my favourite records? Surely I can do this in the comfort of my own home.

figure 2.2
Audience Chart B

Let's look at the model again, only now from the writer's perspective:

DJ   RADIO   LISTENER

SOURCE → MEDIUM → AUDIENCE

WRITER   SCRIPT   READER

The writer writes for the reader. This is where the biblical quote becomes so appropriate. I call it the Screenwriter's Leap of Faith.

How do you know when you start to write a script that you will be able to write a good script? Screenwriting is an art form, and you may not be able to hit it every time.

If you do write a good script, how do you know if you will get it to the right producer – that reader with a chequebook? And if you get it to the right producer, how do you know if he or she will hire the right director? If you wrote a one page script and gave it to ten different directors, would you not get ten very different films? And how about actors? If you asked a director to direct the same one-page script with ten different actors, would you not also get ten different films? And what of the editors, production designers and composers?

You don't know if the right people will get to work on your script, and you have absolutely no control over this. You might get lucky, write a fabulous script, get it to the top producer who hires the hottest director with a cast of talented newcomers, and yet you may still find that you cannot get your film onto a single screen at home or around the world. It does happen.

How do you know what the future holds for your idea for a screenplay? From the moment you decide to commit endless hours of time and energy to writing it, you have to admit that you have no idea what the end result is going to be.

The screenwriter's leap of faith is that amazing belief in yourself and your idea that will sustain you, despite all of these barriers to success! Hence I say that the Biblical quote has never been more applicable.

Hint The goal of a filmmaker is to elicit emotion in an audience. The goal of a screenwriter is to elicit emotion in a reader.

There are four times during this book that I am going to go into downer mode. This is the first and it relates to that miserable word 'misfortune'. There is nothing I can do to teach you about misfortune except to try and educate you as much as possible about the savvy needed for the industry, and thus hope to minimize the odds against you.

Consider these two questions: Is every hit movie good? Is every good movie a hit?

Every year at the Raindance Film Festival, I find a sweetheart, darling, cute film that I really believe is right for the British audience. The film plays to a packed house, including several distributors. After the screenings of these films, the audience bursts into rapturous applause and files out talking excitedly about the movie. The filmmakers are usually there too, and I know how urgently they need a sale.

Usually in cases like this, I stride up to the Acquisitions Executives that I recognize at the screening and ask them what they think of the film. They know that what I am really asking is whether or not they think it is suitable for a UK release. I am usually told 'It's too American for a British audience' or 'I don't think the British public is ready for something as controversial as that'. Misfortune can and will befall you. Learn to recognize it for what it is, and move on. There is nothing you can do about it. You must learn to move on.

From this can be learned one of the most fundamental rules of screenwriting: learn when to let go. Your job as a writer is to inspire the teams of other creatives that are involved in the filmmaking process. Not every idea is going to work. There is nothing you can do about this. So learn when (and how) to let go.

Hint 'Grant me the strength to change what I can, to accept the things I cannot, and the wisdom to know the difference.'   St Francis of Assisi

---

What writers can control

The actors' actions: through description in the screenplay.

Dialogue: through the script.

Setting: by choosing where the story is told.

The story, the story, the story.

But once the screenplay has left your hands, everything can be changed.

What writers can't control

Casting.

Performance.

Editing.

The vision of the director.

Cinematography and the skill of the camerman/woman.

Production Design, Set, Wardrobe, Special FX, and artistry of the craft people.

Score and suitability of the music.

Marketing, poster and trailer – the skill of the market makers and publicists.

The success of the film: Hey! Who does? It is rubbish!

Successful writers write to inspire everybody else, and then let go.

Screenwriters are artists and have a responsibility for the work they create. To create a screenplay that glamorizes or condones gratuitous sex or violence, shows a lack of responsibility. A good example is the recent court case in which Oliver Stone was successfully sued by the families of victims killed by copycat killings from Natural Born Killers.

The Role of Violence and Sex

Every scene, every line, every word in your script should be brimming with violence – emotional violence: tension, contradiction and conflict.

There are three types of violence: Physical violence: the arming of our fellow citizens and the escalation of global conflict. I hate it, even though it is a part of everyday life and likely to remain that way.

Sociological violence: the violence caused by the loss of one's place in society, at work, or at home. This violence fascinates me, partly because I am a voyeur, and partly because I love to study the structures that create such changes, both failures and successes.

Psychological violence: being put in a position where all one's values and beliefs are challenged to the point where one is unable to function. This is my personal nightmare.

How one treats violence is important. Let us look at some classic stories to see how violence has been used. Take the ancient story of Oedipus Rex: How would you describe this story to someone? Write down how you would pitch this story to a development executive in ancient Greece.

What did you come up with? A story about revenge? About jealousy? About destiny? Did you mention the violence? Most pitches don't mention the violence in a specific way.

If I were pitching Oedipus Rex to an artsy film company, it would go like this: A young man, heir to the throne of Greece, discovers that he has travelled both ways through his mother's birth canal and is so distraught that he pierces his eyes. The violence here is both physical and psychological.

Hint If you are unsure, do some research. The Greek classics are wonderful stories that can provide inspiration for your story.

How about Medea? Another extremely violent story where the Queen of Greece discovers she is being two-timed by her husband. She butchers their children, cooks them, and serves them to her husband for dinner. Can you imagine pitching this story to PBS? The violence here is mainly physical with psychological violence at the very end.

Those are ancient stories. Let's move to Shakespeare, considered one of those greats, and one of his greatest plays – Hamlet. Again, this is a story with epic themes of destiny, revenge, and guilt. At the end, the stage is littered with the bodies of the dead and dying.

Even children's stories are extremely violent. Consider most traditional fairytales, and even Disney! Poor Bambi, the cute little deer sees her mother blown away by evil hunters.

Hint Screenwriters should capture the attention of the audience through appropriate use of violence and sex.

So don't forget what we expect when we go to the cinema: at the most that our lives will be changed forever; at the least, that we don't fall sound asleep. Anywhere in the middle is fine.

Finally, everything in the film industry comes down to one thing – a script that can attract a reader. To attract a reader, a script must be great, not just good.

Summary

1. Nobody knows anything. Remember that this book is designed to give you a practical plan; a method for getting your ideas onto paper.

2. The quickest way into the film industry is with a script – a hot script.

3. Never forget the writer's role: inspire everyone else, then let go.

4. You are an intuitive storyteller. Let nothing inhibit you.

Now let's start getting that idea out of your head and onto paper.

3   Getting Your Ideas on to Paper

FOR MOST WRITERS this is the moment you have been dreading. If you're like me you probably remember announcing the fact that you want to write a screenplay to your family and friends. Did you make that specific announcement at some point during the last eighteen months? Do you remember the warm glow of well-wishers patting you on the back saying 'Of course you can write a screenplay – a great screenplay. I can hardly wait to read it.' They know you have talent. You have spent the last eighteen months doing nothing about your screenplay. It's stuck in your head eating your waking moments and, horror of horrors, suppose you meet one of those well-wishers at a party or on the street? The first thing they say is 'How is the screenplay going?'. And you have to lie and say that it's going well, even if it's not.

Take the plunge.

Hint 'A barn full of hay is going to be emptied one fork at a time. And one fork has to be the first.'   Old Amish saying

---

Getting Started – the Basic Premise

Many new writers I meet through my teaching and at the Raindance Writers' Lab in London are ready to give up on writing. They feel this way because their stories have become meandering and muddled, which in turn makes them feel confused and unfocused. This is probably because they did not start with a plan.

The more I think about writing, the more I believe that a plan of attack to getting that idea out of your head and onto paper is the key to success. And this does not apply only to writing: all art forms, whether written, visual or musical, require the artist to approach his or her vision with technique and craftsmanship. And successful artists, painters, choreographers, musicians and writers develop a method, a unique approach, which enables them to produce their work.

Writing a screenplay is a complex job, and a successful screenplay has hundreds of different elements to it.

A great screenplay is a bit like a meal-of-a-lifetime. Learning to read one is like being able to savour a fine meal and being able to taste each flavour, each element, knowing how the chef blended all the ingredients together.

Writing a screenplay is much more than simply typing **FADE IN** at the top of page one and hoping that when you type **FADE OUT** ninety to one hundred and twenty pages, later you will have a marketable screenplay. This is unrealistic.

In order to write a screenplay, just like any other art form, you need to create a plan, a blueprint. The blueprint has to include all the elements of a screenplay: characterization, plot, dialogue, action and setting. Then you need to decide how you are going to incorporate these elements in a bold, fresh and original way in order to enhance the commercial viability of your screenplay. Consider this then as the business plan for the story part of your screenplay: the who, why, what, where, when and how.

Another way to look at the plan is to think of it as the method of writing a screenplay: a process that allows you to combine your creative energy with proven techniques.

A useful reference for current script sales is the website www.donedeal.com. Successful writers keep abreast of industry trends by reading the trade papers: USA: Variety, Hollywood Reporter, Canada: Playback, UK: Screen International.

Successful screenwriters also understand what the market is looking for and learn what sorts of stories are being bought by the people who are buying screenplays. This is therefore a two-pronged approach: you are developing the savvy to market your script as well as developing the savvy to hone your literary skills.

New writers hate the planning part of writing because they want to get straight to the fun bits: writing the first two words of their screenplay – **FADE IN**; their first slug line – **INT: WRITER'S GARRET – DAY**; a couple of lines of description; and then straight into writing dialogue.

In general, the more you plan, the better your script will be. I will show you in Chapter 15 how to capture those impetuous and exciting, creative moments and incorporate them into your script.

A page of screenplay, properly typed, creates approximately one minute of screen time. Thus a ninety-page script is roughly ninety minutes long.

To write without a plan is a bit like this: have you ever agreed to meet a friend or two after work at 6:15 say, and maybe go and do something? Your office might be in an exciting, trendy part of town – close to bars, restaurants, nightclubs and cinemas. The theory is that in the centre of a playground like this, a few adults can surely have some fun. Everyone is excited about the prospect of a night out and the hours at work fly by.

Then you meet. The excitement mounts. The reality, however, is different from what you had dreamt about. First of all, one of your friends is a few minutes late. You have just missed the start of the movie! You all agree that it is a little early to go for dinner – another reasonable option – so instead you pop into the local bar for a quick drink. A few good jokes and stories sidetrack you. Suddenly you realize you have missed the next showing of that great film you all wanted to see. Never mind, you decide to go out for dinner. But what cuisine? Maybe it should be German, Eritrean, Japanese, Somali or French. Before you know it all the really good restaurants are booked out for the night and you have to settle for a burger and a milkshake at a chain outlet and the bus ride home.

If this has happened to you, can you remember the feeling of despond-ency when you got home?

This is how you will feel if you attempt to write a screenplay without advance planning, but with one difference. On the failed night out, your friends will share the blame with you. With screenwriting, you have no one to blame but yourself. And your friends will blame you. Which will lead to a lack of confidence. Which may cause you to stop writing.

Three reasons you won't write your screenplay

1. Lack of confidence
2. Self-destruction
3. Procrastination

Of all the writers I have met who have now given up, lack of planning is the primary reason that they stopped writing. Don't let it happen to you! Let me to show you in the next few pages how simple it is to formulate a really good plan. The more work and care you put into planning your movie, the better it will be.

If you decorate a room without filling and sanding all the little holes, your paint job isn't going to look very good, no matter how witty your brush strokes are. In decoration, like screenwriting: prepare.

Artists in any medium, whether music, painting, sculpture or writing, have various ways of pre-planning their works. Painters sketch, sculptors make maquettes, and dancers use an exercise called 'preparation'.

Creating a Workable Blueprint for Your Movie

1. The premise

One of your first tasks is to distil your idea and work out what is at the core of your story. Some writers arrive at this a little later in the process but, regardless of your route, it is difficult to move on with the story until you are certain of the basic premise.

Writing the idea of your story in a few simple lines will be one of the most difficult jobs you will face in the entire process, so it is important that you take the time to understand this task fully. You should aim to have a three or four line paragraph like this:

This is a story about [describe the main character] who [what she wants more than anything else in the world] but [name the overwhelm-ing obstacle preventing the realization of her goal] and [tease with the ending].

You will hear a saying in the film business – 'Tell me your movie in 25 words or less'. What they want are those three or four lines as above. Like the paragraph blurb on the back of the DVD box.

Hint Do not name the character because your reader will not know what 'Kevin' looks like. Instead say: 'It's a story about a middle-aged Welsh butcher'. This conjures up an image of the character. In the same way 'unemployed banker', 'disgruntled footballer', or 'fiendish housewife' are all better than 'Mary'.

Hint Make the paragraph a tease – you are writing an ad for your movie.

Hint Phrases such as 'situations dictate', or 'only to discover' are useful in shaping the paragraph, but are hackneyed and should be avoided if possible in the final draft.

This is a story about [succinctly describe the main character]:

Who [what he or she wants more than anything else over the course of the story]:

But [describe the main obstacle to your character's getting what he or she wants]:

And [the ending]:

2. The twenty-five words or less

The historical root of 'describe in twenty-five words or less' lies in the TV Guide for American television which, due to space constraints, would only accept twenty-five words or less for each movie listing. Filmmakers and financiers soon realized that if a movie could not be summed up quickly, it would not get mentioned in the TV Guide. Then no one would watch it, ratings would plummet, and nobody could sell advertising.

As a screenwriter, the twenty-five words description is essential. It is the road map that you will tack onto the wall where you write so that you can remind yourself every step of the way what your story is about.

Without this map, you will meander all over town in a fruitless and ultimately frustrating exercise that may get you lost and ultimately deter you from writing forever. Write your plan here:

Can you think of movies you have seen where this happens?

Were they commercially viable?

Hint It is easy to describe the mood, atmosphere and setting without telling the story. Make sure that you tell the story.

3. High concept vs. low concept

The film industry likes stories that can be summed up in far fewer than twenty-five words. Panic In Needle Park was summed us as 'Romeo and Juliet on junk'. Shaun of the Dead as 'a Rom-Zom-Com', The Green Mile was 'Forest Gump on Death Row', Aliens as 'Jaws in space'. A movie that can be summed up like this is called a high concept movie. Name three other movies that can be summed up in one pithy phrase:

There are other movies that are more difficult to sum up so economically. These are called low-concept films, and usually deal with a story where the relationships are of more importance than the story line itself. Often these movies are adaptations from novels or short stories. For example: Cold Mountain, The English Patient or The Constant Gardener. Name three other movies that are more difficult to sum up in a single phrase:

4. Hero's basic action

The basic action is the main thing that your hero will try to achieve throughout the movie/story. Your hero might want to do many different things in the movie, but you must try to pinpoint that one basic action that happens in the middle of the story or which occurs most.

By focusing on the basic action, you will also be able to see clearly the essential struggle that might ultimately change your hero.

For example, in Thelma and Louise, the basic action is that they go on a car journey. The struggle is in the decisions they make during their journey and how they react to the misfortune that befalls them along the way.

In Bee Movie, the hero's basic action is to file a law suit against humans for stealing honey from bees.

What is the hero's basic action in your story?

```

```

5. Details of the basic action

By describing the basic action in more detail you will find additional clues about the forces causing or forcing your hero to change. Look for both good and bad forces, positive and negative. Write them down here:

Positive

Negative

You will probably come up with words like 'jealous', 'indecisive' and 'disloyal' under negative qualities, and 'brave' and 'honest' for positive qualities. Remember that the stronger and more dramatic the qualities are, whether negative or positive, the stronger your hero.

6. Ghost

All good stories have a ghost. The ghost represents the person/event from the past that the hero is still frightened by, paralysed by, or ashamed of. In the horror genre, the ghost takes a physical embodiment. How often have you seen this movie: the hero pacing in front of a white picket fence? It is night. On the hill is a darkened haunted house. What does the writer do to our poor hero? He makes him go up the hill, into the house, and live out his own worst nightmare.

In detective stories, the ghost is referred to as the personal crime. The detective, hired to solve the murder, is also responsible for a murder which occurred before the story started. An excellent example is in the film Basic Instinct, where Michael Douglas's character is nicknamed 'Shooter' for his accidental killing of a German tourist before the movie started.

Name or describe your ghost:

7. Psychological and moral weaknesses

A good story has a character who at the beginning of the story possesses a variety of moral and psychological handicaps.

Hint The larger the weaknesses, the stronger the conflict.

What are the psychological (strictly personal) flaws that keep your hero from achieving his/her goal/goals? For example, indecision or fear.
Write them here:

What are the moral flaws – having to do with acting properly toward others – that keep your hero from achieving his/her goal/goals? For example, irresponsibility, insensitivity, recklessness or greed.
Write them here:

8. Nightmare

Nightmare is that thing in the future that your hero dreads and fears. It is the lowest level to which he could possibly sink.
Write your hero's nightmare here:

9. Struggle

Look at the basic action and the psychological and moral weaknesses of the hero and answer these questions:
What struggle does your hero have to surmount in order to accomplish the basic action?

[ ]

Worst nightmare: what is the one thing that your hero fears most?

[ ]

What is the worst thing your hero could face?

[ ]

10. Hero's potential

How can your hero think, or choose, or how can he behave better, or accomplish at a higher level than at the start of the story?

At the start of your story, your hero has the potential to improve, but has not yet fulfilled this potential for various reasons.

He may be unable to improve because of physical flaws, sociological flaws or psychological flaws. He may be overcome by fear of his worst nightmare.

Defining your hero's potential will allow you to take your hero to higher highs and lower lows throughout the story.

[ ]

11. Final twenty-five words or less

Revise and restate your initial premise, if necessary, in the clearest way possible. Your premise may not change, or it may change dramatically from your original. In either case, you are finding your story.

[ ]

12. Testing the concept

Why wait until your movie is written, shot, edited and marketed to find out if it is going to be a blockbuster? It is much easier to test your film out at paper stage rather than waiting until it is made at the cost of many hundreds of thousands, if not millions. Here's what to do: Try out your twenty-five words on everyone you know now. Every time you meet someone, stranger or acquaintance, you must let him or her know what you are doing. You are trying to get them to ask 'Can I know more?' Tell them your twenty-five words. As you are speaking to them, observe their reactions. It's a good idea to jot them down. If it is a comedy – did they laugh and, if so, how spontaneous was the laughter? If it was a horror story, did your twenty-five words gross them out? Or did their eyes glaze over with boredom. No matter what the reaction, ask them 'what do you think?' Or 'would you like to see a movie like that? Or 'Is there any way I could make this better?'

You are essentially conducting your very own market research campaign coupled with some advance PR about the movie and about yourself. The big advantage to doing this yourself is that you can instantly rectify any story flaws and ensure that, as far as is possible, you are working on a marketable screenplay. If you share your life with someone, this is a great time to incorporate their suggestions and ideas into your twenty-five words. They will probably welcome the chance to be involved in your project – but be careful that they realize that you are not going to be sharing the script credit!

The Raindance reader report I prepared for interns asks the reader to jot down the characters in order of appearance, and then asks the question: 'Would you like to spend two hours in a cinema with this character and, if not, why?' This is a pretty harrowing test for your screenplay.

Three Reasons You Won't Write Your Screenplay

1. Lack of confidence

How many times have you walked up to your computer, filled with inspiration for your screenplay, turned it on and been faced with a giant blank? This is lack of confidence in your idea. Some people call it writer's block, but it is actually a lack of confidence. Never give in to these feelings – you'll stop writing. You are entering uncharted territory. And no one said that your end result was going to be any good – so take away that pressure right now. Forget the pressure of winning an Oscar. Writing this script will be challenging and exciting. Enjoy!

Hint Go back to your basic premise and work and rework it until you are absolutely satisfied that this idea will work for you.

---

2. Self-destruction

The human race is unique on the planet in that we all have our own ways to self-destruct. I know you have yours and I have mine. Let's not go there right now!

3. Procrastination

Among the paths to self-destruction, procrastination is my personal favourite. Ask my editor: We had an initial meeting for this book at the idea stage. What an inspiring meeting! I then had to produce an outline and a sample chapter. The outline wasn't too hard – I put together what was essentially the index. But the sample chapter weighed on my mind for weeks after the deadline. I finally sent the script format and style guide (Chapter 17), which I had written for Raindance a couple of years earlier. So even that wasn't too bad. But then came the task of writing the actual book. I vowed I would write every single day for an hour until I had broken the back of the book. Each night I would turn on the computer and stare at the screen. After a few nights I realized that while 'writing' my book, I achieved the cleanest apartment in London and all the odd jobs at home, such as replacing blown light bulbs, had been done. Apparently I will do anything to avoid writing!

Hint Discipline. A little bit every day is better than nothing. Or be like Hemingway, and leave each day with an unfinished sentence on the page. Those few words will pull you right back to where you left off, and make it easier to continue writing.

Summary

1. Making a plan/premise is your first task and it is the most challenging.

2. Test your premise on everyone that you can.

3. Revise if necessary. Your next task is to create a structure.

Let's put it all together and become a really good yarn spinner. We are now ready for tale assembly.

4 Tale Assembly

TALE ASSEMBLY, OR story structure, is the way that your story unfolds. In this chapter I will describe the various story structure theories currently on offer from the script doctors and gurus such as Syd Field, Michael Hague, Linda Seger, Robert McKee and so on. I will then attempt to explain story structure in my own unique way and, in the next chapter, I will tell you to set aside and disregard everything I have said in this chapter as I attempt to explain the basics of tale assemble and story structure in a very different way – by using the principles of character and character development. I hope I manage to do this with out confusing you. The intent is to explain structure, and then give you a workable plan when approaching your own story.

The phrase 'story structure' is probably the least helpful and most over-used phrase in the movie business. The word 'structure' implies that there is some sort of magic framework that one can purchase or hire; assemble it in one's creative playground; and presto! – Create a story.

While I believe in a structured approach to one's writing, I do not think that there can be anything as simple as a 'story structure' that works for storytellers.

Story is to film what melody is to music. There is a very well known story of Amadeus Mozart as a teenager that explains this concept best. As a child prodigy, Mozart earned a very respectable income travelling from court to court playing his music. One morning, after a particularly late night, Amadeus' mother failed time and time again to rouse him. Imagine her cajoling him with lines like: 'If you don't get up now, you won't have time to get your wig on before the coach arrives.'

I suppose Amadeus was no different than any of us as teens with our parents threatening us with disinheritance if we were late for school one more time.

In desperation, or so we are told, Mozart's mother went to the piano at the foot of the stairway leading to Mozart's room and played 'doh-ray-mi-fa-so-la-ti…' Mozart leapt out of bed, raced down the stairs and finished the thought with a resounding 'doh!'

Story is to film what melody is to music, and scene is to story what note is to melody.

The job of a screenwriter is to create tension and then release it. Over and over again until the end of the film.

Story Structure Paradigms: Three-Act Story Structure

There probably isn't a screenwriting book that does not use the term 'three-act story structure'. It has become the term used by mainstream story analysts and story development executives.

The term 'three-act story structure' is one which I am wary of, for it is easily misunderstood and is too general to be of much use. However, the basic paradigm, despite its limitations, is useful for novice screenwriters.

The history of three-act structure goes back to ancient Greece and and the teachings of Aristotle. He made the revolutionary discovery that a story had three distinct parts: the Beginning the Middle and the End. Furthermore he defined the three elements as follows:

The Ending – that part after which there is nothing, the Beginning, before which there is nothing, and by logic, the Middle is the part in between. This seems very passé by twenty-first century terms but was treated as a groundbreaking discovery by the Greeks of his day.

A few millennia passed and then in 1974 the American script assessor and author, Syd Field, published a book called Screenplay in which the three-act structure was expanded in detail.

There are two types of people who buy content in the film industry: Acquisition executives buy finished films; Development executives buy scripts. Both types of buyers offer creative advice!

figure 4.1
Syd Field's Three-Act Structure

Act I	Act II	Act III
SETUP	CHAIN OF CONFLICT	RESOLUTION

1   30   60   90   120

Three-Act Structure

Get your hero up a tree. Throw stones at him/her. Get your hero down.

This too seems very simplistic in the twenty-first century but, in the mid 1970s, was considered revolutionary work. All major film and television companies made Field's book, and all his subsequent ones, required reading for their script doctors, writers, executives and script development personnel.

Limitations of three-act structure

The concept is based on theatre performances, during which a curtain falls between acts. In movies, development executives talk about 'the second act story curtain'. What can this possibly mean in a movie where there are no curtains?

The concept pre-supposes that there are major plot points at pages 30, 60, 90 and 120 – one at the end of each act, and one in the middle. When was the last time you saw a movie with just four plot points?

The concept does not make any distinction between the different types of genre.

Syd Field's book Screenplay has been seminal in developing and maintaining the notion of 'three-act story structure'. It is perhaps ironic that when I met Syd Field at Raindance in 1995, he told me that his three-act paradigm was out-dated and that it was his publisher who kept proposing ideas for new books based on his now outmoded paradigm. Field told me that he preferred a much more fluid, more advanced story structure paradigm, and that he was that year studying Mexican cinema, which makes the most of advanced story paradigms.

There are nonetheless valid reasons for studying three-act story structure. It is of special interest to novice writers as a guide, and also to story professionals curious to see how their work will be evaluated within the industry. Let us take a look at three-act structure. I will analyse each section, and then show you some tools I have discovered − tools you can use in order to execute your plan more efficiently.

Beginning

The beginning of your screenplay is the most critical part of the story. Agents and producers say that they will read the first ten pages. If they aren't hooked by page ten then they will say the dreaded word 'Pass'. Fortunately there are many tools you can use at the beginning of your screenplay to help distinguish it from all the others.

Your tasks at the beginning

1. Introduce the hero

By 'hero' I mean the person who experiences the events of the movie and through whose perceptions the story is told. In commercially successful films this character is always introduced early. Showing us a character we can identify with pulls the audience into the film.

Heroes are introduced in one of three ways:

Running start − where the hero is already in pursuit, or being pursued. Most action adventure films start this way.

Family or community start − where we see the hero with his/her family, flatmates, co-workers and so on. Everything seems right and normal with the hero, but we know something important is going to happen. The opening scene of Jaws is a good example of this.

Slow burn − do not contemplate this method. The less said the better!

2. Tell us the time and the pace of the movie

There is a big difference between the opening of a James Bond movie and a romantic comedy. There is no science here, but your reader will deduce a lot about the pace of your movie just by looking at the first page of the screenplay. How many scenes are on the front page? Are there three or four scenes (fast paced) or a three-page opening scene (soft romance or drama)? A reader will also notice the percentage of dialogue to descriptive passages and so get a clue as to whether your script is a 'talking heads' movie or is action based. This isn't scientific, no. But it does help prepare the reader for your story.

3. Tell us what the movie is really about

I'm talking here about the theme of the film. Theme is not the story. Story goes before theme. But theme is the glue that binds the story together, and is what your story is really about. This is often the basic mistake new writers make when they talk about their story. They talk and pitch the theme, and not the story. Theme is a unifying or dominant idea or motif. For example, that greed can cause physical harm to others, is the theme of the movie Erin Brockovich. Incidentally, this is also the theme of the movie Jaws.

That duty comes before personal wishes is one of the themes of The Godfather. That love conquers all is the theme of innumerable novels, poems, plays and movies including Guess Who's Coming to Dinner?; As Good As It Gets; and Pretty Woman.

Writing theme is one of the most troubling tasks writers face. My advice is not to write theme at all – ignore it. Finish the first draft of your screenplay and look at it. Maybe then you will see the recurring motif which binds your story together. In order to enhance and develop the idea, perhaps you will think of a line of dialogue or an action that will click your idea into place and reinforce your theme.

Hint Draw a movie poster of what your movie is about. Don't worry if you can't draw or that your characters will look like stick men. Often the dominant motif, your theme, will become obvious through the drawing. Next draw a tableau – a frozen image that encapsulates the theme of your movie.

It is difficult to teach how to write theme. Perhaps the best advice is the zenist advice to an archer: you cannot hit a target by aiming at it; you can only hit it when you feel it in your heart. If you decide your theme too early in the writing process, you may limit yourself. For example, you may decide to write a film with a tragic theme and discover as you go that a dark comedy is trying to emerge. If you are too militant about theme too early in the writing process, you might limit your creative vision and prevent the story from developing. If you can follow your heart and your inner instincts, theme should slot into place making a compelling story.

Hint A clue to theme, whether in action or dialogue, often appears on page three of commercially successful films. See if you can find the line of dialogue that pertains to theme in the following extract from page three of Chinatown (Robert Towne) below:

INT. GITTES' OFFICE - GITTES & CURLY

Gittes and Curly stand in front of the desk,
Gittes staring contemptuously at the heavy
breathing hulk towering over him. Gittes takes
a handkerchief and wipes away the plunk of
perspiration on his desk.

                    CURLY
                  (crying)
          They don't kill a guy for that.

                    GITTES
          Oh, they don't?

                    CURLY
          Not for your wife. That's the
          unwritten law.

Gittes pounds the photos on the desk, shouting:

                    GITTES
          I'll tell you the unwritten law,
          you dumb son of a bitch, you
          gotta be rich to kill somebody,
          anybody and get away with it.
          You think you got that kind
          of dough, you think you got that
          kind of class?

Doesn't this speech sum up what Chinatown is really about?

4. Choosing the correct beginning

Choosing the correct beginning for your story is a potential pitfall for many novice writers.

For example, in the hands of an inexperienced writer, Chinatown would begin with the birth of Gittes, his early days at school, his first job, first love, first betrayal and so on until the point in the actual film which might, in my clumsy case, be well into sixty minutes, at which point it would join up with the original!

A good storyteller knows how to cut as deeply as possible into the story, creating audience excitement without losing pace.

Concrete tools assist one's hands with physical tasks. The tools described in this book are designed in the mind and are meant to assist in the work of writing your screenplay.

Tools which are useful at the beginning

1. Choosing the type of hero

The basic concept of a story revolves around the principal character – the hero (or protagonist). Choosing the type of hero you have will largely determine the type of story you have. What attributes does the character

Online Resources

Choosing the correct social stage is probably the simplest way to give your story the edge that will distinguish it from other screenplays. Read the next chapter!

95% of screenplays fail because the hero is not clearly defined, and/or because the hero does not have a specific want and need.

have? Is s/he strong physically, or weak? Attractive, or homely? Honest or a cheating liar? There are many different types of attributes or character traits that you can choose from.

2. Choosing the social stage of your story

The next chapter deals with the different social stages but, in brief, where you chose to set your story will also pre-determine the type of characters you have as heroes, and pre-determine to a large extent the types of actions they are capable of doing. For example, a story set in the villages of the wild West will most likely result in a John Wayne type hero: usually male, with great skill in physical survival. A story set in Manhattan, a city, will probably suggest that your hero, whether male or female, leads a much less physically demanding life.

3. Who is the hero and what does he want

In order to motivate a script reader to read your script, you must make it crystal clear who the main character is and what it is that he wants. This must be done in the first ten pages, or the script reader will lose interest in your script and stop reading it, and you won't sell your script. During my time as a script reader, I gave a negative report to ninety-five per cent of the scripts I read, and in every case it was because the writer had failed in this task.

There are two aspects to this challenge: What the hero needs (an inner problem) and what the hero wants (an outer problem).

The inner problem can be one involving a character weakness which affects the hero personally (a psychological problem) and holds him back from achieving his goal. An example of this would be the vertigo suffered by Scottie Ferguson in the movie Vertigo. An inner problem can also be a character weakness (a moral weakness) which affects how the character relates to others or which hurts other characters in the story, or affects them adversely. For example the Jim Carey character in Liar Liar.

Or your main character could be suffering from moral as well as psychological weaknesses. What is interesting about these inner problems is that the main character is usually unaware of them until other characters (using what is called moral argument) point them out. For example, Louise says to Ray (the rapist in Thelma and Louise): 'Just for the future, when a woman's crying like that, she's not having any fun.'

The want of a main character – the outer problem – is easier to see, because it is what drives the character throughout the story. The pitfall new writers often fall into at this point, is that they do not make the goal of the main character specific enough. There is a simple test to see if your outer problem is specific or not. Ask yourself this question: Is there a point where the reader can see my main character achieve his goal, or grasp at and fail to do so? A story with the outer goal of 'I want to leave London' is not specific enough and will fail because it is too general. However a story with the goal: 'I need to leave the city by the weekend or suffer dire consequences', is specific because, come Sunday night, we will be able to see whether the main character is still in the city or not.

4. Create empathy for your main characters

The audience (reader) must feel a connection for each and every character in your script. Only then will a reader identify with your story. The reader doesn't need to like your characters, but he does have to identify with them.

Here are some tools for creating empathy.

Firstly, put your hero in a predicament. Nothing draws an audience into your story and creates empathy for a character more effectively than putting him in a predicament. The audience immediately connects with the character and, if you do this successfully, will make the audience fidget and squirm with your character.

Consider the opening of Rainman: Tom Cruise is a complete jerk. But we care about what is happening to him. He is sitting in a car; he is stuck in a traffic jam; his cell phone brings him the news that his business is about to go bankrupt; and his girlfriend is arguing with him. Who hasn't suffered at least one of these calamities?

Secondly, show your hero learning something.

Audiences love to be taught something. This is one of the principal reasons people watch movies: to learn something that they can use in their own lives.

How many times have you seen this in a movie: The assassin is in the tiny room in a parapet overlooking the city square. His target, the President, is about to arrive in a motorcade from the Palace. What does the assassin do? S/he assembles the weapon. We think to ourselves: 'So that's how they do it!' – useful information should we ever need to assassinate someone!

Anything you can do to show your audience how to do something, either by demonstration (as above) or through your character trying to learn, will create empathy for that character. The audience will automatically want to know more. You have succeeded in making the characters in your story personal to the audience.

5. Save The Cat

The American author and screenwriter, Blake Snyder, has developed a very useful story organisation device and he has written two books: Save The Cat and Save The Cat Goes To The Movies. Both books describe the so-called 'Save The Cat' scene in stories. Blake describes the 'Save The Cat' scene as the scene where the main character does something out of his way and, in so doing, shows a kindness perhaps otherwise not evident, thus creating interest in the character. This might also be considered as an additional way to create empathy.

6. Timelock

Timelock is 'an event that must occur within a specific period of time or else dire consequences will befall the hero'. The ticking bomb is the classic example.

When a timelock is used, energy is compressed into a short time space and the drama is significantly increased. It is also a device that the audience is able to relate to through personal experience.

The Bridge On The River Kwai has an interesting double timelock. The first three-quarters of the film are: build the bridge, build the bridge, build the bridge. The last quarter of the movie is: blow it up, blow it up, blow it up.

Hint Successful writers not only use these tools, but do so in a refreshing, bold original and dynamic way. Always try to add a twist if you can.

---

7. The Switch

Just when you think one thing is going to happen, something else does. A switch can be used at any point in your script — in small scenes, or in the larger plot of your story. A switch keeps the audience guessing. They know the ground is uneven. A skilfully constructed switch should not reveal itself as a tool that you have used. The switch is frequently used in advertising — usually for humour — and is very satisfying to watch.

Here is a one page script advertisement for www.raindance.tv written by my partner in the project, Andrew Williams:

```
                    TOO LOUD


INT. SCENE - WHITE SPACE

                    RAINDANCE
          I'm a Raindance film.


                    HOLLYWOOD
          I'm a Hollywood Movie. Hollywood
          is shouting through a loud hailer.


                    RAINDANCE
          Er... Hollywood, why are you shouting?


                    HOLLYWOOD
          What's that? You'll have to speak up
          Raindance, I can't hear you.


                    RAINDANCE
          I said (breath) WHY ARE YOU SHOUTING?!


Hollywood puts down the loud hailer.


                    HOLLYWOOD
          Oh... Why am I shouting? What do you
          mean? That's the great thing about
          Hollywood movies


Hollywood lifts up the loud hailer again.
```

```
                    HOLLYWOOD
          They're very loud! Dolby stereo,
          baby!!! Yeah!!!

                    RAINDANCE
          But what about subtle, intelligent
          dialogue?

                    HOLLYWOOD
          Booooring! Turn up the volume!

                    RAINDANCE
          Atmosphere, intimacy, suspense...

                    HOLLYWOOD
          Dull. Dull. Dull. Surround sound
          explosions, Yeah! 200db - Feel the
          reverb, baby!

                    RAINDANCE
          But I can't hear myself think.

                    HOLLYWOOD
          Exactly, Raindance, Exactly.
```

Notice the brevity of the descriptive passages. Were you able to visualize the scene? Could you hear the hum of the saw or the thud of the hammer?

8. Anticipation

Building anticipation in your audience is one of the oldest and most effective dramatic devices.

I'll explain it later.

9. Stacking and layering

A problem befalls your hero, closely followed by another and another. Stacking.

Sometimes a writer will present the hero with a series of problems which are scattered throughout the story. Gathering several of these problems together and throwing them at your hero one after the other 'stacks' the problems and gives your hero a greater challenge. If you do this effectively, it will make your story more interesting.

Layering the story in different levels is another way to involve your audience. Different audience members notice and pick out layers at different times and, when they do, they feel very pleased with themselves and think 'I wonder if anyone else got that?'. Did you guess the ghost layer in The Sixth Sense before the ending? If you didn't, the ending has a powerful resonance due to the 'Bruce Willis is already dead' layer.

Hint Stacking and layering are real crowd pleasers.

10. Backstory

Sometimes called 'the exposition', the backstory is where you provide the reader with the necessary information to explain to him what happened before the movie started. This information will generally assist in explaining to the audience why your hero wants his/her goal so much – the motivation.

Hint Backstory is what happened to the hero before the movie started and provides information necessary to explain the hero's motivation.

Backstory can be done through a montage (the opening of Tootsie), through dialogue (As Good As It Gets), through narrative (the opening of The Assassination Of Jesse James), or it can be done visually (The Silence Of The Lambs).

Try to find a new, bold, fresh and imaginative way to state backstory.

If you were writing a gangster movie and had to have a scene where the older senior members of the mob explain the ropes to the young Turk, how would you do this?

The cliché is the restaurant scene with everyone sitting around chewing on Havanas.

But if you simply changed the setting to, let's say, the sauna, you would be able to compare the bodies of the old and the young as well as comparing their social power as they sit sweating. It is through novel ways of telling backstory that you will distinguish your writing.

11. Flashbacks and dream sequences

Flashbacks are considered a hackneyed device, and much overused to create backstory. There are two particularly dull flashback techniques: the flipping calendar and the harp music. Decide if there is a better way to show backstory before you write the flashback scene.

Dream sequences are often used to show the motivation of the main character, and to explain his darkest and deepest fears. As with flashbacks, brevity and moderation are, I believe, keys to a commercially acceptable script.

12. The plan

We need to see the basic plan of the hero near the beginning, and we certainly need to know what it is by page ten. Your main character will start with a goal and, in the beginning of the film, will come up with a plan in order to achieve the goal. The beginning shows your hero marshalling all the elements necessary to achieve the goal. But, when he tries out the plan for the first time, it fails. At this moment you are usually in the middle of the film (Act Two).

13. Ghost

It is no longer enough to write a good single genre film. Hollywood does not buy single genre films. Hollywood buys double genre films. For example, romantic comedies and action adventures. Hollywood seeks double or multi genre films like The Sixth Sense

Ghost is that element from the past that the hero must overcome in order to achieve his goal. Without a strong, challenging and painful ghost your story will languish.

Learn how ghost works in the different genres. Study films in the genre you would like to write until you understand ghost thoroughly.

Hint A common reason stories fail is because there is no ghost or the ghost is overcome too easily.

14. Nightmare

Ask yourself: what is the worst possible thing that could happen to your hero, or what is the single most terrible event or situation that could befall your hero? This is not the same as ghost. Ghost is an actual event or person from the past that your hero fears. His nightmare is something that hasn't happened yet.

Nightmare usually takes one of three forms – physical (as in losing health, or life); social (as in losing one's place in society); or psychological (as in being forced to abandon one's beliefs)

Try and see if you can give the nightmare a twist and come up with a new nightmare that will integrate into your story and add depth and texture.

Hint Perhaps your hero's worst nightmare is in fact your own worst nightmare. Have you taken the time to decide what your own worst nightmare is? Can you go further and find an even worse nightmare that could befall you?

15. Foreshadowing

Often a small scene at the beginning of the film foretells the ending of the movie. Or a tragedy is foretold moments before it happens. In Raiders of the Lost Ark, Satipo says 'But nobody has come out of there alive!' Minutes later he is dead. In The Silence of the Lambs, Jodie Foster is told to follow carefully the procedures when visiting Hannibal Lecter because 'you don't want Hannibal Lecter inside your head.'

16. Mirroring

Mirroring is a technique which originated in the theatre of ancient Greece. When the gods were centre stage, they couldn't show emotion, because that would diminish their greatness as deities, so Greek theatre employed a chorus which would mirror the emotion of the audience by chanting: 'isn't the god angry', or, 'isn't the god very sad'.

In movies, when a hero character like Harrison Ford enters a scene and is confronted by, for instance, a rotting corpse, you can't have his character wrinkling his nose and saying 'Gross!'. Instead writers employ a secondary character, a sidekick, who will mirror the emotion of the audience. This secondary character can act out emotional responses which are too large or inappropriate for the hero to respond to, or which he cannot respond to.

Mirroring can be expressed through physical actions or through dialogue. Often a sub-character will mime or imitate the hero's actions.

17. The first ten pages

Agents and producers – the first industry personnel with the ability to purchase your script – will judge your screenplay after reading the first ten pages. If, after ten pages, they like what they see, they will read the next ten, and so on, until they finish the screenplay. The minute their interest in your script founders, they will say 'Next!'. Creating a good beginning is ninety per cent of the battle of selling your script.

In actual fact, industry readers rarely get as far as the first ten pages. They will read the first few pages. If you do not have the reader hooked by then, he will stop reading and your script will not be sold. There are simply far too many scripts in circulation by writers who do know how to hook readers.

The reason that it is so difficult to write an entertaining and compelling script is proven by recent market research in the US which shows how limited the attention span of the American audience is.

In America, it seems that a worker returns home and heads to the medicine cabinet or fridge to get his favourite form of relaxation. He plops down on the couch to surf the hundreds of channels available. The longest a viewer will linger on a channel whilst surfing is fifteen seconds, unless the viewer has a destination programme.

In your script, fifteen seconds represents a quarter page, or about eight lines! In the first eight lines you need to write so compellingly that you entice the reader to commit to reading the next eight lines. Then you have to do it a second and third time. At the bottom quarter of the page there is a new level of writing excellence required: you need to create a sparkling drama so intense that the reader is willing to lift up his hand and turn the page!

The Middle

In the beginning everything seems right and fine with your hero. He has a specific goal, and we see him developing his plan of how to achieve his goal. When he tries the plan the first time, it doesn't work. The hero needs to modify his original plan or create a brand new plan to attain his goal. Then he has to decide whether all of this extra fuss and bother is worth the goal, and he evaluates the amount of energy and commitment required to achieve his goal against the benefits of the goal, if achieved. The hero cannot develop a new goal at this point. If he does, you will be creating a story with a fragmented desire line and the story will fracture.

For example, have you told anyone that you have purchased this book on screenwriting? If you have, did you tell them it was because you wanted to hone your screenwriting skills? Have you told them that you have started reading it? Invariably they will ask you how it is. And you respond with terms like interesting, helpful or challenging.

What would this person say if you said 'I found this screenwriting book good, but have decided to study figure skating instead'? Your friend would roll his eyes and wonder why you have fractured your career line.

Screenplays cannot do this either. When the hero's plan doesn't work he needs to devise a new plan, but retain the same goal.

It is in the middle of a screenplay that the story is played out, where the plot thickens, where the hero's plan is repeatedly challenged, defeated, revised and challenged again. In the middle we get everything we don't expect. Writing the middle is also the most difficult part to achieve – especially if you have not taken time to work out the entire story properly. Know where your story is going, writing the middle will be easier.

Tools useful to the middle

1. Wrinkles and reversal, obstacles and misfortune
The plot thickens. By keeping the audience guessing about what happens next, you create interest in your story.

Tarantino uses this technique in Pulp Fiction but he uses it in reverse. Just when you think everything is fine, the John Travolta and Samuel Jackson characters start reading scriptures and kill someone. Later, they pull out their weapons and, as they are about to kill someone, lose interest and walk away.

2. Predictability
When I read a script and criticize it as being predictable, what I really mean is that it is too predictable, for predictability can be one of the most satisfying of dramatic tools. For example, in Gremlins, the Chinese shopkeeper says that whatever they do they should not get water on the little furry creatures. Of course, what happens?

If you have ever lived with a baby, you will know that babies love to play peek-a-boo. What entertains a baby about peek-a-boo is not that he will make direct eye contact, it is that he just don't know when.

Hint Which is more dramatic? A: You know the hero is going to be killed when he walks through the door, or B: You do not know the hero is going to be killed? The correct answer might be A. Predictability is often used to great effect in the movies as the audience's anticipation of something they know is going to happen creates huge suspense. How many times have you seen this scene: our hero, usually a woman, walks down a dimly lit corridor late at night to her apartment, fumbles with the key and lock; the door creaks open; she enters and is jumped by the villain.

---

3. Anticipation

Anticipation is another useful and powerful dramatic device. By promising something and then making your audience wait, you create anticipation. I will tell you more about this later!

4. Coincidence

Coincidence is another very useful dramatic device, if used skilfully. Audiences will accept one coincidence in a story, but rarely two or more. For example, in E.T., isn't is a lucky coincidence that the little space guy falls to earth and runs into the garden of a house with kids? Next door live some pensioners. Had he run into the pensioners' house, it would have been a very different movie. When multiple coincidences are used, we usually feel that the story is contrived to the point of unbelievability.

Using a coincidence successfully means that you have asked the audience to suspend their disbelief at a crucial point in the movie. If you use a coincidence unsuccessfully your movie will be marred with comments like: 'Great movie until that bit about the spaceman in bed with the mother'

5. Point of no return

Near the middle of the film, storytellers often place a scene where the plan fails yet again, but the hero rallies for another big push to reach his goal. This scene is different from when he first fails however, because the hero realizes that if he fails again, he will be unable to go back to the life he led at the beginning of the story. Attaining his goal has become much more difficult than he imagined and, in order to achieve his goal, the stakes have risen. Failure could result in loss of health/life; loss of social standing (married/divorced; employed/unemployed); or loss of confidence in his or her own ability (crippling self-doubt, or other mental illness). In other words, failure will result in loss in one or more of these three main areas: physical (health, death) sociological (one's place in society – housed/homeless, employed/jobless) or of psycholgical (no self confidence or lack of respect by one's peers).

6. Big Gloom

The big gloom is the point where your hero is so far away from his goal that he wants to give up. But he can't of course, because that would be the end of the movie. But we believe that he will give up. At this point, another character – usually a mentor, a guardian angel or wise old man – comes along and encourages the character to continue.

The big gloom is the low of lows. Christopher Vogler in his excellent book, The Writer's Journey, refers to this scene as the Visit To The Underworld – or Visit To Death – where the demise of others with similar ambitions can be seen, or where the hero sees a vision of his own death, should he fail. Often this is so overwhelming that the hero contemplates giving up.

Writers who exclude this scene automatically make the climax (which generally follows this scene) less dramatic. The best way to create a high is to contrast it with a low.

Endings

Short films are often different. Shorts are often cyclical stories that start and end at the same place. But if, after a minute or two, you don't know what it is about, trouble ensues. With a short, one doesn't have time to recover.

The task of the ending is to wrap up the story promised on page ten, and to tie up all the loose ends.

Often you will see a movie which was pretty good, but you hear yourself saying 'That was a pretty good movie, but what happened to the Danny Devito character that disappeared halfway through the middle of the film?'

This demonstrates a case where the writer has not tied up all the loose ends.

There are two types of endings.

Firstly, cause and effect – usually in stories in the masculine mode or right hand stories. The majority of films have cause and effect endings.

Or secondly, ambiguous endings. This type of ending requires the audience to work harder, making it a less popular ending among industry filmmaker and movie moguls who regard this sort of ending as a riskier financial venture. Did she pull the trigger or not? Did they fall in love or not?

Moguls suggest that adults attend the cinema to seek a sweet seductive falsehood, a bed-time story, and that ambiguous endings make the audience work so hard that they lose interest. Ambiguous endings are therefore harder to sell because they are harder to finance.

Ambiguous endings seem more popular during periods of civil unrest. The Vietnam War era spawned numerous stories with ambiguous endings. My favourite from this era is Easy Rider. In this film, the physical action at the end is very clear – they all die. But what is ambiguous is what the film is saying about social values – reflecting perfectly the ambiguity in the mood of the times, and explaining this low budget film's popularity.

One's ultimate aim at the end of the movie is to create resonance, similar to the resonance in a concert hall as the conductor cuts off the last note of the orchestra. The last chord drifts around and around the hall for a few seconds, creating wonderful resonance. Then the applause starts. No one want to leave their seat.

In the movies, resonance is called buzz. Buzz is the conversation that breaks out (or not) after a screening. Perceptible above the music track over the closing credits, and certainly obvious as the patrons stream past the popcorn stand after a performance, buzz is a highly sought after phenomenon which signifies commercial success or failure.

It was the discovery of buzz that led me to my theory of screenplay structure and my buzz structure theory has helped my own writing.

The Buzz Structure Paradigm

My office is about a twelve-minute walk from the large first-run cinemas in Leicester Square. One of the few advantages of running a film festival is the opportunity to see films on one of the largest screen in Europe. If I have a ticket to a screening starting at 6:30pm, I know I can leave my office at 6:35pm, walk to the cinema and take my seat, missing the trailers and commercials, arriving just in time for the opening 'pop'.

I hate missing the opening few seconds of a film. I have kicked off so many screenings at the festival. I introduce the filmmaker, listen to their introduction, wait for the applause to stop, and usher them up the stairs to the rear. On the way I wave or nod to the projectionist to start the show. I turn halfway up the stairs to see the first frame of the movie hit the screen. I almost hear a 'pffit' as it does so.

After seeing about a hundred films, I noticed that I always arrived at the cinema needing to go to the toilet. Having squeezed every last second into my workday at the office, I was often in considerable physical discomfort by the time I arrived at the cinema. But I didn't want to miss the pop. So I would take my seat in the cinema, sit down, wait for the pop and then find a suitable break in the action to head for a comfort break.

I noticed that in certain movies I left after a few minutes, others after ten minutes, others after a half-hour, and, in some movies, I would sit in physical agony for the entire two hours. I then compared story structure to this experience and realized that a story, two hours long, needs to be pegged in nine different places, or the story will sag. People will hit the toilets or popcorn stands if the story sags.

Have you ever been to a movie with a friend and decided to excuse yourself? When you come back to your seat a few minutes late, what do you say? 'Have I missed anything?' If they say 'No', it means that the writer hasn't achieved his goals.

Here are my nine basic steps to story structure: One page of properly typed and formatted screenplay equals approximately a minute so the numbers below can refer to screen time or page count.

Page 1 – set up the time, the pace and the setting (see next chapter). There is a big different between the opening page of Terminator and that of a romantic comedy like Notting Hill.

Page 3 – say something which refers directly to the theme of the film.

Page 10 – by now you must be able to answer the following questions: who is the hero, what does he want and how does he plan to get it?

Between pages 10 and 30 we see the hero prepare to execute the plan.

On Page 30, something happens that throws the story into a 180-degree swing. The hero's plan does not work.

The hero then attempts to come up with a new plan of action. Remember that the goal cannot change, or you will fracture the story line.

On Page 45 the hero's plan fails again, but perhaps not as dramatically as in the page 30 scene. It is not as traumatic because the hero has already been disappointed once, and now realizes that the achievement of his goal is going to require a much greater commitment than on page 30.

The page 45 scene is more of a psychologically upsetting scene – a bit like when you returned to your parents' house a few weeks after you first moved out. When you went into your room, your clothes and bed were still there, but your father had turned your study desk into a hobby table, and your mom had taken down all your posters. You can still come home and live there if you want to. In other words, you are still able to return to your life as it was on page 10, even if it feels uncomfortable. You

Short Films

Shorts are to features what haikus are to ballads. Shorts have a variety of interesting structures. The principal one is cyclical: where the story starts and ends at the same place.

will probably decide not to, in part because you fear that returning home will make you look weak.

The page 60 scene is very dramatic. The hero realizes for the third time that his plan does not work. If he is to achieve his goal, he will have to enter a strange land so far away from what he knows, that he might not be able to find his way back to his life as it was on page 10 if he fails yet again. This is the point of no return.

Hint The threat of loss of physical well being, one's place in society, or severe psychological damage, makes the point of no return more compelling to the reader.

The hero then takes a huge breath and clenches his fists and heads off with plan number four. Suddenly, on page 75, he realizes that this new plan won't work either, and now he is isolated and/or lost with little or no hope of succeeding. Plus, he is now faced with the prospect of losing everything.

I call this point — the point where the hero is as far as it is possible from his goal — the Big Gloom.

Hint Sometimes referred to as the visit to the underworld: where the hero looks around and sees the corpses of others who have tried to write a screenplay and failed; or the visit to death — where one's own death is foretold.

Suddenly in the midst of his despair, a guardian angel, or a kid on a skateboard comes by, and finds out what the hero wants. This person offers a golden titbit of advice. 'So that's how you do it'. Your hero heads off towards the ultimate test with plan number five. The page 90 scene is the Final Battle. Winning means success, losing means losing everything.

Hint Your hero stands to lose in any or all of three different categories in the final battle: Physically, sociologically, psychologically.

The last pages are the resolution, where the story is summed up. It can vary from a few lines in length, as in North By Northwest, to several pages, as in Castaway or The Assassination Of Jesse James.

It is important to note that these page numbers are guidelines only, and can be moved backwards and forwards in a fluid way. You can also reorder the key scenes, although most commercially successful storytelling lays out the scenes in this order.

figure 4.2
Elliot Grove's Nine-Step Structure

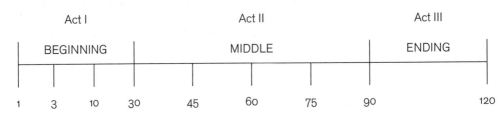

Syd Field writes that the page
30 scene should fall on or about
page 30. Robert Mckee teaches
that it must be on page 27. I
have met many writers suffering
from various personality stress-
related disorders because,
no matter how many times
they have played with the line
spacing, their page 30 scene is
landing on pages 26 or 28.

European vs. US scripts

American movies tend to be 120
pages/minutes long. European
scripts are closer to ninety. In
a European script, the page
30 scene is generally closer to
pages 20 – 24, the point of of
no return as early as 45 to 50.
But pages 1, 3 and 10 scenes
are similar in European and
American scripts.

Interestingly, the page 30 scene
in Thelma and Louise (the rape
scene) is on page 22.

Nobody knows anything. Trust
your instincts.

In order to explain how buzz works, let us look at three different kinds of movies: A movies, B movies, C movies.

In a C movie, you sit down and watch the movie. You may leave the cinema several times to make telephone calls or buy popcorn. You probably will leave before the final credits start to roll if you feel you can guess the ending. As you leave the cinema, you almost forget that you have seen a movie. When you get home the telephone rings. You answer. It's your best friend in the world asking you what you did today. You reply with news from the office, the fact that you bumped into so-and-so, comment on a story you saw on the net, and oh yes, you forgot. You saw a movie. What was it like? You can't really remember.

B Movies are different. You probably stay in the screening for the entire movie. At the end of the screening, you pause and turn in the aisle to look at the credits for a moment. When you get into the street, you are still pondering one of the penultimate scenes. When you get home the telephone rings. The first thing you say is: 'I saw a movie tonight'. What was it like? 'Pretty good. There is this really interesting character (usually played by Danny Devito) – you have got to see it – but the character just sort of peters out after an hour.' In other words, the writer missed one of the structure points.

Have you seen a B movie or a C movie?

Hint Most screenplays fail because the reader cannot see a hero with a clearly defined goal in the first ten pages.

An A movie is totally different from a B movie or a C movie. You are glued to your seat for the entire time, no matter what physical discomfort you are in. At the end of the movie you lean over to your friend and comment on it. Everyone else in the cinema is doing the same. You stay and watch the credits, allowing the last dregs of ambience to wash over you. You contemplate the movie the entire way home. When you get home you rush to the telephone and call your best friend in the world. 'You have got to see this movie!' And it is the first thing you are conscious of when you wake up the next morning. If you are the author of such a script, the money movie moguls will be beating a path to your door.

Hint Box office is determined by word of mouth. Good buzz or, good word of mouth, will do more to sell tickets or DVDs than advertising, marketing or publicity.

Other Structure Ideas

Often your story will be coming together, but you will feel unsatisfied with the way you are telling the story. Here are some ideas about finding a so-called structure that will enable your story to unfold.

1. Laundry lists

I do a great deal of public speaking these days. When I started, a friend lent me a book on how to prepare for public speaking. It suggested creating 'laundry lists'. You have probably seen laundry lists in newspapers and magazines: The Seven Secrets to Financial Freedom, The Three Ways to Improve your Love Life and so on. Indeed, in this book you will see a whole series of laundry lists.

There are times when such a laundry list will assist you in structuring your story. The advantage of a laundry list is that you can immediately create a sense of purpose and reason within your story that is very helpful, especially if you are skipping over huge expanses of time or geography.

You might have noticed a title card halfway through a movie, something like 'Moscow, three days earlier', for example.

A student in the Writers' Lab was wrestling with a story involving reincarnation: one character over seven key ages of civilisation. The individual stories were shaping up nicely, but the challenge was to try and hook them together so that they made sense, and permitted the reader to suspend disbelief.

We came up with the idea of having a laundry list – in this case seven meals, seven different time zones, and seven different days: Monday, Tuesday and so on. First up was dinner with Cleopatra, next was a meal in a Roman palace, then there was a scrap of bread in a Nazi concentration camp, and finally, coffee in a Manhattan coffee shop. An elegant solution to the challenging opportunity, we thought, and one that would break down a reader's resistance to the topic.

2. Navajo story circle

This technique springs from the traditional oral storytelling tradition practised to this day by the Navajo. Each evening the men sit around a fire and relate their version of the day's events. Perhaps one of them was riding high on the plateau and saw a speeding car travelling down on the plain. Perhaps another one was walking down the road when the car sped by covering him in rocks and dust. And maybe a third was actually in the car pleading with the driver to slow down. Soon, all the stories and people connect, with each individual's version of the event adding new depth.

This technique is widely used in episodic television shows like 24, Murder One, and Lost. Movies where this has been employed include 21 Grams and Jim Jarmusch's Mystery Train.

3. Natural storytelling Dogme style

Every screenwriter has, at one point or another, suffered through the torturous hours of attempting to tap into the mines of creativity. There is so much pressure to come up with something fresh and interesting and, most importantly, an idea that no one has ever come up with before.

Mogen Rukov, head of scriptwriting at The National Film School of Denmark, developed a tool called The Natural Story to relieve the tormented souls of writers and provide a deceivingly simple solution for coming up with creative ideas for a script. One need look no further than the familiar rituals of everyday life to find inspiration – life is unpredictable and dramatic and yet nothing more than a series of familiar events.

'What is original is just a small change in the deeply familiar... All that is deeply familiar to us is a series of stories, stories whose mechanics we understand completely. It is a prerequisite for creating something surprising or interesting that the foundation is something we know the mechanics of.'
– Mogen Rukov

Making a cup of coffee, driving to work, even falling in love are all natural stories – stories in which we know the events that will unfold. Great ideas don't appear to successful writers out of the depths of the cosmos but from the reflections of their own lives, routines and traditions.

Rukov encourages his students to use their natural stories to find subjects to write about. But, in order to maintain creative stamina, Rukov preaches humility. Listen to critique; new ideas are often better ideas and don't be afraid to lose sight of the original concept. Try and avoid the trap of new writers who are afraid to engage friends and potential producers. The end product is all that matters.

Anders Thomas Jensen and Suzanne Bier talk of writing Dogme style: 'Writing a Dogme film isn't that different to writing a normal script. You're not allowed superficial violence and action. There are some things that you can't do'.

Susanne Bier: 'Dogme tends to lend itself to realistic story telling'. The limitations actually add to the work and sharpen your perceptions of what you're dealing with.

And the Dome 95 co-founder Kristian Levring: 'For example, you can't use flashback. Or solve problems with visuals – purely visual storytelling is difficult with Dogme – you can't use slow motion. For example.

'Lars Von Trier worked closely with a professor at the Danish Film School, Mogen Rukov, developing a theory called "natural" or "organic story" – the idea being that events in the story should flow from the story's inner life. A stripped down method of story telling.'

Many writers I now work with find this approach to be very stimulating and freeing. Stories that spring from so-called natural story can have a freshness and zing lacking in scripts produced by formula.

4. Nature

This might be too obvious or simplistic for your story, but nature gives many lessons on structure. Trees have branches – there are branching stories like Richard Linklater's Slacker. Whirlpools are spirals and spiral stories suck you deeper and deeper into the story, like The Usual Suspects. Streams move slowly, taking you over little eddies and whirlpools where you swirl down and examine relationships for a while, only to bob up a few yards downstream. The Thin Blue Line is an example of this. Perhaps you will find inspiration for your story by observing nature.

5. Tubes and trains

Have you ever stood in front of a train or tube map in a major city like New York, Tokyo, Paris or London trying to figure out how to make connections? Did you notice the major stations where several lines intersect and, by cutting from one line to another, you will get to your destination?

What if each train line represents a character – the red line the hero, for example – and the other lines representing the other characters. What if each station represents a scene, and in each station some of the other lines (or characters) intersect? Sometimes the story will switch from one line to another at one of these junctions. Or, if you like, you could keep on one line for the entire journey, because it is the most direct.

Why not try to plot out your story structure like a tube or a train map?

Planning Your Structure

The words Story Structure can be baffling to screenwriters. Structure is the term used to describe the way a story unfolds. In real life, structure could be used to describe the way human beings solve real life problems.

Fill in the following blanks as a planning tool to assist in plotting the essential elements of your story.

Online Resources

1. Problem/Need

Problem - the predicament your hero is in at the start of the story.

Need — the inner problem, which is preventing your hero from having a better life.

2. Goal

The test of a suitable goal is when you can see an actual moment when your hero achieves or loses it.

What your hero wants more than anything else and seeks over the course of the story. This cannot change. Be specific. Make sure we can see a time where the hero achieves their goal, or fails to.

3. Motive

Why your hero wants the goal

4. Stakes

What happens if your hero fails or succeeds?

Hint The stakes must be high and put the hero to the supreme test. If he loses, he must lose big. Physical. Sociological. Psychological.

5. Opponent

The relationship between the hero and opponent is the single most important relationship in your story. The opponent is the person who is competing with the hero for his goal, and/or is the person who stands in the way of the hero.

Describe how each opponent will attack your hero.

6. The Plan

Characterization

Notice how often this section refers to specific elements of character. You should re-read this chapter after you have read the following chapter on Characters.

The plan is the set of guidelines the hero uses to overcome the opponent and achieve the goal. Since the opponent is the main obstacle to the hero's goal, we also need to see what the opponent's plan is.

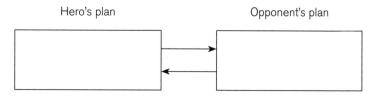

Next, try to list the action and reaction between the hero and opponent as each character tries to achieve his goal.

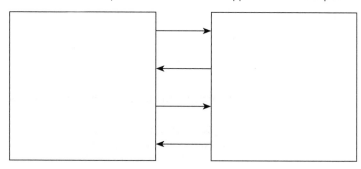

7. Battle

The final battle is where the opponent and hero fight, and the outcome determines who achieves his goal.

List the characters in conflict. You would be surprised how many screenwriters aren't sure who should be in the final battle. This is a definite sign that the character essays are incomplete. If this is the case, you need to stop now and go back to the character essays.

8. Convergence of space

This refers to the narrow space, or gauntlet, where the final battle takes place. Note how many climax scenes are on a rooftop, a ledge, or in an alleyway – anywhere that is small or confined. Squeezing that final battle into a tiny space heightens the emotion and ratchets up the drama of a scene.

Where will your final battle take place?

9. Similarities between the hero and the opponent

A good battle exists when both the hero and the opponent share attributes. Often the opponent is stronger than the hero. See if you can list these similarities.

[ ]

10. The Big Gloom

What is the lowest point of the conflict?

[ ]

11. Self-revelation

What is it that your hero learns about himself or herself by going through his/her struggle? Just as in our own lives we learn as we achieve or fail to achieve, our goals.

Psychological revelation – what the hero learns about himself.

[ ]

Moral revelation – what the hero learns about treating others.

[ ]

Moral decision – where the hero proves his moral revelation by actually doing the right/wrong thing.

[ ]

Finding the Ending

One of my daughters is a ballerina. I attended a rehearsal to watch her learning a new dance. The choreographer asked the pianist to play a section of music, about twelve bars long. He placed the dancers in their final positions, and they practised getting into that position. Listening to the music again, he would again place them in their starting positions.

He didn't move on until they knew where their 'story' ended, and where it started. He then showed them the three or four positions within the beginning and end, and let the dancers flow them together until it looked seamless.

I think this is an excellent working practice to follow as screenwriters. If you really want to know where your story is going to end, you really need to know where it is going to start. And often the best way of knowing where a story is going to start is by deciding boldly and firmly where it is going to end. Then work backwards and choose the beginning that best enables you to tell the story.

Comedy writers often work backwards from the punch or payoff line.

Summary

1. Find the basic Premise for your story.

2. Be prepared for change.

3. When you are stuck ask yourself what the hero's worst nightmare is.

4. Test your premise on your friends.

5. Change, revise, rewrite. You are finding your story.

6. Make certain you do this in parallel with finding out who your main characters are.

You are now ready to explore characterization.

5 Characters

THERE ARE TWO ways to approach developing a story idea: The first way is to come up with a concept – a short five to eight word phrase that sums up the entire idea for a movie. The second way is by creating memorable characters.

Think back to the last time you went to see an A movie (see previous chapter). When you got up the next morning, wasn't the ambience and essence of the movie still hanging over you? And what did you remember from the movie? The plot points? Or the people you met the previous night at the cinema? Of course you will remember a couple of the major plot points, but aren't the people you met at the cinema more memorable than the details of the story line? Have you ever watched a movie you really loved again a few weeks or months later? Do you not think to yourself 'I remember the character, but I forgot that particular scene'.

My greatest learning in the seven years since I wrote this book, is that characters are the meat and bones of any story – of any movie. In fact it might not be a bad idea to ignore the previous chapter on structure, for I believe that structure and characters are completely interwoven. Any discussion of structure that ignores characterization is very unhelpful. A good story will have fascinating and interesting characters whose personalities help create the structure of the story as surely as the people you know best in your personal life each have their own stories, and so create the narrative 'structure' to their own lives.

Most screenwriting books will labour the point about characters growing and developing (usually with a line drawing zigzagging up the page), and suggest that a successful screenplay must have characters who grow and develop. Occasionally, to explain a movie like Leaving Las Vegas, they concede that a downward spiral might also qualify as character development. Structure without truly great characters is unlikely to create an interesting story.

Isn't structure the way your character's story unfolds? In other words, at the beginning of a movie we usually see the hero in a predicament. We also see that he has a specific goal. The hero then develops a plan, which, based on his or her experience, he considers to be the most likely way to achieve his goal. Of course, the original plan rarely works, and the hero is forced to make new plan after plan based on new information and new experience.

We, the audience, love to watch this story because we hope to find a new way to solve problems in our own lives. It is very similar to your plan in life. Let's say your overriding goal is to write an excellent screenplay. All the rest of us aspiring screenwriters are desperate to see what techniques and tools you employ in order to create a great screenplay. You try this series of tools and techniques and we say 'What a great idea!' or 'Ooops! That doesn't work for me'. In our excitement, we just know that this alternative plan will definitely work. But our hero, in his/her naïveté, has chosen this route, a route condemned to failure. But do you know what? It almost works. And so on until the end of the story. At the very end we either say: 'So that's how you write a great screenplay!' (happy ending) or 'I told you that wouldn't work!' (sad ending). In this case the way in which the hero tackles the problem at hand creates the structure for the movie as we follow the hero's ups and downs.

Creating Characters

How many times have you read in movie fan sites about the unlikely casting of an actor (it's usually Danny De Vito) in a part deemed unsuitable for him by the great and the good? What inevitably happens is that this actor gets an Oscar nomination.

Let's talk about getting Oscar nominations for the actors (characters).

Casting your movie

The first step is to do what any casting agent does for a movie: create a list of the principal characters needed for your film. As you work on the basic premise, you will develop a list of characters. Start a blank page for each character. Remember, you may end up with some characters that you don't use – almost like an audition. These characters may not be needed for your movie but might nevertheless shed some light on the main characters. Treat these characters with great respect. You never know when you might need to call one of them as a witness!

Resumé

Casting Agent Ros Hubbard does exactly this when she is looking for actors.

Summarize the character's role in a brief paragraph. Pretend you are placing an ad in a newsletter for auditions that goes out to actors.

Role

Each character can be described as a friend or enemy of the hero – opponent, ally-opponent, opponent-ally or sub-plot character.

RAINDANCE WRITERS' LAB: WRITE AND SELL THE HOT SCREENPLAY

In order to develop strong and compelling characters, describe each character in a series of different ways. Use additional paper if necessary.

Traits

Character traits come in three flavors; Physical (blind, limps, stutters, strong), Sociological (homeless, rich, married, ill), and Psychological (lies, has vertigo, claustrophobic, cocky).

Traits are what make your characters distinctive. Giving your character interesting traits is what breaks down the stereotypes normally associated with Hollywood movies.

Traits are the best way for a writer to break down stereotypes.

All bankers are not bald, fat and dressed in a three piece suit. But, if there is a banking character in your movie, and the director casts a short fat bald actor to play the part, and orders wardrobe to place him in a three piece suit, then we pretty much have the stereotypical banker. But what if you use the character traits tool and give your banker a love of acid jazz? Immediately the stereotype is broken.

Hint Use the technique of magnification: give your character a trait and then make it more and more obvious. For example, in Good Will Hunting, Matt Damon plays a janitor at a university. Our pre-conceived notion of janitor is that they are not too bright. The university professor is perplexed that someone is solving complicated equations, but none of the students admit to it. It is then revealed that the mathelete is the janitor himself. And the final twist, the final magnification, is that he has taught himself. Beware, however, the risk of magnifying and failing to get the audience to suspend its disbelief.

List all the traits that make your character unique and which break the preconceived notions your audience may have about your character.

Ghost

Ghost is that thing from the past which your main character is still afraid of, or embarrassed by. Ghost takes different shapes in different genres. For example, in horror, the ghost takes a physical embodiment. In detective stories ghost is called personal crime. In Basic Instinct the Michael Douglas character plays a cop who accidentally shot and killed a German tourist about eighteen months before the movie started. His

Look into your own life to see if you can find something you are hiding. Confront your own ghost and see if you can use it within your story. Chances are, if you are able to tell us what your ghost is, we will be magnetized, and there is a chance you might overcome your ghost in the process.

Can there be a better reason for writing a screenplay?

nickname is 'Shooter' – a name he abhors. When he visits Sharon Stone for the first time, he sees all the newspaper clippings from his past laid out on a table. She enters, greeting him as 'Shooter'. At the end of the movie, he shoots and kills a hooded figure he is certain is the killer. When he pulls back the hood, he sees that he has shot his girlfriend. This gives that moment a very deep resonance.

Hint The ghost must be painful to the hero, and something which is not easily overcome.

Write your character's ghost here.

Nightmare

Online Resources

Nightmare is that event in the future of which your main character is terrified. What is the very worst thing that can befall your character?

Values

What are the qualities that are good about your character?

What are the qualities that are bad or weak about your character?

Writing exercise

This is the fun part: getting to know your characters. At the risk of repeating myself, remember that successful writers never skip this next step. Create a blank page for each character and write the character names

figure 5.1
Characterization Chart

Resumé 1 Character Name

Role

Resumé 2 Character Name

Role

Resumé 3 Character Name

Role

Resumé 4 Character Name

Role

and descriptions. Then create a free-form essay about the character – either in point form, or as a story. Push the boundaries of what you know about each character until you know them as intimately as you know a best friend in real life. A good exercise is to buy a newspaper, open it at random, and ask: 'How would the character react to this headline?'

Now summarize the main attributes and traits of each character in a line or two.

Now go back to the cast list on the previous page and try to incorporate this new information as concisely as possible into each character's resumé. When you have finished the character essays, give yourself the quiz below. You should be able to answer all of the questions, without hesitation, in under sixty seconds:

1. How old is your character?

2. What star sign are they?

3. Where were they born?

4. Where did they go to school?

5. What grades did they get?

6. What does their father do?

7. Who is their closest friend?

```



```

8. Which is their favourite TV programme?

```



```

9. If they were a magazine, which title would they be?

```



```

10. What would they wear to meet you at the theatre?

```



```

11. What is their favourite music?

```



```

12. If they were to buy their lover a spontaneous gift, what would it be?

```



```

You are likely to meet very interesting characters while researching your main characters. What to do if the main character's uncle is more interesting than the main character himself? Simply take the main character aside, thank him for his time and effort, tell him you admire his work and that you hope to work with him on your next project.

You should know the characters in your movie so well that you are able to answer these questions immediately. If you take longer than 60 seconds to answer these questions, it probably indicates that you do not know your characters well enough. Go back to your character essays and write some more! The writing part is fun, because it is in doing so that you are meeting new people.

You may want to try writing your character essay in prose. Here are the first few lines of a ten page character essay I wrote for a project: Larry Raine is tired of hearing everybody saying 'What a Loser' every time he steps out of his office. Out of money, but not out of his dream, Larry is determined to get his movie 'The Big One' made.

Until I wrote this, I had never considered the main character from his own point of view – only from others. This exercise really helped me.

Creating empathy

Unless a reader can connect or identify with each of the main characters, he will not be drawn into the story. This does not mean that the reader has to like the main characters. But he does need to feel involved in their personal issues. A useful technique for creating empathy is to personalize the character to the audience. Successful storytellers typically do this in two ways: either by showing the character learning something, or by putting him in a predicament.

Hint Successful stories make the audience care for each and every character on the screen, even the ugliest and vilest of them.

Avoiding stereotypes

Not only are stereotypical characters boring, but they also promote prejudice. The stereotypical characterization of black people in Hollywood movies has taken over two generations to live down, and is still a problem.

Stereotypical characters in movies do exist – usually because Hollywood production companies, encumbered by major stars, rewrite characters in their movies to suit the business and entertainment profiles of the stars. Tom Cruise will only appear in movies where he plays a certain type of role. Stereotypes exist in everyday life as well. When considering your characters, you most likely will think of them in terms of their occupations. This is similar to your daily life. You may have forgotten the name of the person you met at a function or social networking session last night, but you probably will remember the person's occupation.

A collection of characters listed by occupation will spark stereotypes in a reader's imagination.

For example, a lawyer, carpenter, nurse, or homeless person will all bring to your story pre-conceived notions about the character that might not be suitable for your story. Probably the easiest way to break stereotypes is by looking at the traits of your characters.

Here is an exercise I did in the Writers' Lab – the evening script workshop I have run at Raindance since 1995.

Give each of these character stereotypes a trait we wouldn't expect.

Character stereotype – traits that break the mould

A master of character trait is Charlie Kaufman. Look again at his movies, in particular Being John Malevich and Eternal Sunshine of the Spotless Mind, and note how skilful he is with the use of character traits.

Banker – bald, fat, wears a suit, loves acid jazz.
Homeless person – dirty, a working knowledge of medieval literature.
Politician – dishonest, flirtatious, an expert sport referee.

The key to creating successful traits for your characters is to fit a square peg into a round hole.

Hint When a reader reads your character's traits and says 'Wait a minute. I don't buy that!', you have failed to get him to suspend his disbelief.

Tools For Creating Character Development

Pared down, stories are very simple. E.T. falls to earth and has to get home. Character development makes your story complex. How your characters grow will depend on their goal and the plan they develop to achieve their goal. It will also depend on how they learn to cope with the changing demands of their conquest, and by their ability to adapt to the challenges that oppose them.

1. Goal

The most common flaw of the 2500+ scripts I read and analysed is that the hero did not have a clearly defined goal. A clearly defined goal is one where you are able to see a moment where the hero achieves (or loses) that which he aspires to.

New writers often present me with scripts where the goal of the main character is 'I want a better life' or, 'I want to move away from the city'. These are too general. A story with these types of goals means that the hero is involved in much internal thought and reflection making this a story more suited for a novel.

Instead of 'I want to leave the city', the goal should be 'I have to leave the city in a week or else dire consequences befall me'. This is a more specific goal because, at the end of the week, we can measure how successful the character has been in achieving his goal.

A different tack would be to find another hook you can hang your storyline on — a hook that would give you the chance to explain why you think your hero wants or needs to leave the city.

As mentioned in the previous chapter, another common fault of new writers is breaking the storyline by changing the goal half way through the script. A storyline can bend, but not change. For example, if you told your friends and relatives that your goal is to write a screenplay, they would not be impressed if you suddenly announced that you had decided to become a guitarist instead. But if you tell them that you are first going to hone your writing skills on a short story, your friends will forgive you, as this is still a creative writing exercise which is consistent with your ultimate goal.

2. Inner need

Personalize your story. Give your hero a second problem to solve at the same time as he is trying to attain his main goal. This is a deep inner problem, difficult to describe (unlike the main goal). Doing this will add a dimension to your story and give it an emotional base. The strangest thing about writing is that you may not realize what true emotional need, what inner problem, your hero has. To find a truly powerful inner problem see if you can look at your own life and see what your own inner problem is. This can be a painful process as you delve deep inside yourself and confront your own ghosts and nightmares. Through writing you may discover what your own inner problems are, and you might be able to solve them. Surely this is a result worthy in its own right of the effort to conceive and finish a screenplay?

If you do not know what your inner problem is, or fail to identify a strong inner problem for your hero, it will be apparent in your script.

One of the first scripts I read was a story set on a mythical island in the Caribbean. The story was based on the American invasion of Granada. The General and his wife were sent by Washington to quell the rebellion, and were accommodated in a five star hotel. Once I accepted this fact, I noticed that whenever the General and his wife were in the hotel suite, they had no physical contact. When the General had to leave in the morning to go downstairs to battle, he would bend over and peck his wife goodbye with a very tentative kiss. I called the writer (a forty-something male from a small northern city) and told him that he had to resolve the sexual relationship between the husband and wife. At this point he broke down and told me that, after sixteen years of marriage to a good woman, he had told his wife he was gay, and they had just split up. If he had included this gay element to his military story, it would have had so much more power. And the story would have been timely. It was written about the time of Bill Clinton's inauguration and the gay controversy sweeping the military at the time.

3. Weaknesses

Inner problems can also be defined as two distinct types of weakness.

Firstly, a psychological weakness – a weakness that holds the hero back, but affects only himself. These weaknesses come in three types: physical (blind), sociological (single), and psychological (shy).

Secondly, moral weakness – a weakness that hurts other people, an immoral act or series of acts that the character might not be aware of, or for which has created a false justification which hurts other people.

4. Revelations

Another interesting point is that the hero will not be able to achieve his outer goal until he has solved or deals with his inner problems. And how can anyone solve a problem unless he knows what the problem is?

At the start of your story, your hero will not realize what his inner problems are, but, over the course of the story, there will be moments when the light bulb goes on and he says something like 'So that's how I got here!' (psychological revelation) or, 'That's what I am doing wrong!' (moral revelation). These 'light bulb' moments are called revelations, either psychological or moral. One can have many such revelations in the screenplay, but ideally you should aim to build them in intensity towards the end of your script.

The best way to illustrate this is to look at your own life: you will not achieve your outer goals until you resolve your own inner problems. I am the perfect example.

Audiences love to learn details from the screen that they can incorporate into their own lives. Writers have something to give to an audience. Basing your script on your own life makes it personal and valuable.

Much has been made of the fact that I started Raindance Film Festival on my own with a hundred dollars. The festival grew to a certain size, but my goal was to make it the best independent film festival in Britain – if not Europe and the world. But my progress ground to a halt after five years. I just couldn't figure out how to make it any better. I tried everything, and worked like a dog in the process. My goal was thwarted, not by an opponent, but by my own inner problems, both psychological and moral. But I certainly couldn't see them. I didn't even know that I had a problem until I switched the lights on one Tuesday morning after a long weekend and, by some miracle, was able to see the Raindance office in a new light. Papers were stacked to the ceiling. Desks were over flowing with files, unpaid bills, paid bills and memo pads with important telephone numbers. The mail arrived and with it a warning letter from the tax man. Then it hit me. I had to get organized. That was the thing that was holding me back. My inner problem was that I didn't force myself to do the one thing I hate – paperwork. I went to work. That day I threw out sixty bags of garbage. I hired an accountant, registered the company, and got everything organized. In that process I also discovered a moral problem: I hadn't been paying people on time either. Since then, Raindance has flourished to the extent where I can see it approaching my outer goal. And, other than dealing with my inner problems, I haven't actually done anything differently.

Hint Your hero will only achieve his outer goal when he is able to conquer his inner problems.

5. The plan

Your hero will have a clearly defined goal 'I want to…' and this must be specific. Avoid the common flaw first-timers make with their scripts when the hero does not have a clearly defined and specific goal. As in real life, any character without a clear plan to getting what he wants is uninteresting to the reader/audience. Make the plan as concise as possible.

Hint A goal is something that your hero reaches at a specific moment in time and either achieves, or loses. 'I want to rob a bank' is not particularly specific. But 'I want to rob that bank on the corner before he does' leaves your audience in no doubt as to your hero's goal.

The plan can be physical, like the map in the opening of Raiders of the Lost Ark which shows the location of the cave where the idol lies.

The plan can be a physical object that needs to be attained or delivered, such as the FedEx package in Castaway. The plan can be social, such as Dustin Hoffman needing acting work in Tootsie. The plan can be psychological, as in most love stories.

The plan can either work or not work. If the plan does work, then the drama in the story comes from the hero trying to find out how to make it work.

If the plan does not work then the hero is challenged to find a new plan. In the process the hero discovers that the goal is even more difficult to achieve than he or she thought and he has to commit further to the quest for the goal, or else abandon the goal. By choosing to commit further, by trying to find a better plan, the hero has to expose him/herself to risk.

Hint If you abandon the goal then the story is over. If you change the goal, you fracture the story line. You can however change the plan and continue the story.

---

6. Ghost

We have spoken earlier about the ghost in a story. A satisfactory ghost is that thing from the past which is difficult and painful for the hero to overcome. Stories without ghost lack depth and texture.

7. Motivation and desire

Why your hero wants something is important too. Try to find out the motivation of your hero.

There is outer motivation, as in Witness, where Samuel Lapp witnesses a murder. It is the motivation to discover the villain that propels the story along.

There is inner motivation to action too. Sometimes your hero will react to a situation based on his or her inner problems. This can be because of fear, or a deep-seated belief of what is right or wrong within the context of the morality you have defined in your story.

8. Characters on the brink

Building characters that matter to an audience is made easier if you show characters on the brink. It is also a great tool to use in order to create empathy for your characters. List the brink scenes in your own life: childbirth, marriage, divorce, homelessness, bankruptcy, getting a windfall, illness, death, redundancy, addiction and so on. A story has more power if the characters are on the brink at the start of the picture.

For example, in Ghostbusters, the main characters have just been made redundant. In Gone With The Wind, the nation is on the verge of war.

Relationships of the Hero

One mistake new writers make is placing their hero alone without relationships with the other characters. This results in a weak hero, cardboard cut out opponents, and uninteresting minor characters. In many ways, a character is defined by who he or she is not. This can result in passive characters which are more suited to novels. That's why the single most important step in creating great characters is to compare all of the characters to the hero. For added contrast, complexity, and excitement, make sure that the entire cast of your movie is as different as possible from each other.

Every time the audience sees your hero compared to, or relating to, another character, they see the hero in new ways – this adds dimension and texture to your story. It is the same in life. The reason offices organize parties is so the heroes of the workplace can be seen in an informal atmosphere with their loved ones thus shedding another ray of light on their characters. By doing so, the secondary characters are also forced to become complete human beings who are as complex and interesting as your hero.

1. The hero and the opponent

The most important relationship in your movie is the relationship between your hero and his/her main opponent. How these two characters interact with each other determines the drama of the story. It is curious that many new writers ignore this relationship.

Another common flaw is choosing the wrong character as the opponent. This is the result of not exploring the entire cast list through the characterization essays.

2. Creating a good opponent

A good opponent is a double of the hero. Which means that the opponent is human too – human with weaknesses, failings and strengths, just like the hero. The opponent will have moral weaknesses preventing him/her from acting properly towards others. The opponent will have an inner need, based on the moral weakness, as does the hero. The opponent will have a goal, preferably similar to that of the hero.

The opponent will be stronger, smarter, more cunning, better looking, (depending on your story) than the hero. This allows the opponent to put pressure on the hero, forcing the hero to stretch beyond his normal ability. For example, I would not be a suitable opponent for Stallone in Rocky, because the outcome would be a foregone conclusion.

3. Values

We all live life according to certain values. Your hero and his opponents do as well. Each of your characters base their actions on a certain set of values which they believe is right, even if these values contradict your own personal values, or the values of society and the culture we live in. Good stories set up the values of the hero with the values of the opponent. We watch the movie, waiting to see which set of values is superior within the confines of the story. Thus we can watch a movie like True Romance and cheer for Christian Slater, the bank robber.

A wonderful element about writing a story is that you get a chance to explain your own value system to the reader. Sometimes your story will be constructed to portray your values directly. Other times, the story can directly oppose your personal values using tools like parody.

4. Moral argument

Stories with an evil opponent are rarely as compelling as a story with an opponent who possesses both good and bad qualities. Evil opponents operate in a mechanical and inhuman way that alienates us. Again, true life serves us well. There is rarely a situation with clearly defined good and evil, right and wrong. Good stories have characters who believe they are right and can argue their cases to each other, and to the audience.

5. Achilles heel

The opponent should be the one person best able to attack the hero. The opponent should know the hero and his weaknesses so well, that when he attacks, the hero either has to overcome his weaknesses or be destroyed. Often the hero knows the opponent. Furthermore, the hero often is not aware of his weaknesses until the opponent reveals them.

Hint The hero learns from the opponent.

Think of drama as a football match. If the best team in the world is playing a bunch of high school dropouts, then the best team will score every time they get the ball and the audience will be bored. If, on the other hand, the best team in the world is playing the second best team in the world, each team will have to play their best game ever, and the audience will go wild. Similarly in drama, the hero and the opponent should drive each other to greatness.

6. Creating contrast with the hero

If two runners are told to deliver a package to the same address, which is more interesting? If they take different routes, or the same route? If they follow the same route, it becomes a race against each other, with all the drama and excitement of a competition, because the audience can compare the two runners.

Similarly, in a good story, the hero and opponent will share many of the same qualities and attributes. We can then compare the hero and opponent trying to achieve the same thing, and can see which method works best. The Bible has a marvellous tale about Moses. Moses needed to get some soldiers together to go fight the enemy. When he asked for volunteers he was flooded with applicants. Not knowing what to do, he took the men to the river and asked them to drink. The men drank from the river in different ways – some lapping, some scooping water with their hands. He chose the men who stood and scooped the water because they had an eye out for danger and they became his elite. The contract between the hero and opponent is powerful only when both characters have strong similarities. Each then presents a slightly different approach to the same life problem. It is in the similarities that the crucial differences and the instructive differences become clear.

Another advantage of making your hero and opponent similar, is that you keep the hero from being a totally good guy, and the opponent from being totally bad. This allows greater audience identification.

Hint The conflict between the hero and the opponent is not about good and evil. It is about the two well rounded characters who have strengths and weaknesses.

Stage of the Relationship

Sometimes it is useful to explore the stage of the relationship between the two main characters. Often the length of time they have known each other will provide a useful clue as to how the relationship has developed, along with a few hints as to where your writing can take it.

I have been working on such a stage for a love story, and have developed the following theory of how a male-female relationship could develop over time.

Blending (first year to 18 months)

Blending is the first stage of being together – a stage where all differences are overlooked. Using the same toothbrush, drinking from each

Characterization resources can be found in the unlikeliest places like newspapers and magazines such as Hello, OK! and The National Enquirer. These are full of true life stories that document character traits of heroes and opponents.

others glasses, being together all the time are all things that are deemed sexy. Blending is all about new experiences and self-improvement.

If one person loves classical music then the other will immerse himself in it to learn what the other person appreciates so much. This might start in a process of sharing and lead to a lifetime of enjoyment.

I have a friend in multi-media whose partner went to university and was studying for some sort of very difficult degree. He told me that he actually felt cleverer because his new girlfriend took such an interest in everything he was doing – to the point that he gained in confidence and spoke up at work.

During blending, partners appropriate qualities from each other and integrate them into their own personalities.

The intensity of togetherness means that each partner feels as though they understand the other and, if they survive this period, look back at it as a time full of madness and magic. Can it be any different? How else would you be crazy enough to let a complete stranger into your life?

Common problems and challenges
– Each is frightened of letting go
– Each is frightened of upsetting the other partner
– Each is frightened of love being withdrawn
– Blending couples have no experience of falling out and making up again so their arguments tend to be huge and dramatic
– One partner in particular is afraid of losing his identity

Skill
– It's hard, but you need to learn to surrender to your feelings
– Blenders put two fundamental instincts at war: we all long to be close and to be held, to hold and to be held by the other person, and yet we want to be masters of our own destiny

---

Hint Successful relationships strike a balance.

Nesting (second and maybe third year)

This is the stage where they decide to move in together, creating a new home. Sharing in this new experience becomes a new way of expressing their love for one another. Previously when they visited each other's places it was easy to decide who did what, but now their arguments are over who does what. And sex becomes less frequent.

It seems that everything is becoming mundane and routine. And differences between the individuals are highlighted to the point where one can ask 'Who is this person I thought I knew?'. Many nesting couples worry about their emerging difference to the point of 'I love you but...' and need reassurance that there is nothing wrong with their relationship. It is just changing and developing into something new.

Common problems and challenges

- Familiarity can breed annoyance. Those quirky eccentricities you once thought charming have become nasty habits
- Rows often centre around male and female roles around the house regardless of how 'liberated' the couple. Moving in together can re-awaken role models developed in childhood
- Arguments go round in circles
- During blending, couples have eyes only for each other, but nesters have many people who re-enter their mutual lives and this can cause tensions

Skill

- Since arguments often revolve around simple domestic matters such as 'You ruined the laundry with the wrong temperature', some nesters try to avoid these arguments altogether. But these arguments are worth having as it is through them that couples learn how to resolve their differences. Far better to learn how to resolve one's differences than wait until something big and unavoidable comes up, which might really damage the relationship. By learning how to confront these differences, you will grow and develop as a person. Anyone watching or reading your story will be drawn by the wisdom you impart.

Hint Remember that relationships do not stand still. Keep asking yourself: What are the best things that can happen from being with him/her? What are the worst? Confront these fears and really stare them in the face to see if they are real or not. Only then have you a chance of going to the next stage.

Self-Affirming (third and or fourth year)

During Nesting and Blending it is all about sharing and working together. In Self-Affirming it is about being confident enough to let the other partner go and do something on their own. Self-Affirmers will get as much pleasure from knowing that their partner is off doing something on their own as in doing it together. It takes a new kind of love to allow this to happen, to allow one's partner the freedom (real freedom) to do what they want to do without possessing them.

Common problems and challenges

- If one has no special skill, or lacks confidence, it is easier to hide in a relationship as part of a couple rather than to develop and establish one's own parallel identity
- One partner will often think that the other's time alone is a threat to the partnership
- One partner is unable to voice his own independent needs
- Power struggles emerge

Skill
– If the couple has learned how to fight during nesting, then they will be better equipped to delve deep into their problems at this stage. In the first two stages, the arguments are about basic human needs. In this stage, the couple will try and negotiate as much personal time as permissible. This negotiation can be exhausting

---

Hint Compromise is important. Some individuals never learn to compromise because they think it is a sign of weakness. But compromise can be a sign of great strength. Sometimes, one of the couple will suddenly stop compromising in order to prove a point. It can be considered a form of betrayal when compromise is withdrawn. Compromise only works when there is something of equal benefit for each party, so look and see what the other person has sacrificed or benefited from and ask yourself over and over again: was this fair?

Collaborating (five to fourteen years)

Couples use the security gained from their relationship over the first three stages to embark on new projects. This stage is called collaboration because of the huge amount of support the partners have to give each other. The excitement and freshness of the projects or ventures breathe fresh energy into the relationship.

Alternatively, the couple may embark on a joint project using complementary skills. The most common is having children together. Or they might start a business together, or travel together. Whatever the choice, whether it is an individual or joint goal, it imports new energy to the relationship and avoids stagnation.

During this stage, reliability and dependability replace the insecurity and fear of losing the other one (present in previous stages). Couples have earned their easy familiarity and have developed complementary skills. A shared shorthand is used for sorting out differences rather than spending hours of negotiation.

Common problems and challenges
– Taking each other for granted
– One partner developing faster and risking leaving the other behind
– If there is poor communication, one partner can get wrapped up in an outside project and neglect the other
– There is a line between separate activities and achievements which enrich a relationship, and those which cause a couple to grow apart

This is probably the most difficult stage. In the UK most relationships end after 11.3 years. Common folklore refers to this stage as The Seven Year Itch. Sucessful relationships learn to balance the familiar with the new, fresh and bold.

RAINDANCE WRITERS' LAB: WRITE AND SELL THE HOT SCREENPLAY

Skill

- Lack of possessiveness is important. This is especially hard when one partner launches into a new project when the other isn't quite ready for the change. Couples at this stage need to be generous enough to bless each other's projects and believe that they will succeed, rather than that they will undermine the relationship

Typical scenarios

- 'It's not practical.' Forget the practical – anything is possible in a dream
- 'It won't bring in any money'. Dreams feed your soul and express who you are. Your project doesn't need to bring in money if it means that you learn something new about yourself
- 'I'm not talented enough.' Dreams are about enjoying yourself, so it is not always important how well or badly you do something, just that you do it

Adapting (years 15 to 24)

These couples are adapting to the changes thrown at them rather than dealing with the internal changes in the relationship. These problems can vary from children leaving home, to the ageing or death of parents. By now each partner has given up the idea of what the other might have become and tends to think: 'He/she's always been like that and probably always will be.' What's the point of nagging about his bad habits? They are actually quite endearing. It is ironic that, when you let someone go like this, this is when he is most likely to bend and change. Couples at this stage feel contented and companionship is important. With increased confidence, and caring less what people might think, this is often a period of sexual reawakening. The downside of accepting a partner, warts and all, is that it can make change seem impossible. This viewpoint can quickly change from reassuring to depressing. Couples need to take a fresh look and transform any stalemates to positions of possibility.

Common problems and challenges

- Taking each other for granted
- Not showing emotion
- Thinking that the partner is incapable of change and that splitting up is the only option
- During a crisis, one partner will try to return to an earlier stage: ie a guy who has been fired might turn to home improvements as during the nesting stage; women who have shouldered most of the responsibility of caring for children and ageing parents may return to self-affirming
- One partner thinking that the other has enough to worry about and so ceases to confide their own problems
- Sleeper problems, like the death of a parent, can reawaken reassessment of one's childhood with a knock-on effect. These problems are hard to spot

Skill

– Couples will assume that they know each other well and will hear what they have known about the person from the past, and not really listen to what the other person is actually saying about the present or the future. It is best to listen, really listen, to what is being said or unsaid.

Renewing (years 25 to 60)

Often older couples are the most romantic and the closest. Closeness at one stage was based on the promise of a future together. Now the bond is based on the reality of a lifetime together. Renewing partners look inward to common experiences: shared jokes/stories. They are the least likely to split up.

Common problems and challenges

– Sometimes at the renewing stage one partner is afraid to voice his concerns, especially when other people start encroaching on the couple's time together, for example if the couple's children expect the couple to spend too much time looking after grandchildren
– Health worries can be isolating and turn closeness to claustrophobia

Skill

– As we grow older we start to become caricatures of ourselves. For example if you have always been known for being late, you might start doing dry runs of journeys to make sure you arrive on time. Patience and understanding are key for negotiating through these insecurities

---

Hint It's pretty hard to hate someone on another continent, or in a different state. Believe it or not, I have read a number of scripts where the opponent is plotting his counter-attack from across the ocean. Long-distance relationships will not work. In real life you would tend to get as far away as possible from someone you really dislike. Try to create togetherness for your hero and opponent. Squeeze them together. Make them occupy the same space. Force them to cohabit. The energy this creates will make your script glow. Good stories show the values of the opponent conflicting with the values of the hero.

Conflict

A compelling story contains more than one main conflict between a hero and an opponent. It contains a series of conflicts between the hero and a variety of other characters, and the values they stand for. A successful writer avoids the pitfall of beginning writers and understands what the conflicts and values are, and learns how to amplify these over the course of the story.

Simple stories show the hero attacked by one opponent. Although the value structures between these two main characters can be simply and powerfully stated, these stories lack the depth and texture expected by a sophisticated audience. It is by the interaction of different characters that your story will become more complex and challenge your audience.

In the best stories, the hero is assailed by a range of opponents – the main opponent, and two or three sub-opponents – creating a powerful series of attacks and counter-attacks. This collection of characters allows the writer to show the hero attacked in a variety of ways. This gives you the chance to layer your story in a series of subtle and complex ways that will delight the reader.

The characters also form a society in which the writer can examine more complex beliefs. The trick to making a story dense with conflict is to have each character attack each other as well. In doing so, each character becomes important to the story, and has a reason for existing, other than merely to attack the hero.

You can also repeat this structure on other levels in your story – the family, the workplace or society. Each level gives you another opportunity to state your beliefs, your theme, and the underlying values of your story. Writing a screenplay is your chance to state your values firmly.

You can choose to layer your conflict in one of two ways:

1. Lateral conflict

Two characters of approximately equal power or ability fight for the same goal. The writer with this structure is able to explore how these two opposing values create conflict. Sometimes both of the main characters will discover something about themselves and their values will blend together. The blend consists of the positive aspects of both sets of values, allowing the writer to state what he considers to be the best rules for living.

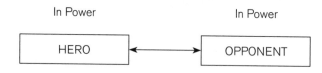

In Power   In Power

HERO ⟷ OPPONENT

2. Perpendicular conflict

Perpendicular conflict suits stories that examine power structures within the society of your film. Adding a perpendicular structure increases the conflict exponentially and gives your story depth and power. Perpendicular conflict concerns the opposition between those in power versus those out of power.

figure 5.3
Power Structure Chart B

A story with a horizontal and vertical opposition would look like this:

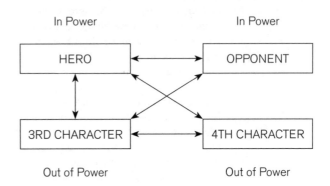

The conflict among the various characters and the values they represent tend to happen in two ways — horizontally and vertically.

The third and fourth characters can be described as follows:

Ally-opponent: at the start of the film aligned to the hero but, as in real life, betrays the main character and allies with the opponent. Have you ever had a best friend who stabbed you in the back?

Opponent-ally: at the start of the story he is discredited by the hero and aligned with the opponent, and then switches allegiance to the hero. Have you ever had an acquaintance at work or school whom you ignored? Then, a couple of years later, you meet him at a social function and decide that not only is he a decent human being, but then you become best friends.

Hint The world must come from your hero. In other words, who your hero is will define where the story is set.

The Staging

To create the world of your story, you must first place the story on a stage. The stage is the basic space of drama. It is a single, unified place surrounded by a set. Everything on the stage is part of the story. Everything outside the stage is not.

Hint If you cut from the stage of your story, the drama will disintegrate.

The challenge is to find a stage that will grow and develop along with your story and enable you to create a strong visual element that will also provide clues to the story. In a sense, good staging is really like a subplot. It adds substance to your story. Look for staging that will enable you to tell the story you want to tell.

The seasons

Frame your story

A builder would never build a house without putting up a frame. A writer must also put up a frame before starting to build the story. The easiest way to frame your story is to determine exactly where your story will end. Then decide where you want your story to start. With these two firm points, it is much easier to spin your tale.

When you need to show passage of time or a change in pace, consider using the seasons. The changes in the seasons give the audience a physical reminder of time against which to measure the decay or growth of the hero.

Classic literature uses seasons with certain probable meanings that you can either go with, or go against. Using the seasons in an unconventional way can add another dimension to your tale.

Classic season staging
– Summer: your hero exists in a predicament, or lives in a world of freedom that is vulnerable to attack
– Fall: the characters begin to decline
– Winter: the characters reach their lowest point
– Spring: the season of rebirth and rejuvenation

Writing against type would show a character at his lowest point in the summer, and his highest point in the depths of winter. This change to the natural order helps keep an audience from knowing what to expect next, adding suspense to your story.

Holidays and rituals

Using universal holidays and rituals helps establish the mood of your story quickly. This means that the writer can set up the wedding, or a Christmas story, or the baptism, with a minimal amount of preparation. The writers of short films – where economy is of the essence – often use this technique.

Rituals and holidays have their own rhythm and drama that can add texture to your story and allow you another way of expressing emotion. If the holiday expands to a national level, then it becomes political as well as personal, giving yet another layer to the story. The more layers in your story, the more complex it will be. If handled well, these layers enhance your tale.

Hint Understand the philosophy of the ritual you want to use and decide whether or not you agree with it. If you are unfamiliar with the ritual, make sure you research it carefully. This will enable you to attack or defend the holiday and all the meanings associated with it. Add to this the season it is in and you will be maximizing the stage setting of your story.

Nature

Choosing a natural setting should be done after you evaluate the meaning associated with each setting. The forest, the ocean, mountains and the wilderness all have different meanings. Try to find one that suits the story you want to tell. Perhaps you can choose a natural setting that cuts across the grain of your story.

For example, if you see a character alone in the desert, you instantly know that his or her immediate overwhelming concern is to find water and to survive.

Weather

Story telling has long used the weather to create a powerful visual representation of the inner turmoil of the hero. Like setting, you can use weather in the obvious way, or twist it to add irony. It is no accident that rain, lightning and thunder precede events most foul in Shakespearean drama. Similarly, the weather can be used to add drama to your story, and provide the stage for your characters.

Classic associations of weather
– Lightning and thunder: passion, terror, and death
– Rain: sadness, loneliness, boredom, and coziness
– Wind: destruction, desolation
– Fog: confusion, misery
– Sun: happiness, freedom, or corruption hidden below a warm exterior
– Snow: sleep, serenity, death

Symbols, Symbolism and Metaphor

A symbol is something that represents something other than itself. Symbols in your movie take on new meanings in addition to the meaning they had to the audience before the movie started. A symbol can be an object that already has a meaning, like a cross or a flag, or it can be a neutral object to which meaning is given by your story such as, for example, the lipstick in Thelma and Louise.

Society

Placing your story in a society gives your story more definition. The simplest way to do this is to say 'London. 1880'. Every story has a definition such as this. It is a concise way or providing information about the characters and the setting, but is flawed in that it relies on the reader's preconceived ideas of Victorian London. A more precise way would be to define the culture of the times. But defining all the nuances of Victorian England would be difficult. It would be like asking Michelangelo to carve David with a toothpick, and of course, the audience would get bored.

Institutions

Placing your story in an institution has many advantages. Institutions like the corporation, the hospital, the mob, or the factory represent society in microcosm. In the example above – Victorian London, 1880 – a writer could take pages and pages to set up the scene and to explain all the social and cultural nuances of that particular time. But if the story was set in an institution like a Victorian hospital, we would see the status of the nurses contrasted with the patients, the relationships between the doctors and the rest of the staff, as well as how patients fared in relation to their social classes. Try to find an institution that fits your story.

Hint Great writers twist an existing symbol to give it new meaning.

Community

A writer can fine-tune the staging even further by placing the characters within a community. We can then see how the hero relates to other individuals in the community. This technique is also useful in allowing the writer to express his concerns or beliefs about a society, represented in microcosm by the community. Witness was a famous Oscar winning film about community (in this case the Amish community) and how it was used as a foil for the forces from the evil city.

Metaphor

Since a screenplay is such a pared-down art form, simply placing your characters in a society, or even an institution, is still daunting. You cannot write pages and pages of description to explain your staging to your audience. Narrowing down the structure of your stage even further will enable you to get more information to the audience in a visual way. Cinema is a visual medium, a fact often neglected by screenwriters and filmmakers. The often repeated phrase about a picture is worth words.

The trick is to look for a means of organizing your setting in a way that allows the audience to reach the right conclusion for your story.

Many writers use the metaphor of the city as jungle – a terrifying place, where danger, even death, lurks around every corner. Your characters can be attacked from above, from below, and from the side. No one can be trusted. Populated by 'animals' and filled with hunters and the hunted, this city is not a fun place.

Being John Malkovich is an example of a unique setting. The simple act of setting the story inside someone's head transformed the entire story.

The challenge to modern screenwriters is to discover new metaphors, as yet unused, as a way to tell the story. This is the best way to distinguish yourself and set yourself apart from your competitors.

Hint Elevate your story by creating a unique metaphor for your setting.

Setting the Social Stage

Social stage is the point to which the society of your hero has developed. All societies evolve through distinct social stages. Choosing a specific social stage allows you to communicate a great deal without resorting to dialogue.

Civilizations tend to develop over time. There are four key stages. Allow me to use the example of the Roman Empire. In the beginning the people were nomads, traveling alone or in small bands. Then they discovered agriculture and settled down into villages. Some of the villages became so large that they turned into cities and, after time, city life became corrupted to the point where the rules for living were altered out of all recognition into a state called the oppressive city. The inhabitants then suffered a series of attacks by barbarians and the civilization sank into the Dark Ages.

Without turning this book into a dissertation of cultural development over the millennia, let's simply put the social stages into four unique areas — each with a particular type of hero, a unique breed of opponent, special concerns, and particular values.

Wilderness and the super-hero

There are no buildings in the wilderness, and the hero travels alone or with a band of disciples. Nature is vast and all-powerful, threatening the existence of everyone. The hero is a super-hero because he is the only character capable of fighting the forces of nature and surviving. Death comes early and quickly to the weak. Roving bands of barbarians circle the group as they travel in search of water and food. The main concern is to survive, to reproduce, and to be in harmony with nature — using the knowledge and strength of the super-hero.

At the end of wilderness stories, the super-hero leaves his group (sometimes called disciples) at the foot of a steep cliff or mountain, and climbs up into the clouds where he (super-heroes are always male) receives divine inspiration which he writes down. Upon his descent he shows these words to his disciples and they become new rules for living that change forever the way men live. For example, Moses and the Ten Commandments. Most religious stories fall into this category.

Hint If you were capable of writing a story set in the wilderness, where your hero receives divine inspiration, which he could write down and show us, you would no longer be known as a screenwriter but a religious prophet.

Village and the classic hero

I define a village as a small settlement. You can stand at one end of the village and see all the way to the end. Perhaps there is one traffic light. The buildings are single story, and there isn't a great deal of difference between the structures. The general store, courthouse and a private dwelling aren't that different and usually they are built with the same materials. In the back gardens there is a wooden fence, generally under construction, or falling into disrepair − symbolizing the barrier between civilization and barbarianism. As the buildings are single level, so too are the villagers. They are all roughly of the same social status although, if a stranger arrives in the village, one of the villagers will speak on behalf of the villagers − the priest, the sheriff, the schoolteacher or the judge.

Society has evolved to the point where man has created basic shelter that will survive the seasons. The social structures of the village are young and developing. The village is surrounded by wilderness and is exposed to the forces of nature (although nowhere nearly as strongly as in the wilderness), and the villagers are prone to attack by roving bands of barbarians. The villagers mistrust anything from the wilderness, to the point that anyone they do not understand, or who is different from them, is considered to be a barbarian too. The barbarians want the village destroyed because the village represents the new, and it encroaches on their freedom to roam. The barbarians do not understand the changes in society that have created the village.

Into the world of the village comes the 'classic hero'. Almost exclusively male, the classic hero does not come from the village, but arrives into it. Larger and physically stronger than the villagers, almost barbarian-like, the classic hero relies on martial arts to survive. Sometimes the villagers mistake the classic hero as a barbarian. In other stories, the villagers see in the classic hero their only hope of defeating the barbarians.

The classic hero will use his talents as a warrior to help the fragile community deal with the savage forces they cannot physically or morally handle themselves. Society has not reached the point where discussion and verbal skills are the tools for solving problems. The village does not have a courthouse and the jail is generally a very simple one.

Village stories share a sense of good and evil, black and white. Although the values of the villagers and the classic hero may not be correct, according to our principles, the basic premise is that everyone inside the town is good, and everyone outside of this village is a barbarian or savage for whom destruction is the only option.

By warring with other characters from his own social stage, the classic

Have you ever been driving in the countryside and stopped off the beaten track for a drink in a local establishment? Do you notice how the locals looked at you when you entered? You were considered a barbarian, bringing new and possibly evil things to the village.

hero is a doomed figure. He (classic heroes are predominantly male) is used by the villagers to destroy barbarians in order to allow the village to grow and prosper. The classic hero has no place in the village and once his task is done, he leaves or is forced to leave. Many screenwriting books talk of the need for a character to grow and develop. In a village story, the hero does not change, he 'rides off into the sunset' unchanged. What has changed are the villagers who are now at a higher level, because he has saved them from the roving bands of barbarians, or they are at a lower level, having had their wickedness and corruption exposed. An excellent example of this is John Dahl's Red Rock West starring Nicholas Cage and Dennis Hopper.

Examples of the classic hero include the pioneer, the samurai and the westerner. The qualities of a classic hero can be incorporated into a hero set in a different social stage. For example, super-cop, who lives in a city filled with barbarians, is discarded once his task has been fulfilled.

City and the average hero

At some point as the village grows and spreads out, it reaches a physical boundary and can no longer spread horizontally. It must now spread vertically. The village develops into the city. Contrasting with the social stage of the village, the city is a place of hierarchy, rank, privilege and vast differences of wealth and power.

This is the world of the average hero, of everyman and everywoman who is ordinary in every way – no stronger, brighter, dumber, or wealthier than anyone else in the city.

The average hero is concerned with the nesting instinct (creating a place in society, providing a home, raising a family). He or she is concerned with equality and justice (making sure that everyone follows the same rules for living). He or she is probably also concerned with avoiding the slavery of bureaucracy and government.

Some examples of the average hero can be found in Michael Dorsey in Tootsie, Karen Blixen in Out of Africa, Frank Galvin in The Verdict and Dorothy in Wizard of Oz.

Oppressive city and the anti-hero

When the city grows so dense, so tight, so technological and bureaucratic, it becomes a place of enslavement. It once was intended as a place of nourishment where its citizens could expect to have a decent job and a decent life. It once was a place where the arts flourished hand in hand with commerce, making for a dynamic community. Now, however, the city has knotted together so tightly that it can no longer help its citizens. Instead it uses its citizens to further itself, devouring them in its thirst to sustain its bulk. Often the controls of the machinery driving the city are held in the hands of the powerful and mighty few. Stories set in this stage feature the anti-hero. The anti-hero can have two distinct traits.

He could be the person who will not be beaten down by the oppressive city and who is therefore sent into exile. A variation on this is the citizen who discovers or witnesses a crime by accident, and holds the key to keeping someone in power. The result is this citizen being hunted and pursued, often to the death. Examples include Blade Runner, Cool Hand Luke, Patriot Games and Twelve Monkeys.

Or, he could be the person who stays and is beaten down – the incompetent, the bumbler, and a character who is unsocial or anti-social.

Examples of the anti-hero include Chauncey Gardner in Being There, early Woody Allen characters, Ratzo Rizzo in Midnight Cowboy, Travis Bickle in Taxi Driver, as well as Jim Carrey in Pet Detective and in Me, Myself and Irene.

The next development of society is for it to crumble under its own weight and the citizens (who survive) are returned to the wilderness – for example Lord of the Flies.

Hint As society gets larger, nature and the hero get smaller.

Using the Social Stage

A huge challenge for screenwriters is to explain how it is possible for nature, society, and the individual to coexist and prevent the evolutionary cycle from repeating.

Usually the most effective way of marking time and placing the hero within a society is to place him/her in a particular social stage. People living in the wilderness tend to create main characters who are gods or super-heroes. In the village world, the hero is the 'classic' hero. Stories set in the city world feature the average hero, the everyman or everywoman. The main character in a story set in the oppressive city is the anti-hero.

The option of where you set your story will to a large extent determine what your hero will do and how he will react. Here are some interesting options.

Cross stages

Taking a character from one social stage and plunking him into another social stage can create a dynamic story. For example, what if the stereotypical city character, like Woody Allen, is plopped into the village stage a century and a half ago? Suppose our hapless Woody rides into a western village, ties his horse up to the hitching post and accidentally feeds his horse the oats and water belonging to John Wayne. John Wayne bursts out of the saloon hollering. How would Woody Allen try to resolve this misunderstanding in the crude setting of the village? Would he succeed against John Wayne's 'fastest draw in the west?' Similarly, what if John Wayne is in the city, parking his car illegally while he runs into a corner store for one of those famous cigarettes and when he gets back he has what he perceives to be an undeserved parking ticket? Would John Wayne be able to resolve his disagreement with the parking attendant by using the pistol-brute-force of the village?

Look again at Crocodile Dundee and you will see that is exactly what they did: village hero in the city. And to great effect.

On the cusp

Setting your story on the cusp between two social stages is a great way to add dimension to your story and give your self a platform for your own personal view of what is right and wrong. Nothing is more fascinating to an audience than a transition between social stages, particularly our own social stage – as this affects the health, prosperity, and comfort not only of ourselves, but that of our children as well.

My favorite example of a movie set in a transition stage is Butch Cassidy and The Sundance Kid. At the start of the movie, Butch and Sundance are robbing banks in the village stage. How they succeed is by scoping a village, and then setting fresh horses every two hours distance from the village. This allows them to outrun the sheriff and his posse. Then one day they rob a bank, not realizing that the railroad (from the city social stage) has been laid. The soldiers can now keep up with them, and they realize that their old livelihood has become unsustainable. At this point they should have taken a decision: give up, spend some time in prison, and then move to the city to take up white-collar crime. With their skills and imagination I am certain they would have been very good at this. But they were unable to see to the next social stage, and so were destroyed.

Find a present day parallel

We have just discussed Butch Cassidy. How about our life? There can be valuable lessons learned from everyday occurrences in our own lives. Large and small.

At the time of writing this chapter, the British public was transfixed by story after story of the failing health care system and one particular incident where hospitals stock-piled organs from stillborn babies for medical research without first obtaining the permission of the parents. One couple was shown leaving the hospital with the internal organs of their child, pickled in several lab jars, in stomach-turning scenes straight from the oppressive city.

How about the terrible events of the 9/11 terrorist attacks? At what point are we in the civilization wheel? City? Oppressive city?

I am pretty negative by nature even though I am constantly congratulated for PMA (Positive Mental Attitude). I believe that the terrible attacks of 9/11 were the first attacks by barbarians on our tightly woven and overcrowded oppressive cities. Do you remember George Bush on CNN that night, and on every other station around the world saying: 'We are fighting a new kind of war with a new kind of enemy. We do not know who they are, but we will find and destroy them.' Bush and his misguided politicians and military strategists decided, like Butch and Sundance, to use the forces of the current social stage in order to fight the forces of the next social stage, with largely unsuccessful results.

Find a historical precedent

If you can tie your story into an ancient story which supports your view of the stage at which our civilization is on the social-stage wheel, you will probably be able to garner critical, if not commercial, acclaim.

A friend of mine in London claims that the fall of the Soviet Union was caused by Jerry Seinfeld, and not by enlightened politicians of the era. In the late 1970s, the first satellite broadcasting TV was launched over Europe. Geo-blocking, the computer software that controls where you watch programmes, is an expensive but necessary part of the rights management of popular programming like the Jerry Seinfeld Show. However, at that time, there were so few televisions in the Soviet Union, that it was agreed that it was pointless to geo-block this territory on commercial grounds. Imagine now, yourself as a Soviet citizen of the time, being told that Westerners are evil. There was, coincidentally, a terrible economic recession and food was at a premium. You hear that your neighbour ten blocks away has just finessed a television, and you rush over after work, just as Kramer is skidding into Jerry's kitchen, opening the fridge and guess what? It's full of food. Perhaps being an evil Westerner isn't so bad after all – at least they have food.

Or this: In the last eighty years leading up to the fall of the Roman Empire, were not the spectacles in the Coliseum – the feeding of Christians to lions - the equivalent of reality television today?

Social Metaphors

When writing for a pared-down form, such as screenplay, it is always useful to draw upon universal experience in order to create the setting quickly. This enables your audience to see your story within the context of something that they already understand.

When writing a short film, or a film using a very limited budget, creating a metaphor that is instantly recognizable is crucial, i.e. the wedding, the funeral, graduation day, the hen party. Our audience will then be able to see your story clearly, and be able to understand the details you bring to this setting.

The family

Everyone in the world is part of a family. The family is the basic unit of drama and of human life itself. The family provides the first relationships for the hero. The relationships that the hero forms with parents and siblings will powerfully shape the story. Through these relationships we will see and judge the hero's ability to grow and develop.

Hierarchy

You must consider the power structure of the family – who is in charge, who has the most influence, who uses this power, and who abuses it. As soon as you place your hero somewhere in this power structure, the audience will observe how the hero's position changes relative to the power over the course of the story.

Municipality

As in real life, where you or your characters live can have great impact on your audience. If you live in a luxurious flat overlooking Buckingham Palace, the audience will read one lifestyle. If your hero lives in a cardboard box outside Buckingham Palace, the audience reads a completely different lifestyle.

Homes range from the very small and humble, to the huge and grandiose. Each home will help to express the character. And you can also cut against type.

Obviously, each social stage has different types of buildings, and the audience will understand the social stage in part by the types of buildings you show them.

Wilderness/Village

As the village life is threatened by extinction, stories set in the village will become increasingly nostalgic.

The wilderness and the village are almost always shown in relation to one another in a story since it is the contrast between the two that emphasizes the change of the hero. In the village we see only essential buildings, because the village represents a society at its most basic state – the livery stable, the jail, the saloon, the dry goods store, the schoolhouse and the church. Some of the buildings should be unfinished to accentuate the growth and the forces of change that are continually overcoming the wilderness. Villages often feature wooden fences that separate the village from the wilderness. Made of wood, fences represent the fragile barrier between the old and the new, and visually suggest vulnerability to attack.

Town

As villages become larger and more successful, the social order starts to change and diversify. This is represented by the buildings, which are taller and denser than the buildings of the village.

Three-storied buildings are common in the town. The layers suggest a society that is becoming established, with the social layers not present in the village.

A strong sense of community is a feature of town life. Although the buildings can be multi-story, they are still small enough so that someone on the street can talk to someone leaning out of the upstairs window.

Nature is interspersed through the town. The society has not become so artificial that nature is driven out. The characters in the town live in harmony with nature, and respect it for its power.

City

The city is organized vertically. Everyone living in the city is classed by how high up they are — either in the physical structures, or where they are in terms of personal power or wealth. The contrast between the dizzying heights and the subterranean passages is extreme.

As most of us live in the city, see if you can find a way to bend or distort this setting to add impact to your story.

The classic way of demonstrating the difference in power and wealth is to place the rich and powerful in penthouses at the top of skyscrapers, the middle classes in the middle floors, the poor and the vanquished on the street, and the criminals in underground lairs.

Thus every time you see Batman's opponent, you are led to an impressive room deep in the bowels of the city. Audiences identify with the subterranean room, and the writer is able to create texture for the story without having to resort to more than the actual description of the set.

Buildings in the city are divided into compartments. In the village, buildings tend to be one large room, where all the action takes place. Town buildings, although multi-layered, tend to focus on a single room too. But stories in the city divide buildings into a series of compartments or rooms. These function not only to allow people to congregate, but are also used to divide and isolate people one from another. Thus, while stories in the city deal with positive values like creating love, nest building and justice, they can also range through the negative values of intrigue, secrecy and injustice.

Unlike the village or the town, there are no communal bonds in the city. People communicate using messages and move from place to place. It is highly impersonal.

Pain

Which hurts more: banging your head on a corner of a cupboard or being zapped by a ray gun? Obviously the ray gun. But what exactly does that feel like? Have you ever been hit by a ray gun? On the other hand, how many times have you banged your head? When you see an actor do that you go 'ouch'. If you see an actor being melted by a ray gun, you have no connection with the pain.

Always try to make pain personal to the audience. A great example is in Die Hard when John MacLean, played by Bruce Willis steps on broken glass.

Summary

1. Structure is the way your character's plan unfolds.

2. Make sure that your hero has an outer goal and an inner problem.

3. Choose a social stage that fits the character of the story you tell.

4. Never forget the instinctive storyteller lurking inside you. If you find anything in this chapter that confuses you, set it aside and return to it later.

You are now ready to start piecing your screenplay together.

6 Scene Writing

CHRISTOPHER VOGLER CALLS a scene a 'deal between the writer and the audience'. Blake Snyder describes a story or a scene as a journey that you are going on, and never coming back — a door you go out of, and come back changed, or a train you get on from a station never to return. Apt as these descriptions are from both of these Raindance tutors, I am looking at screenplay and scene writing in much more practical terms.

A screenplay has two parts — the dialogue and the descriptive passages. The descriptive passages in a screenplay are called 'the black stuff', referring to the amount of space they take up on the page. Dialogue margins are much narrower.

Script readers frequently reject scripts because they contain too much black stuff. A script with a high percentage of black stuff comes across as verbose and ponderous.

But script writing is a visual medium and so your script will probably have more description than dialogue.

The irony is that in the trade they say that the agent and producer (hopefully the first two people to read your script) will never read the black stuff. Instead they read the dialogue and, when they don't understand what is happening through the dialogue, only then will they resort to reading the descriptive passages. But only until they understand what is going on, and then they immediately return to the dialogue. This, by the way, explains how experienced producers can read a script in half-an-hour!

It is a bit like going into the cinema and requesting a screening of, say, Gone with The Wind, and asking the projectionist to put a board in front of the lens, turn a magic switch and play you the entire movie without the picture, the sound effects, or the musical score. When the story is not carried by the dialogue alone, only then do you go to the projectionist, ask him to rewind a minute (page) or two, and replay with the pictures until the dialogue makes sense.

Script readers always approach a script with the three 'ums'.

When they pick up a new script, the first 'um' is when they check the length of the script. The next 'um' is as they open the script at random to see if it is properly and professionally typed. The last 'um' is as they flick through the pages for an idea of the amount of black stuff to dialogue.

There is no science to this but, by fanning through the pages, one can get a rough idea of whether or not the script is a talking heads movie or a descriptive piece.

We do this ourselves when we browse through a bookstore. You probably did this when you picked up this book. Did you pick it up, and flick through it to see how dense the type was, and how many illustrations it contained? Maybe you started to read a chapter to judge the writing style and quality of the ideas.

Writers often forget what a sparse and cut-down form screenplay is. It is also quite easy to forget that, as a screenwriter, you are denied many of the literary tools afforded to novelists, poets and lyricists. Simile, metaphors and rhymes have little or no place in screenplay.

However you arrive at your scenes, you will need to know how many scenes you have and in which order they fall. The more work you do at this stage the better.

The Basic Rules

You can only write what you physically see on the screen

You cannot write:

```
Elliot is depressed.
```

How would you show that visually? It's impossible. Think about how you can show Elliot depressed. You could say:

```
A tear splats at Elliot's feet.
```

Hint If your screenplay has too many interior thoughts, perhaps the story is better suited to a novel, lyric or poem.

A writer's job is to describe all the action on the screen

I often see the following line of descriptive action:

```
They make wild passionate love.
```

Remember that a page of screenplay is a minute of screen time. The writer assumes that this love scene will take a minute, yet, by the script description, it will be over in a few seconds. I always ask the writer for more details: Who is on top; what are their hands doing, where are their lips? I also want to see the choreography of the scene – any trick pelvis moves – who knows? I may learn how to improve my sex life.

With your minute, or page of screen time, you have to decide how long you are going to take to describe the love scene. The same holds true for car chases and fight sequences. How long is it going to last in the mind's eye of your movie? A minute is a very long time. And if your car chase or love scene is two minutes long, you now have two minutes/pages to show us a chase scene from hell or the sex of the century. Don't wimp out. Show us every visual idea you have. Inspire us. Titillate us. You are the writer. It is your responsibility to create the blueprint for the scene.

Hint When you start writing a new scene, sit back and try to imagine yourself sitting in a cinema in front of a blank screen. What do you see? Choose the words that will spark an image for a reader.

Beware of overwriting

A common mistake new writers make is to needlessly overwrite descriptive passages.

I recently read a script as a favour for a friend. If you had a spare $25 000 to spend on a venture, would you write a cheque for this?

```
Elliot sits on a stool, his left leg crossed and
supported on the ring. He reaches for a coffee in a
shiny blue mug embossed with the word HOLLYWOOD in
gold and which is sitting on the shelf to his left.
He brings the coffee forward to his lips. He sud-
denly passes the coffee from his left hand to his
right as the telephone RINGS...
```

Not only is description such as this overwritten, it is confusing to follow and gives the actor too much detail. It is also dry and boring, and fails in the writer's first task – to inspire everyone on the shoot.

I rewrote the passage as:

```
ELLIOT fidgets on a stool.
Coffee splashes from his mug.
The telephone RINGS.
```

Structure of a scene

A scene must have its own structure and, like the whole movie, a beginning, middle and an end.

The plot devices discussed in Chapter 3 also pertain to scene writing – goal, reversal, stacking, the plan, and the switch. Use them to your advantage to create a spell-binding read.

Developing a strong personal style

The knack of writing descriptive passages distinctively is acquired through practice, and through reading scripts of commercially successful movies that you admire. Once you have developed the ability to write compelling, descriptive passages, your career as a writer will develop fast. Remember too, that you are at all times writing for the reader – the person with a chequebook. It is this person that you must inspire first.

This scene doesn't appear in the finished film for nearly a minute, and when it does, it is cross cut with the courtroom scene. But it is the opening scene of the movie.

Let's consider the following example of an excellent descriptive passage. It is the opening of Frank Durabont's Shawshank Redemption based on the novella by Stephen King.

```
A dark empty room.

The door bursts open. A MAN and WOMAN enter, drunk
and horny as hell. No sooner is the door shut than
they are all over each other, ripping at clothes,
pawing at flesh, mouths locked together.
```

There are four movies that are created during the filmmaking process:

– the one you write
– the one the director directs
– the one the actors create
– the one the editor makes

```
He gropes for a lamp, tries to turn it on, knocks
it over instead. Hell with it. He's got more impor-
tant things to do like getting her blouse open and
his hands on her breasts. She arches, moaning, fum-
bling with his fly. He slams her against the wall,
ripping her skirt. We hear fabric tear.
```

Now imagine again that you have a spare twenty-five grand to invest in a movie. Can you see the advantages of the example above? Did this scene turn you on? Did you get images of the setting and action in the scene? Most importantly, would you like to read more? This is the sort of scene you need to write to get a deal.

The method of scene writing

Online Resources

This is a plan I have developed for writing a scene. It involves getting a piece of paper for each scene and drawing a chart.

Hint Keep the description brief. Make every word count. Be very clear about what the point of the scene is.

Write the scene down from start to finish. Remember we are not writing dialogue yet. If you have an idea for dialogue, make a note on the back of a piece of paper, or write it in the margins.

Do this for the entire script. Then look at the script and ask yourself of each scene: is there a briefer, faster , fresher way that I can say the same thing?

figure 6.1
Scene Writing Chart

Scene no.	12
Previous endpoint	Bob hits the bottle in the local bar
Cast members in scene	Bob, Mary
Point of Scene	Mary and Bob break up
Goal of main character	Bob goes to Mary's office to propose
Endpoint	Mary tells Bob that it's over
Conflict	Mary is tired of waiting for Bob to propose
Twist	Bob shows Mary a ring

Write the scene, what happens, without dialogue

Make the necessary revisions until the entire script flows.

Have you ever been typing into a long document when suddenly you feel that you may be repeating yourself but you can't remember whether or not you have typed these words before, and so now you have to scroll up and down a lengthy document? If you are like me, this is one of the most boring and irritating jobs to be confronted with as a writer.

You may want to use the action flow chart.

Action flow chart

How many times have you started writing a lengthy document, and after a few pages asked yourself 'Have I written this before or not?' This tool is intended to provide you with an easy way to keep track of your story as well as the different characters and settings.

A good story is not just about one character trying to reach his goals. It is about numerous characters all trying to achieve their goals, sometimes working together, sometimes working against each other.

This chart is a visual aid to assist you in keeping track of the actions of the different characters.

List actions that the reader or audience cannot see, so you can fully develop each character. Each character must be completely motivated and active throughout the story. You can also log scenes to keep track of how many violent scenes or love scenes you have, for example. The result is a story with multiple lines of action perfectly choreographed with well-defined characters.

Make up a chart with the following headings:

Tag
The type of scene: conflict, love, violence, jealousy etc.

Scene
A short description of the scene (five to eight words).

Hero
The actions the hero takes to reach his goal.

Four character columns
The actions of the main opponent and the other key characters.

Three open columns
For tracking the actions or objects of any character or story element.

Symbol
List up to three symbols that can be found in that scene. Remember that more than three symbols can get confusing, and that you do not need symbols in every scene.

See figure 6.2 opposite.

figure 6.2 Action Flow Chart

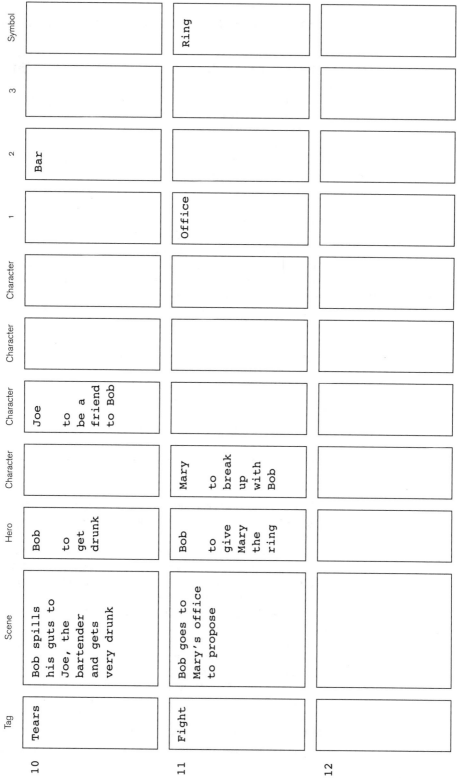

Tag	Scene	Hero	Character	Character	Character	Character	1	2	3	Symbol
10 Tears	Bob spills his guts to Joe, the bartender and gets very drunk	Bob to get drunk		Joe to be a friend to Bob				Bar		
11 Fight	Bob goes to Mary's office to propose	Bob to give Mary the ring	Mary to break up with Bob				Office			Ring
12										

The Eighteen Tricks and Traps of Successful Description

1. Write action, not description

Don't think of writing description, think of writing action — movement. Describing an inanimate object is boring to write and boring to read. And especially boring to the reader with the chequebook!

Remember, your job is to inspire the entire cast and crew. One of the key people on the crew who has to visualize your script is the Production Designer. It is the Production Designer's job to create the actual sets you have described. Sometimes the log line of the scene will do it:

```
INT. RAINDANCE OFFICE — DAY
```

Most screenplays are static and the scenes do not flow. Writing movement into a scene makes your script more interesting to read, immediately distinguishing it from ninety-five per cent of all the other screenplays in circulation.

From this simple line, the Production Designer will know to create a room with desks, telephones, and computers. The Props master will add further details, like the clutter and knick-knacks. Here is where you, as a writer with the biblical quote, can use your creativity to inspire.

It is not your job to describe the clutter, the furniture, and knick-knacks, unless required by the plot.

If the slug line says **INT. RAINDANCE OFFICE — DAY** the reader will imagine desks and office furniture. You do not need to mention them.

If the slug line doesn't convey all of the information necessary, then you need to add some simple description:

```
INT. RAINDANCE OFFICE — DAY.

A puddle of water is growing in the middle of the
floor.
```

Now we have some important information we need about the set, but it is still open enough to allow for the collaboration of the Production Designer and Props Master.

Once you have all the necessary description of the scene, you move on to action. You are still writing description, but you are creating pictures with movement in them — your characters and objects moving in their world. By creating movement you will also enable the reader to visualise the scene. Getting your reader to visualize will enable him to see your movie playing in his head.

You aren't describing things, you are describing things happening. When we use our words to paint pictures, we are painting moving pictures — and that is interesting to a reader. Which means that you have a better chance of selling your script.

Hint Action is the element between patches of dialogue.

---

2. Attention to details

There are times when `INT. RAINDANCE — DAY` is too general and the reader needs additional information. The trick is not to bore the reader by completely describing the setting. This could lead you to an overwritten scene — one of the fatal flaws of scene writing (see overwriting below). Instead, find the one (or two) details that give us clues, and let the reader's imagination fill in the rest.

```
INT. RAINDANCE OFFICE — DAY

Files and half empty coffee cups litter the room.
```

Or

```
INT. RAINDANCE OFFICE — DAY

A lonely paperclip partners a vase of flowers on
the boardroom table.
```

These are two very different offices. How is the first office different from the second? Imagine yourself as a Production Designer. What sort of table lamp would you use in the first place? How would that differ from a lamp in the second office? The carpet is different, the curtains are different, the pictures thumb-tacked to the wall in the first are very different from the lithos and expensively framed posters in the second.

Hint Carefully select a detail which implies other details. Try to distil the entire situation. You can also sum up an entire room in one short sentence while giving clues to character as well. Notice how there are two very different Elliots in the following two scenes.

---

3. Paint movement

If you describe people and objects as moving pictures, you can hide the descriptive passages within the action and within the movement. Instead of a boring, static still life, you give the reader the excitement of action.

```
INT. RAINDANCE OFFICE — DAY

ELLIOT slumps amongst the cluttered files and
trash.
```

The reader is focusing on Elliot, and doesn't even notice that you wrote the description of the office. No static words in this scene — just movement.

4. High school English

Readers in the industry are accustomed to an easy read. The language used is of the same level as in a high school English essay. Avoid complicated words and convoluted descriptive passages.

5. Maximize your vocabulary

The key to economical and dynamic writing is word choice. During your first draft, you may write a dozen words to explain a situation. Later, you may hone it down to one or two that explain exactly what you mean. You have hit two birds with one stone: you create quick, easy-to-read sentences coupled with greater impact than your puffed-out original.

6. Avoid wimpy verbs

`Elliot walks into the room.`

Walks is not specific. Walks is too general. How many words can you think of for the word walk? Does Elliot limp in, stride in, jump in, sneak in, jog in, slide in?

If Elliot saunters in, strides in, struts in, strolls in, marches in, paces in, or bounces in, not only does this give us a specific type of walk, but adds to the action and character while removing clichéd words from your script.

7. Classified ad

Screenwriting is a very pared down and sparse art form. The challenge for a writer is to create the greatest possible impact with the fewest possible words. A novelist can spend pages and chapters describing the minutest of details. A screenwriter has just ninety to one hundred and twenty pages to get a complete story across.

Hint Economy is the creative challenge.

Economy is not only the most important part of a screenwriter's job, it is the most difficult to learn.

How do you learn lean, compact and dynamic writing?

One of my tasks at Raindance is to write copy for the various ads we use to promote the film festival. As you know, newspapers charge by the word. A good trick when you start to write a scene is to imagine that you are writing a classified ad for a newspaper, and that you only have a limited budget – say $10. This particular newspaper charges 0.75 per word. Try to see if you can describe the scene and leave yourself enough change to buy yourself a coffee! While writing or rewriting, I will take apart every single sentence and try to find a bolder, fresher, quicker way of saying the same thing. In a first draft, I might have six or seven words that end up being replaced by one. I try to recognize every time I have used unnecessary words or am beating around the bush. You will learn how to get directly to the point.

Try to write the scene description like you are writing a classified ad.

Hint Scene writing is like writing a haiku where you have a very limited number of words. Try to use words that imply other words.

---

8. Find the emotion

Don't describe how something looks, but how it feels. The Production Designer will decide how the set looks, the Casting Director decides on how each character will look. The writer describes the attitude of the scene, the feel, and the emotion.

One of my favourite writers, William C. Martell, writes dynamic description filled with emotional resonance. Consider the opening of Hard Return:

```
EXT. URBAN JUNGLE, 2019 AD — EVENING

The wreckage of civilization. Crumbled buildings,
burned out cars, streets pockmarked by war. Downed
power lines arc and spark on the street.

This place makes Hell look like Beverly Hills…

Except the battered twisted metal sign reads
BEVERLY HILLS.

Night is falling. Fingers of shadow reaching out
to grab anyone foolish enough to be in this part
of town.
```

The only time the future is mentioned is in the slug line. Every other word in this scene describes how the future, this scene, feels: frightening, ugly, and dangerous.

Did the skin on the back of your head crawl when you read this? Did you get a visual image of the scene? If you were the Production Designer, how many different possibilities would you have in order to recreate this scene?

Suppose you were an actor who had to walk down the street? How would you do it?

Hint Well-written descriptive passages describe the scene's emotion.

---

9. Avoid poetry

Imagery, alliteration, homonyms and other forms of word play can make your script more interesting. But overuse these tools and your script will end up looking cutesy.

Avoid asides to the reader. Your job is to involve the reader in the story, not to impress him with your verbal dexterity.

Good screenwriting is both interesting and apparent. Word play should service the script, not show what a good education you have.

10. The four-line rule

If you want to whiten your script, a good rule is the four-line rule. No passage of action should last longer than four lines.

If you have a big action scene, which lasts a page or more, break it up with spaces. Every four lines put in a blank line. This instantly adds more white stuff to your script!

Another quick trick for long action passages is to have at least one line of dialogue on every page – even if it's just a character yelling 'Watch out!' This breaks up the page and gives the reader a break from reading descriptions of action.

11. Style on the page

Try to make each page look attractive and easy to read. Develop your own personal style in writing descriptive passages.

Experiment. After a few scripts, you will develop your own style and your own voice in descriptions. Developing a voice is an important step in taking command of the page (more on that later).

12. Characters

Do you think you could completely describe a character in three words? John Dahl managed that amazing feat in his script for Buffalo Girls, titled

The Last Seduction.

This is a wonderful example of clear succinct writing.

BRIDGET GREGORY, bitch-ringmaster-goddess.

He manages to convey Bridget's occupation and attitude, which allows us to imagine details about everything from the number of tattoos to hair length, personal grooming and wardrobe, in a mere three words.

13. Active verbs

Use active verbs. Elliot doesn't try to sit on a chair, he sits on the chair. Better yet, he crashes into the chair, or, slouches/wriggles/slumps in the chair. Try is an energy-sapping verb: it saps power from the active verb. Other pitfalls to avoid are starts to, begins to and ...ing — walks is stronger than walking.

14. Avoid widows

Typesetters call the last word of a sentence that carries over onto a new line of print a widow. A single word, which takes up an entire line of space. In the rewrite process, kill all the widows. Rework the sentence until it fits entirely on one line. You should aim for a widow-free script. Another benefit is that this discipline will force you to choosing the correct words and eliminate any unnecessary words. As a result, your widow-free script will look cleaner on the page.

15. No ands or buts

In real life, pain hurts. Screenwriters merit the attention of an audience by making an emotional connection with them. By making an emotional connection with the audience, you allow them to participate in your story.

And and but are often unnecessary. See if you can do without them.

16. Confidence

An experienced writer knows exactly what each page has to say and he knows how to say it. Write strong sentences with strong visual image, and remember that the page belongs to you. Write with such clarity that anyone can open your script at random, read a passage, and know exactly what is going on. Don't fill your pages with energy-sapping adverbs or adjectives in long, run-on sentences. It's your script. It's your idea. You are the writer. Write with confidence.

Hint Remember the three reasons you won't write a screenplay: Lack of confidence is the number one reason!

---

17. Page turners

View each page as its own unique drama. At the end of each page, you must have built up enough suspense that the reader is actually willing to exert the energy to raise his or her hand, grab hold of the page, and turn it.

Build a page-turner into each page of your script.

Add extra spaces or trim entire lines just to end a page on a moment of suspense. If there's a moment where the hero is about to be killed but saves himself, put the about to be killed bit at the end of one page so you have to turn the page and keep reading to get to the part where he saves himself.

William C. Martell even adds artificial suspense to the end of a page to keep those pages turning. One of his thriller scripts has a scene where the hero comes home and his girlfriend suggests they go out to dinner.

Boring! The hero enters his apartment on the second to last line on the page. So he added:

`Hands reach out from behind the door and grab him!`

At the top of the next page, we find out that it's his girlfriend. Lines like this not only turn your script into a page-turner, they add suspense, reversal, and excitement.

18. Editing

If you think your description is a little overwritten and could use some trimming, be brutal. Kick out every word that is not earning its space.

Design the page so the eye is drawn down, and make sure that you have a page-turner at the end of each page.

Exercise for Writing Descriptive Passages

Online Resources

This simple exercise can be used in a variety of situations, and will enable you to hone your descriptive passage writing skills.

1. Take a careful look around the room you are in at the moment and describe everything and everyone in it, including you.

2. List the movement in the room. If there is no movement, try to recall how you entered the room.

---

3. See if you can include some of the objects in the room in the description of movement.

---

4. What is the emotion of the room?

---

5. Imagine you are sitting in front of a blank cinema screen. What must you tell the production designer in order for him to achieve the look of the room?

---

6. See if you can sum everything up in four lines – the look, the movement and the feel of the room, including any character description.

Summary

1. Organize yourself. Know which scene comes when, and what the source of conflict is. Use the charts provided.

2. Write out the action and keep it as brief and dynamic as possible.

3. Develop your own individual style.

4. Never forget to draw on your instinctive storytelling ability.

We are ready to tackle dialogue.

7　Dialogue

CREATING DIALOGUE IS the last step in the screenwriting process. Dialogue writing should not be attempted until the story outline and the character studies have been thoroughly completed.

Writers who attempt dialogue before the story has been planned in detail usually find that the act of writing dialogue is such a pleasant diversion from the nitty-gritty of character study that they forget that story, not dialogue, is the major issue, and they find that the characters take charge of the story and dictate the terms of play to the writer.

It is easy to spot this in a script: writer finds himself boxed into a corner by his unruly characters and, in order to compensate for their behaviour, the writer simply adds a new character in a desperate attempt to drag the story back on course. This new character normally arrives at about page thirty, with the additional pressure to pull off one of those McKee 'plot points'.

This never works, and the script is ultimately doomed to oblivion (assuming the writer has had the fortitude to complete it).

Writing instructors and screenwriting books are filled with ironies when discussing dialogue. One thing everyone agrees is that the best dialogue is minimal dialogue.

Here is the ultimate irony: As we discussed in the last chapter, agent and producers don't read the descriptive passages – just the dialogue, unless they are confused about what is going on and need to refer to the descriptive passages for clarification.

A picture is worth a thousand words. Think about it, by this reasoning, the best dialogue would be no dialogue at all. Movies are a series of pictures with sounds. The sound is composed of three elements: music, effects and dialogue. Listening to a movie with solely the dialogue playing would make it a very different experience, would it not? Yet agents and producers, those two types of professionals with chequebooks, do just that when they read your script.

The next irony is the common adage 'Don't talk about doing something, do it'; or 'Actions speak louder than words'. Again, no dialogue seems to be the way to go.

People love to watch a story. A story consists of a person with a plan. It doesn't need to be a good plan or a clever plan, but audiences love to watch to see if they can learn something new by how this plan unfolds.

These are just a few examples of the paradoxes facing a screenwriter embarking on writing dialogue.

When approaching a scene in preparation for dialogue writing, you should have the following available to you:

- The character studies for each of the characters in your head. If the characters cannot speak to you outside of the scene, or if you cannot ask them a question and actually hear (or feel) their responses, then you do not know your characters well enough. You cannot continue until you have this.
- Scene outlines along with clear in and out points (Chapter 5)
- Any twist or reversal you might have for the scene.
- A list of which characters are in the scene.

See if there might be better way to tell the story or make the point of the scene. Often a new idea will spring to mind, or you may recast the scene with different characters from your cast list (don't make up any new characters).

Dialogue Tracks

When you are ready to proceed, imagine yourself in a recording studio. Write dialogue as if you and your characters are in a recording studio – by laying down tracks. Write dialogue for the entire script, once for each track. Take your time, be patient, and create clear tracks for story and moral argument. You may not have key words or moral argument for each scene. Later, when your dialogue writing session is complete, you will be able to mix (edit) the tracks to create powerful and satisfying dialogue.

Write these tracks – story dialogue; moral argument; key words.

1. Story dialogue

The talk about what is happening in a scene.

> SWEET-FACED WOMAN
> I'm just going to get some flowers,
> dear. I'll be back in twenty minutes.
> It's tulip season today. I'm so happy.

(Mark Andrus and James L Brooks, As Good As It Gets)

Hint Write story dialogue for the entire script, without worrying about how it sounds at this stage. You will be mixing it later.

Online Resources

It may be helpful to construct a simple chart to track the following in each scene:

Goal

Figure out which character's goal is driving the scene. That character's goal will be the spine of the scene.

Conflict

Who opposes the character's goal?

Plan

The character with the goal now comes up with the plan that may call for either direct or indirect action within the scene.

Twist

Scenes with twists are more exciting than scenes without.

Endpoint

A firm statement or a completed action or a surprising revelation make good endpoints.

figure 7.1
Story Dialogue Chart

Scene no.	
Goal	
Conflict	
Plan	
Twist	
Endpoint	

Write the scene, what happens, with dialogue

2. Moral dialogue

Describes what is worthwhile in life, along with what is right or wrong, within the context of the morality you have created for the world of your story.

Values
Let your characters speak openly about their values and what they like or dislike. This allows you to compare different versions of how to live.

>   LOUISE
>   Just for the future, when a woman's
>   crying like that, she's not having
>   any fun.

>   (Callie Khourie, Thelma and Louise)

Moral argument
Two or more characters come into conflict about what is right or wrong on the grounds that a particular course of action will hurt someone.

>   MELVIN
>   (to Simon)
>   What I know is that as long as you
>   keep your work zipped up around me,
>   I don't give a fuck what or where
>   you shove your show. Are we done
>   being neighbours for now?

>   SIMON
>   (to Frank)
>   Do you still think I was exaggerating?

Frank can only smile

>   FRANK
>   Definitely a package you don't want
>   to open or touch.

>   MELVIN
>   Hope you find him. I love that dog.

Simon, terminally non-confrontational, still finds himself compelled to turn back toward Melvin.

>   SIMON
>   (directly)
>   You don't love anything Mr. Udall

Simon closes his door leaving Melvin alone.

                    MELVIN
         I love throwing your dog down the
         garbage chute.

         (Mark Andrus and James L Brooks, As Good As It Gets)

3. Key word and catch phrase

Words that carry certain meanings which may mean something different to the audience. When embedded in a story, key words provide the snap, crackle and pop. You may want to repeat a key word or catch-phrase several times over the course of a story, with each situation casting a new meaning and new shading to the words.

Famous key words that have leapt from the screen to popular culture include: 'Show me the money'; 'A man's gotta do what a man's gotta do'; 'Make my day punk'; 'Yada Yada Yada'.

4. The final mix

Now it is a simple matter of taking the three different tracks you have created and, like a sound engineer in a music studio, mixing them down into one track. Some scenes will need mainly story dialogue – in them you will raise the level of the moral argument – and every now and then your sound engineer will spike in some key words.

The Fifteen Tricks and Traps of Dialogue

1. Keep it simple

Writing dialogue becomes fun and simple when you know your characters really well – through your character essays. When you achieve this, your characters will actually 'speak' to you.

No confusing words or difficult names. If your script has an African character name or is a sci-fi picture with technical jargon, remember that your script is being written for a reader. Try to keep it simple. A good screenplay is written in high school essay style and vocabulary.

2. Keep it short

Find the shortest and most direct way to express your thoughts.

There is a marvellous moment in Escape from Alcatraz when the child psychologist, a fellow prisoner of Clint Eastwood, asks how his childhood was. 'Short', was the terse reply. No one actually speaks like this but, in this moment, we learn volumes about Clint Eastwood's character.

3. Make each character speak with an individual voice

Each character should have their own individual way of speaking. Often a writer, so accustomed to writing each character's voice as they themselves would speak, forgets that each individual in the world speaks a little differently.

This flaw is actually the easiest and the most fun to correct. Deciding the individual voices of the characters and then doing a dialogue rewrite is amusing and entertaining.

4. Forget dialect

A script written in a dialect will be considered a script by a rank amateur first timer.

I had to read a script written in a heavy West Yorkshire accent. It was almost impossible to understand the colloquialisms. I even asked some vintage Brits in the office to translate, but they also found it difficult. Remember that dialects may be quaint but are difficult to understand and make your script hard to sell.

When Trainspotting played in Scottish in America, it was subtitled. Even my British friends find the thick Glaswegian accent difficult to understand.

Scripts are best written in clear and simple English. The choice of words will tell the reader if the character is cockney, street urchin, or southerner.

Casting directors will also dislike your script if it is written in dialect. Simply by writing your female lead as cockney means that you have limited the choice of actress to those who can pull off a cockney accent. You have encumbered your script.

On the set, your cockney accent further eliminates the possibility of collaboration with the actors – the dialect is preset.

If you want your character to speak in French your choices are:

```
             ELLIOT
          (in French)
    It's 10 a.m. I'm still drunk.
```

or

```
             ELLIOT
    Dix heures du matin. J'suis
    toujours bourré.
    (It's 10 a.m. I'm still drunk.)
```

5. No difficult words

You have to be easy on the reader. Any time you drop in a difficult word, or a word that you have invented (to explain some new-age technical concept, for example) you slow down the reader. The reader has to look the word up, call someone, or skip over it in the troubling knowledge that they don't really know what you are saying.

6. Don't underline

Have you ever, in a speech of dialogue, in order to emphasize a word, underlined it? Don't do it. You look like a rank amateur first timer, and you have eliminated the possibility of collaboration with the actors. You are also directing from the typewriter, which is not your job. Well-written dialogue should speak for itself. Pauses and key moments should be obvious. Only underline a word if you think that the reader and the actor who reads your script are so stupid that they won't otherwise get it.

7. No '...'

Have you ever, in a speech of dialogue, in order to denote a pause, used '...'? Again you are directing from the typewriter, eliminating the possibility of collaboration with the actors, and making yourself look like a rank amateur first timer. There are exceptions to this rule.

Firstly, only use '...' if you feel that the plot hinges on this specific point, and/or you think the reader or actor won't be clever enough to get it.

Maybe you should limit yourself to five '...'s per script.

The second exception is the interrupted speech:

JOANNE
How old is Elliot? I'll bet he's...

BERNICE
...thirty-six.

You can use this as often as you like in your script.

8. No parenthetical directions

Do you put in actor's directions such as 'whispered', 'angrily', or 'shouted' under the character name?

ELLIOT
(angrily)

Again you are directing from the typewriter. Well-written dialogue will show how it is to be spoken.

If a professional actor receives your script with parentheticals, they will cross them out with a heavy black pen. If you put these directions in, you are eliminating the possibility of including their creative input.

I once worked as a touch-up artist on a film where in one scene a huge, Rambo-shaped man was arguing with his petite wife. Instead of hitting her, the script, with parentheticals, called for him to go to the kitchen door and smash it so hard that it splintered. We rigged a stunt door and, during the rehearsals, the actor pretended to hit the door. We rehearsed the scene over and over again until we were ready.

At the moment of the take, the actor went to the door on cue with his massive arms knotted for a killer blow, whereupon he sighed and gently stroked the door.

The response from the crew was spontaneous. At the end of the take we all applauded. The power and energy of the actor, and the fact that he could have easily demolished the entire house, if not the door, with his bare hands, and yet was rendered powerless by the emotion of the scene, made the scene memorable for its intensity. Although we later did a take with the actor physically smashing the door (as per the parentheticals), it was the first take that the director kept.

9. Musical beat

People speak with their own rhythms. By speeding up, slowing down, and emphasizing key words, people speak with a natural beat. Even though you have edited and honed your dialogue, you must make certain that your dialogue sounds like real speech. To do that you must restore the musical beat.

10. No long speeches

Try and remember the four-line rule. It applies to dialogue as well as descriptive passages. Certain masters of the screenplay write dialogue that goes on for pages. Tarantino opens True Romance with a monologue that is three-and-a-half pages long.

Writing dialogue like Tarantino on your first script will earn you derision. When you are at a level like Tarantino, you can write what you want.

There are times, however, when you will want to write a speech longer than four lines. You could double space after a few lines:

```
                 QUINTO
         You used to laugh at me and my
         little jingle — Got a problem?
         Someone not treating you right?

         Owed a bit of cash? Call Quinto.
         The professional prick. Here I am,
         couple of years down the road.
         What do I find? You.
```

(Elliot Grove, Table 5.)

Or you could add stage directions to break up the dialogue:

                        LARRY
          I'm trying to get the cash. Everything
          I do these days has to do with cash.

Ramona flings the script to the floor.

                        LARRY (cont'd)
          And the weather doesn't help, either.

(Elliot Grove, Table 5.)

11. No funny punctuation

Screenplays are written in a standard screenplay format (see Chapter 16). The correct way to use punctuation is standard English punctuation. In my days as a script reader I encountered screenplays submitted with a whole series of punctuation styles, such as the triple exclamation mark!!! Using punctuation such as this makes your script look like a comic book. Avoid.

12. No on-the-nose dialogue

By on-the-nose dialogue, I mean obvious dialogue which telegraphs the action, for example:

Elliot reaches for a glass of Perrier.

                        ELLIOT
          I am thirsty. I think I'll get a drink.

On-the-nose dialogue is story dialogue track without sound editing. Most of what you write in your first 'track' will be on-the-nose.

13. Start late, end early

Of each and every line of dialogue ask yourself 'Is there a briefer, fresher, quicker, more dynamic way to say the same thing'?

14. Avoid reality

New writers are tempted to include the humming and hawing of real speech in their dialogue. Such additions ignite the 'first time amateur' light bulb above your head. Experienced actors are trained to know where the 'you knows', and 'mmms' are to be included in the dialogue. Leave them out! Again you are precluding collaboration with the actors, and you don't want to do that!

15. Start on page three

As a script reader, I've read a script, sometimes two, every single day for nearly six years. Most scripts submitted to me came as a 'T'.

figure 7.2
The T Script

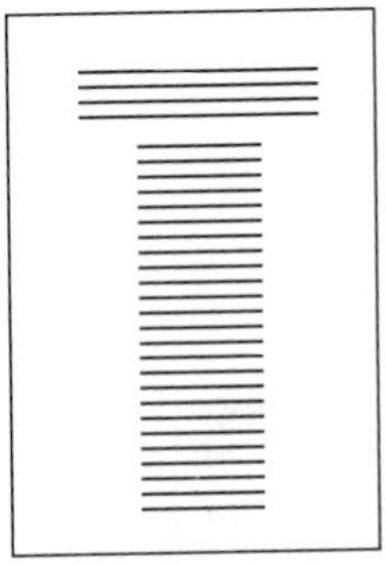

figure 7.3
The I Script

About one in ten came as an 'I'.

You can imagine the drama at my home a few seconds after the thud of the mail on the front steps. I could hear the footsteps of my partner racing to the door, and listen for the rip of the envelopes.

'What have you got?'

'A T.'

'An I.'

Wow. Such drama.

It would seem that one of the easiest ways to distinguish oneself in a fiercely competitive market is to start your dialogue on page three.

Certainly, agents and producers are obliged to read the black stuff for the first few pages. But how good are you? Could you manage to write three pages of compelling action? That's just three minutes of screen time! If you manage this, you will catapult yourself into the top one per cent of screenplays written in the English language this year. In the fiercely competive business, sometimes it comes down to this.

Hint Great dialogue should either move the story or reveal something about the character. The best dialogue is no dialogue. A picture is worth a thousand words.

Writer's Block

Do you suffer from writer's block?

Writer's block has absolutely nothing to do with lack of creativity. It has everything to do with lack of confidence. Look at your life and try to identify any recent situation which may have undermined your confidence, and then ignore it. Believe in yourself. You are at your own page seventy-five. You will feel much better and write better dialogue.

Dialogue Diagnostic Tool

Organize a table reading with friends or actors so you can hear what your dialogue sounds like in voices other than your own.

Organizing a table reading

There are many ways of conducting and organizing a table reading of your script. The first time you do this, you may find the whole process somewhat scary. The basic trick is to create an environment where you and the readers feel comfortable and safe.

Finding actors

Do you have trouble writing dialogue? Pull out your character essays. The chances are that you have still not fully researched your characters.

Remember to write the tracks. If you still have problems, try writing the story track only and then organize a table reading. Chances are the actors will have valuable suggestions as to how the dialogue can be made more life-like.

Actors are usually happy to do table readings. It is an informal opportunity for them to meet other actors and writers and to practise their craft. Ultimately, the actors might even be considered for the role. Place notices in the backstage entrances of theatres, acting schools and the net.

Setting a time and place

Evenings are a good time, especially early in the week. Arranging a table reading for a Friday night when everyone is either exhausted or in a party mood is usually unwise. A neutral venue, like a rehearsal room or church hall, is great if you can afford it. If not, have people into your home. It is also advisable to let everyone know what the timing is. If the reading is to

start at seven and finish at nine, write that in all your notices, so participants know what the time demands are. And be punctual.

The ground rules

Please be aware that nowadays people are very suspicious of meetings
with strangers. Do whatever it takes to make everyone comfortable with
you, and never take advantage of anyone!

Styles of reading

You can cast the script with actors, and have them just read the dialogue
scene by scene. Some actors will put in basic gestures and follow stage
directions if asked. I think that it is most useful to hear the dialogue only
at this stage. It is also a useful reference to tape record the dialogue for
later. Make sure you have the actors' permission.

Another type of circle reading is the round circle – especially useful if
you do not have enough actors for all the character parts. Simply start off
reading the first paragraph of descriptive passage until a line of dialogue,
all of which are read in turn around the table. This technique is useful
because you hear the dialogue read by several different voices.

Saying thank you

Actors do not expect to be paid, but it is polite to offer some form of
refreshment. It doesn't need to be fancy or expensive, just considerate.

A day or two after the reading, put a simple 'Thank you' card with a
considered note in the mail to each participant. You will be amazed how
readily they will agree to work with you again!

Afterwards – the rewrite. Collate all the notes from all the table readings and incorporate the suggestions and ideas into another rewrite.

Summary

1. Write minimal dialogue.

2. Preserve the musical beat, and make it sound like people talking.

3. Write three dialogue tracks – story, moral argument and key words.

That's the theory! Before we put it all together, let's look at writing
shorts.

8   Writing for Short Films

SHORTS ARE TO features what sonnets/haiku are to novels.

A short film script can be a great calling card for a writer, and it can be a great calling card for a director and a writer/director team. In order for it to become a great calling card, you need to make your short script as perfect as you possibly can. The audience for a short will be far more critical than that of a feature.

Short films are not a lesser form of cinematic storytelling – you are unlikely to make money from them. Although TV broadcast opportunities may be limited, they do get shown in cinemas, they do win awards, and they do work as an introduction to talent. Many of the best writers and directors started out with shorts.

A short can be anything from thirty seconds to thirty minutes in length – and this means they can do and be a great many different things. However, if you want to get your short into a festival, then keep it to no more than ten minutes. A film longer than ten minutes is difficult to show in front of a feature film. Remember: you can tell a great story in as little as 30 seconds. And chances are, the longer the short, the more expensive it will be to produce.

The great thing about shorts is that they can be about anything – the only limit beyond the cost of production is that of your own imagination. So don't be hemmed in – let your imagination fly. Play with your ideas. Play with the form. Experiment with ideas. Every short can and should be a unique vision.

Film is about telling stories in pictures, which is the most economical way of telling a story – and in the making of shorts, economy is everything. Remember the golden rule of filmmaking: show, don't tell. A good short can be more like a visual poem than a play, or a short story or trailer for something bigger to come. The idea and story can be focused enough in scope to exist entirely in the viewer's head, and so logic and time can play a much smaller role in the journey from beginning to end than in other formats.

The best short films are often a moment that is played out, but one that has a story at its heart – a conflict that has to be resolved, where there's a deadline to the action, where there's a choice that a character has to make. You should always try to tell a story. Short films aren't an excuse to 'break all the rules' – but they are an opportunity to push the boundaries of what cinematic storytelling can do. from these scripts and films you can learn much that will serve you well in longer formats.

It's worth thinking about the simplicity, clarity and economy of the storytelling; the vision of the piece, and its visual images; making every element pertinent; making everything exist in sympathy with everything else. Make your story coherent.

It's worth being careful of conflicting and incoherent worlds; ideas that are too concept-driven; the lack of narrative engine and story; the lack of engaging character; the lack of focus and concision; action and repetition without meaning; descriptive dialogue; extended jokes with (usually unsatisfying) punch-lines. Again, make your story coherent.

Think about how your film will play to its audience. Does your story have a potentially universal appeal? What will the audience know and when will they know it? What will they be guessing? What questions will they have which need answering? And what can you show without having to explain things away?

The impact of page one is crucial. Are we emotionally engaged? What is the vision and world of the film? Is it original? Do we inhabit the characters? Do the world and story of the film have integrity and authenticity? The last moment is also crucial – it's easy to come away feeling very little about a short, so work towards a meaningful, satisfying ending.

Be careful of cliché, because there are so many of them in short films (hit-men for hire, post office heists, people seeing themselves die, children representing innocence, dysfunctional abusive relationships, films about writing or making films, in-jokes and navel-gazing). Write what you know and feel passionately about rather than something second hand and culled from watching other films. Use the form to be fresh and original and unexpected – you don't get that opportunity very often in your writing career.

Think about the practicalities of writing your script so that it can be shot with a low or limited budget – there's never enough money around to spend on making shorts. Remember that digital technology is freeing up what filmmakers can do, and what they can afford to do. But remember also that a low budget short doesn't need to look 'cheap', unless of course you want it to do so.

One potential pitfall for writers can be directing their own scripts. Many of the most talented filmmakers write their own stories. But be careful of directing your own work because you want 'control' over the project. Creative collaboration can be a hugely rewarding experience – and if you're not a natural filmmaker, there's a chance you will spoil your writing with inexperienced filmmaking. Go to film festivals, meet filmmakers – find people with whom you can collaborate.

Spare a thought to the presentation of your script. It isn't hard to make it easy to read, and it's always worth the effort of rewriting and editing in order to make your story shine. There are no excuses for your script to not be as perfect as it can be.

Watch as many short films as you possibly can. There is no replacement for knowing what work is already out there, and knowing what you as an audience (as well as a writer) think and feel about it.

Short Story Writing Tools

1. Create a branding brief for your short

Short stories usually deal with bold concepts, but seen in close up. Sucessful writing will portray these concepts in a minimalist way which catches the eye. This is a technique used in advertising. Pretend that you are a copy writer hired by an advertising company to write a series of print ads and television ads for a product. Imagine what the key elements are of the story you are trying to 'sell' and see if you can come up with a branding brief. Here is an outline of a branding brief used by an advertising production company in London.

The Goal

Brand Identity and Brand Values

Ideal Brand Position

The Message

Notable Product Characteristics

The Target Market

Tone

2. Writing one-liners and topical gags

Often short story ideas come from a one-liner. Here are some hints if you want to try writing topical one-liners.

1. Read the newspapers. Not as daft as it sounds, sometimes a sentence jumps out at you and you come up with an instant punchline.

2. Try and avoid the obvious or the ongoing old story − if there's another joke to be had out of the teddy called Mohammed that hasn't been done yet it'll take you too long to think of it.

3. Look at the quirkier stories in the news − you can find them in newspapers, on the net, even on ceefax. Often there'll be a simple gag off the back of them.

4. Try and be different. Go off on a tangent, find a topic where you hear the same obvious jokes being made and try and look at the story from a completely different angle.

5. Listen to shows like News Quiz and The Now Show, the current topical shows on the radio. You can catch up with them on the net. Watch Have I Got News For You. Don't nick the jokes (instant disqualification, because everyone else will have heard them), but get the feel for the structure of a gag, and listen to how the professionals tackle the week's stories.

3. Retell a joke or oral story

Have you ever been at a party or family or other social function when someone asks 'You won't believe what happened to me yesterday?' Often this can be a motherlode of ideas for a short film.

In Sweden doing a screenwriting class, I was asked by a young Norwegian filmmaker (in English) if I would like to see his three minute short. It was lunch time, and I was tired, and was trying to watch anything. I asked him if it was in English, and he said 'No'. Before I knew it, I was watching a short film in Norwegian on my lunch break. The film was beautifully shot, and consisted of a camera moving slowly around a elderly couple in an elegant restaurant.

After the screening (from a laptop) he knew I hadn't understood a thing, so he told me the story:

A couple go out to celebrate their fiftieth wedding anniversay. She asks him 'Do you still love me?' 'Of course I still love you darling, or I would have left you ages ago'. Then she asks: 'If I were to die before you, would you still live in our house?' 'Of course I would', He said. 'I've just paid off the mortgage'. 'If I died before you, and you were living in our house, would you still sleep in our bed?' 'Of course,' he says, 'it's a really comfortable and expensive bed.' Then she asked: 'Would you take all of my pictures down?' He answered: 'I might.' 'Would you marry someone else?' She asked. 'I might' he answered. 'OK,' she asks, 'If I died before you, and you were sleeping in our bed in our house, would you let your new wife use my golf clubs?' 'No, he said. 'She's left-handed.'

He then told me he had been told this story by his grandfather. His movie screened in many film festivals and on Scandanavian television.

Perhaps you will have a family story like this which you can adapt into a short film script. These types of stories have already passed the marketing test. If they didn't work orally, they wouldn't be repeated.

4. Use a song

Occasionally you will find a musician with a song, for which they want a dramatic short made to illustrate their song. The British singer Robbie Williams did just this in 2006/7. On tour, he was too busy to shoot conventional pop promos. His record company created a competition for filmmakers to come up with short films using any one of his ten songs as a starting point. It wasn't necessary to use the entire song, just make a story surrounding the film. One of the films was fantastic. It is called Goodbye To the Normals, and has had huge numbers on YouTube. The writer was paid out of the competition budget.

Remember that will need clearance of any music for your film, and make certain you have this before you start writing.

Writing for the Internet

Movies on the internet have become the next hot thing. Everyone wants in: the hedge funds, the studios, the television networks and the websites themselves.They are all gagging for quality content. They have the money and the infrastructure or hardware. What they all lack is content. This is where you have a golden opportunity to literally cash in.

Writing for the internet falls into two categories. Films which succeed and get lots and lots of 'hits' or views, are either existing film content, or newly created content.

Successful web content is content which is brief, succinct and has a good payoff line. Web viewers tend to browse and surf, lingering on a clip or film which immediately grabs their attention. At our newly launched www.raindance.tv we have discovered that seven seconds is the most someone will linger unless hooked in.

That is about three script lines.

Filmmakers in Britain are focusing on short form content for the web. Where an idea is greater than a couple of minutes, they are strung together, soap-opera style, in series called webisodes. These series are designed for the lucrative mobile telephone market

A typical webisode series might consist of:
1. Two young teenagers in Liverpool decide to become pop stars
2. They try and find a guitar player
3. They try to find a lead singer
4. They rehearse
5. They decide to go to London
6. They get into a van which breaks down
7. The van breaks down again
8. They finally reach London etc.

Hint Think of yourself as a visual communicator. You can write features, shorts or web movies, dependeing on the market you are pursuing. Design your scripts to take advantage of the medium that is going to want to buy your script.

How short films make money on the internet

There are two ways films make money on the internet. Firstly, viewers can agree to pay money to watch the films by entering their credit card into a website shop software. This method is called, variously, Pay Per View (PPV) or Video On Demand (VOD). Secondly, by watching it for free knowing that the film is going to have ads surrounding the film from which a portion of the revenue is split with the film rights holder. This method is called ad revenue share (Rev Share). Obviously, this is the method most popular on the internet.

Keywords
In order for your film to be seen by as many viewers as possible, filmmakers rely on two things: the publicity generated by the website carrying their film, or by search engines picking up a key word in the title of the film. The word 'samurai' is a top key word on the internet, so obviously this word in the title of your film will bring it up more often.

Keywords will become more important to screenwriters as the new voice recognition software, developed by the revolutionary site www.blinkx.com, becomes common place. Google is desperate to acquire this technology as well. For example, if you type in the phrase 'Show me the money', this software search function will take you to the precise moment this dialogue is spoken

The challenge for writers is to find top internet key words and incorporate them into dialogue, knowing that voice recognition software will pick them up.

The best places to find top-rated key words is to look at the eBay and Google AdSense sites. This information is free. Recent top keywords on eBay include the rather creatively challenging 'Britney Spears', for example. Make a list of the top 100 key words from eBay and Google and see if you can incorporate them into your dialogue.

Story Design in the Short Fiction Film

While attending the excellent independent film festival in Aarhus – the second city of Denmark – I met an ex-patriot American, Richard Raskin who has spent his entire career writing about short stories and short films. He kindly agreed to contribute the following article to this book.

Introduction

Born in New York in 1941, Richard Raskin teaches screenwriting and video production at Aarhus University in Denmark, where he is also the editor of p.o.v. – a Danish Journal of Film Studies, and organizes an international short film symposium every year. He has served as jury president at international film festivals in France, Belgium, India, Holland and Denmark, and frequently lectures on storytelling in the short film at film schools and film festivals throughout Scandinavia and elsewhere. He has written a number of books, the most recent of which are A Child at Gunpoint: A Case Study in the Life of a Photo (2004), The Art of the Short Fiction Film: A Shot by Shot Study of Nine Modern Classics (2002) and Kortfilmen som fortælling (2001). His articles have appeared in such journals as Zeitschrift für Kunstgeschichte, Film History, Journal of Media Practice, Asian Cinema and The Canadian Journal of Film Studies.

The purpose of this article is to propose a non-formulaic model that can be used as a set of guidelines when writing scripts for short films.

Unlike sequential models, which focus on a series of steps a story is presumed to pass through as it unfolds, the present approach is based on the view that short film storytelling can best be described in terms of opposing properties that balance and complete one another in a dynamic interplay. An approach of this kind is not only more open than other narrative models, but also better suited to catching the most common beginner mistakes in designing short fiction films.

Seven forms of interplay or balance will be described here, some requiring a more ample presentation than others, but all equally important – and all proposed not as rules that must be followed but rather as opportunities for increasing the likelihood of effective storytelling.

Finally, just as short films are at their best when they follow the 'less is more' principle, I will make the present discussion as concise and to the point as possible. Readers interested in a more extensive discussion, applied in some detail to concrete examples, are referred to my book, The Art of the Short Fiction Film: A Shot by Shot Study of Nine Modern Classics (McFarland, 2002).

Character-focus – Character-interaction

Whose story is it?

The best short films generally make it clear from the start whose story they are telling. Once we as viewers know that, we have a 'home-base' within the film, a means for keeping our bearings and for knowing how to gauge the relative importance of anything that happens.

Generally a short is one character's story. But it can be the story of two (or more) main characters, in which case the challenges are much greater and the chances of success correspondingly diminished. Beginners are therefore well advised to make their short films one character's story.

However this property, which we will call character-focus, takes on its full value within a short when it is balanced by character-interaction – by having the main character interact with other characters at key points in the story. This is what gives a short its vitality and a short lacking in interaction – a common beginner's mistake – will not easily capture and hold our interest.

The interaction which breathes life into a short does not have to be conflictual. There are excellent short films that are entirely free of conflict. And this important difference between the short film and longer narratives is often overlooked because of a widespread tendency to take it for granted that all cinematic storytelling is necessarily conflict-based.

This first form of balance, then, involves an interplay of character-focus (clarity as to whose story is being told) with character-interaction (having that character interact with other characters at important moments in the film). A short in which either is lacking can still be excellent – but despite rather than thanks to its management of the properties just described.

Causality – Choice

Theoreticians such as Gerald Prince (1973) suggest that any story must include at least two events, one of which causes the other. And while it is true that causality must be a part of any good story, it is only half the picture. Consider William Golding's account of an incident he experienced while serving in the Royal Navy during the Second World War:

The Germans used to have a very long distance plane. And if we were escorting convoys back across the Atlantic, this plane would come out, and it would circle the convoy, perhaps five miles away from it, round and round and it was wirelessing to submarines saying where this convoy is. So you knew that this plane was sending your position.

I remember one moment at which the captain of the escort got in touch with the plane. He flashed it up on an Aldis lamp, you see – and said, 'Please, will you go round the other way. You are making my head ache.' The plane turned round and started going round the other way, like that, you see. There was this kind of insane contact between people.

It could be argued that causality is in play here, with the British captain's message as the cause and the reversal of the German pilot's flight direction as the effect. But what makes this an interesting story is that the German pilot chose to fly the other way, and for that matter, that the British captain chose to contact the pilot, violating wartime protocol which prohibits frivolous contact with the enemy.

Here we have characters making things happen, rather than characters things happen to. In other words, causality flows from the choices characters make and this is what drives the story forward, while at the same time making those characters more interesting in our eyes. As John Gardner wrote: 'Failure to recognize that the central character must act, not simply be acted upon, is the single most common mistake.'

And what is true of Golding's story and Gardner's observation applies in spades to the short film, where the only characters likely to earn our interest are those who make choices and thereby shape their own story.

The bottom line then with respect to the properties discussed in this section is that an interplay of causality and choice in a short is preferable to storytelling in which causality overrides or precludes choice rather than flowing from it, and in which the main character is too passive or helpless to take charge of his or her own story.

Consistency – Surprise

In the best short films, it is usually in a matter of seconds that the characters are presented and defined for the viewer, and once defined, they remain consistent with their initial definition. At the end of the film, they may have learned or experienced something meaningful but they are still the same people they were at the start; only their situation has changed. And this is another important difference between the short film and longer narratives.

In the feature film, generally spanning considerable stretches of time, the main character is expected to undergo some fundamental change in the course of the story. In the short, in which story-time and screen-time often coincide – so that a film with a running time of seven minutes generally depicts an event lasting the same seven minutes, characters remain consistent from beginning to end. Unfortunately, student film-makers writing short film scripts are sometimes told to bring their central character through some basic transformation by teachers who fail to distinguish between the kinds of storytelling appropriate to short and feature films.

In the short film characters remain essentially the same throughout.

But that doesn't mean that the viewer should ever be able to guess what will happen next. And paradoxical as this may sound, characters can continue to exhibit exactly the same attributes from start to finish and yet behave in a totally unforeseeable manner.

Striving for this kind of interplay of consistency and surprise is well worth the effort when designing the characters and story for a short.

Sound – Image

That the visual possibilities of the film medium should be exploited to the fullest is something that beginners rarely forget when designing their short film stories. But that the action might be as interesting for the ear as for the eye is often overlooked.

In those short films which make the most of the storytelling possibilities inherent in sound, characters produce sounds or are responsive to sounds. In these films, sound is not merely an auditory backdrop for the action, but rather at key moments in each story, actually becomes the action. In this way, an interplay of sound and image is a way of taking full advantage of specific storytelling opportunities inherent in a given situation.

Character – Object

In one way or another, it is essential for any short film to bring the viewer inside the thoughts or feelings of its characters, and preferably without the use of voice-over or inner monologue, which rarely results in a successful film.

Allowing the dramatic context to suggest what must be happening within a character while the camera dwells on the character's face, is one of the most effective strategies for bringing us inside a character's mind. As Gabriel Byrne has aptly stated:

Essentially I believe by some mysterious alchemy which we really don't understand, the camera photographs thought. I think it photographs emotion and that it photographs thought. And if you're thinking it, the camera will pick it up. And I don't think directors understand that enough. They're always cutting away at crucial moments and you think 'Oh God, stay with the actor. He'll tell the story.'

One particularly interesting way to heighten our experience of a character's subjectivity is to evoke those thoughts and feelings through the character's relation to some physical object that is charged with meaning for him or her. Such an interplay of character and object helps to establish at one and the same time both the inner life of a character and some privileged focus in the physical setting, and this convergence of inner and outer, of subject and object, is perfectly suited to the short film since so much substance can thereby be carried in a single moment.

Simplicity – Depth

'The one thing I try to do in all my books is to leave enough room in the prose for the reader to inhabit it... There's a way in which a writer can do too much, overwhelming the reader with so many details that he no longer has any air to breathe.' – Paul Auster

A short film that tells a simple story is more likely to be experienced as an inviting space for the viewer to enter and linger in than a short film filled with clever twists from start to finish. Paradoxically, simplicity enhances depth in short film storytelling, by making the film a 'habitable space' within which the viewer can explore and construct possible meanings.

Correspondingly, a short film that confuses or overwhelms the viewer with too complex a plot or too many details, is likely to hold the viewer at a distance. As editor and sound designer Walter Murch (1995) stated: 'Past a certain point, the more effort you put into wealth of detail, the more you encourage the audience to become spectators rather than participants.' This applies even more to the short film than to longer narratives.

Furthermore, too complex a plot in a short film can draw attention away from the characters, while a simpler plot can give the viewer the time and space needed to enter into the lives of the characters.

It is by keeping the story simple and resisting the temptations of cleverness that a sense of depth can be achieved in a short film.

Economy – Wholeness

If in making a short, the filmmaker chooses to follow the 'less is more' principle by cutting to the bone and ruthlessly killing every darling, this concern with economy in storytelling will serve the film – strengthening it by keeping it lean and concentrated.

Beginners sometimes think that the longer their short is, the closer it comes to being a 'real' film. Hence the temptation to stretch it out and make it fill as many minutes of screen-time as possible. When this happens, what might have been a good six- or seven-minute short often becomes instead an excruciating twenty-minute ordeal for the viewer, as anyone who has served on juries at international short film festivals has probably experienced.

Although in general, cutting should be tight, with shots kept as trim as possible, the camera should also be allowed to dwell unhurriedly on a face at moments when something important is going on within the character, and shots of this kind should be allowed to run their course. Alternating in this way between tight cutting through much of the short and looser cutting when shots can bring us inside the mind of a character, also guards against too uniform a rhythm in the editing of a short.

But by and large, the 'less is more' principle should be followed in weeding out everything that isn't necessary to move the story forward or to bond us to the characters.

At the same time, however, when a short film ends, the viewer should be left feeling not only that the film is complete but also that returning to it again and again would be rewarding. How is it possible to cut to the bone and still leave the viewer feeling that there is abundance in the film?

Part of the answer concerns the ways in which closure is managed. If for example the film ends by returning to its point of departure, only with some element changed as a marker that something irreversible has occurred, that can help the viewer to feel that the story has come full circle and is complete.

Another important closural strategy involves placing, just before the film ends, a symbolic gesture or event – perhaps the most significant moment in the film. That way, when the credits appear on screen, the viewer can be left with something meaningful to replay in his or her mind, and if that happens, there is a good chance that the film will be thought of as whole and inexhaustible.

Conclusion

There is no consensus as to the maximum running time for a film to be considered a short. Festivals differ widely in their criteria, ranging from a maximum length of 15-minutes at Cannes to 60-minutes at Uppsala. And the same variations can be found in the literature on the short film.

One of the problems involved in defining the short is that an intermediate form is often overlooked. The French use the term moyen métrage to describe a form lying between the short and feature film. And in Scandinavia, that in-between form of fiction film is usually called a novellefilm (that is, the equivalent of a short story). Typically 25- or 40-minutes long, films of this kind are really miniature feature films, though scaled down to simpler plots, fewer characters, etc.

The true short film on the other hand – the poetry of filmmaking – is typically only six- or seven-minutes long, and in my view has a maximum length of 15-minutes.

Beginners making their first short films should be encouraged to aim for a running time of six-or seven-minutes, if at all possible. That would increase the chances of producing a film that has the kind of density and concentration found in poetry, and in this connection I would like to quote a Chinese master, Wu Qiao, who wrote:

'The [writer's] message is like rice. When you write in prose, you cook the rice. When you write poetry, you turn rice into rice wine.'

The mediocre short – dilute and tediously belabouring a story that seems to go on forever – is like cooked rice, while the best short films – holding back while teeming with substance – are pure rice wine.

Schematic Overview

1. Character-focus – Character-interaction
Letting the viewer know whose story is being told, yet keeping the main character interacting with others; unless we know whose story it is, we have no 'home base' within the film; at the same time, interaction can provide the vitality needed to capture and hold our interest.

2. Causality – Choice
Making cause and effect relationships central to the story, but having the causality flow from the main character's deliberate choices; main characters who make things happen, driving the story forward, are more interesting to the viewer than are characters things happen to.

3. Consistency – Surprise
Keeping behavior consistent with each character's definition, yet utterly unpredictable; unlike longer narratives, the short fiction film is not good at depicting a character's transformation; while the situation at the end of the film differs from that at the start, the characters remain essentially the same.

4. Image – Sound
Designing the action in such a way that it is as interesting to the ear as to the eye; sound, in particular, should be an integral part of the action rather than simply an auditory backdrop for the action; characters can produce sounds and react to sounds; sounds can trigger events or can in themselves constitute events.

5. Character – Object and Décor
Having characters interact with meaningful objects and with their physical setting; in this way the inner lives of characters can be connected to the physical world; subjectivity and interiority are balanced by external, material things.

6. Simplicity – Depth

Keeping the story simple enough to be habitable by the viewer; stories that are too complex hold the viewer at a distance, in the role of an observer rather than a participant; simplicity can best enable the viewer to enter the story and to explore and construct its meanings from within.

7. Economy – Wholeness

Balancing the trimming away of all superfluous moments and detail so that the film is a concentrated distillation, with the viewer's need to experience the film as a whole that is richly textured and teeming with life; only dwelling on characters' faces (eyes) takes precedence over cutting to the bone; closural strategies can play a major role in leaving the view feeling that the film is complete and inexhaustible.

References

TV interviews

Byrne, Gabriel. Episode 84, Season 7 of 'Inside the Actor's Studio', originally aired in the U.S. on the Bravo network on December 10, 2000.

Golding, William. Interviewed on Danish television by Werner Svendsen in 1980, and broadcast on October 6th, 1983. Golding is best remembered as the author of The Lord of the Flies (1954).

Cited texts

Auster, Paul. The Art of Hunger. New York: Penguin, 1997; p. 282–3.

Barnstone, Tony and Ping, Chou (trans.). The Art of Writing: Teachings of the Chinese Masters (Boston & London: Shambala, 1996); Wu Quao cited at p. 90.

Murch, Walter. In the Blink of an Eye: A Perspective on Film Editing (Los Angeles: Silman James Press, 1995), p. 15.

Gardner, John. The Art of Fiction: Notes on Craft for Young Writers (NY: Vintage Books, 1991), p. 65

Prince, Gerald. A Grammar of Stories (The Hague & Paris: Mouton, 1973), p. 26

Raskin, Richard. The Art of the Short Fiction Film: A Shot by Shot Study of Nine Modern Classics (Jefferson, N.C.: McFarland, 2002).

On the Short Film

Adelman, Kim. The Ultimate Filmmaker's Guide to Short Films: Making it Big in Shorts. Michael Wiese, 2004.

Beairsto, Ric. The Tyranny of Story: Audience Expectations and the Short Screenplay. Vancouver Film School, 1998.

Cooper, Pat and Dancyger, Ken. Writing the Short Film. Focal Press, 1994.

Cowgill, Linda J. Writing Short Films: Structure and Content for Screenwriters. Lone Eagle, 1997.

Elsey, Eileen and Kelly, Andrew. In Short: A Guide to Short Filmmaking in the Digital Age. BFI, 2002.

Hendrykowski, Marek. The Art of the Short Film. Ars Nova, 1998.

Jensen, Niels. Kort om korte historier I litteratur og film. Den Danske Filmskole, 2007.

Johnson, Claudia H. Crafting Short Screenplays That Connect. Focal Press, 2000.

Levy, Edmond. Making a Winning Short: How to Write, Direct, Edit, and Produce a Short Film. Henry Holt, 1994.

Phillips, William H. Writing Short Scripts. Syracuse University Press, 1991.

Poulsen, Henrik. Den korte film. Copenhagen: Gyldendal, 2004.

Raskin, Richard. Kortfilmen som fortælling. Systime, 2001.

Raskin, Richard. The Art of the Short Fiction Film: A Shot by Shot Study of Nine Modern Classics. McFarland, 2002.

Raskin, Richard. 'On pacing in the short fiction film.' Journal of Media Practice. Vol. 7, No. 2 (2006), pp. 159–160.

Riis, Johannes. 'Toward a poetics of the short film.' p.o.v. – a Danish Journal of Film Studies no. 5 (March 1998), pp. 133–150. http://imv.au.dk/publikationer/pov/Issue_05/section_4/artc1A.html

Rudnicki, Jean-Marc. Écrire un court métrage. Dixit, 1999.

Thurlow, Clifford. Making Short Films: The Complete Guide from Script to Screen. Berg, 2005.

Yeatman, Bevin. 'What makes a short film good?' p.o.v. – a Danish Journal of Film Studies no. 5 (March 1998), pp. 151–162. http://imv.au.dk/publikationer/pov/Issue_05/section_4/artc2A.html

Summary

1. Shorts can have commercial value.

2. Choose the story line that will lend itself to a short.

3. Heighten the story by using archetypes where possible.

4. Be brief.

With all of the prevailing screenwriting theory summed up, let's try to develop a workable Writer's Blueprint.

9 The Writer's Blueprint

SO MUCH FOR the theory and the discussion of screenwriting technique. The time has come to start putting it all together. Where I grew up there was a colloquialism which translates as: 'Time to stop chatting, roll up your sleeves, and get your hands dirty.'

I have purposely skipped over formatting and typing rules. These are discussed thoroughly in Chapter 16. Many writers get to this point and then actually fail to write because they are afraid that their lack of knowledge about the finer points of formatting will interfere with their creative process. I get calls all the time from talented writers who want to chat. After I discern that they are healthy physically and mentally, I ask them how their latest script project is going. They always hesitate, draw a deep breath and wonder aloud if they can ask me a deeply significant question like: is 'gunshot' capitalized or not?

Hint Worries about formatting are one of the devices used by writers to procrastinate and put off writing their script. Procrastination is the third reason you will not write your script.

The Writers' Lab: A Recap

Here we are, faced with the excitement of writing a screenplay. Probably you have told a friend or two that what you would really like to do is write a screenplay, and they too are interested in how you progress. So there is the pressure of actually producing work.

Here is the first secret — a tip I found out the hard way after wasting months and years of time. Any successful craftsman has a method of approaching his craft — whether it is the way a potter measures and kneads the clay, or a carpenter sizes up the grain of wood, or a painter stretches and prepares the canvas. I believe that there is a great deal of craftsmanship in screenwriting and it doesn't matter to me which system you use, as long as you develop and hone a system. Once you have mastered the system, then you will be ready for the magic of creativity that can turn your craftsmanship into art of the highest order. I am going to tell you my system.

I have developed this step-by-step system over fifteen years at the Writers' Lab. For me it certainly works. I believe that if you follow these steps, in order, you will end up with a well-structured screenplay. I have devised this system as a complement to your own intuitive storytelling ability. If these steps do not work, you have my permission to disregard them. I would appreciate any of your comments on how to make them better.

Here we go! Do you have an idea for a movie? Terrific. I thought so. Everybody has an idea for a movie. The problem is that it is in your head. The journey from your head to a piece of paper may only be eighteen inches, but it may as well be a million miles. In fact, mankind in general probably finds it easier to land a man on the moon than to get an idea across those eighteen terrible inches and onto a piece of paper.

Hint You need a plan, an approach, to the idea in your head. If you don't have a plan, plan to be confused.

The Seven Steps to a Successful Screenplay

Step one – ideas

Ideas are the bricks and timber of screenplays. An astute writer will carefully create a stockpile of ideas and organize them in a way that makes retrieval easy. We are each different and ideas come to us in different ways. Some excellent idea-generation techniques are discussed in Chapter 15.

Idea storage is an important consideration. Like any organization system, retrieval is the key. Just because you have every Welsh newspaper published since 1933 doesn't mean you have anything of value. It is only of value if you can effortlessly retrieve the newspapers published exactly one week before JFK's assassination, if that is the story you are working on. That has value.

This is how you store ideas: jot them down. To carry an idea around in your head is dangerous and unhealthy. Dangerous because you may lose it. Unhealthy because an idea in your head will create stress that will gnaw away at your self-confidence. An idea in your head is merely a thought. Once it is written down and stored properly, it can be retrieved at will, reassessed, juxtaposed with other ideas, and developed.

I recommend jotting the idea down on a recipe card, or on a page in a small, pocket-sized notebook. You should attempt to write the idea down in as few words as possible – three to eight words. The words should be just enough to jolt you back to the state you were in when you thought of the idea. At this later moment, you will be able to work on the idea further.

Once you have a collection of ideas that you would like to develop for a film, the ideas can be collated in accordance with where they might fit in the movie. Of course, the beauty of this approach is that, when you have a handful of ideas stored on index cards, you can stand the cards up on a table, flip them down one after the other, and see your entire movie from beginning to end. It is also dead simple to order/reorder/edit the scenes.

As a professional writer, your work and the merit of your work rest on the quality and quantity of your ideas. And getting ideas is the fun part. When I graduated from art school, I moved to the UK and got a job as a sculptor's assistant with Sir Henry Moore – the British sculptor of monumental pieces. Every morning he would come to the studio shed where up to forty assistants were working, to make sure we weren't doing any damage. He would then wander along the stream in the front of his property, picking up pebbles and bits of bone. One morning I was sent in to deliver a message and came upon him having breakfast and sketching these pebbles. I asked him why he, sculptor of monumental sculptures, was sketching pebbles. He said to me that he was building up his vocabulary of shapes.

Hint Don't be afraid of bad ideas. Ideas come in many forms – both good and bad. Try to be open to all your ideas. Go with the flow.

Step two – the basic premise

Online Resources

Create the basic premise. For full details see Chapter 2. Ideas are the bricks and timber, the building materials of a screenplay. Your next step is to create an architect's sketch of what the finished building/screenplay will look like. This is an idea boiled down into a few lines. This will become the blueprint to which you constantly refer in order to make sure that you are on course.

Hint The paragraph should read: This story is about [describe, do not name] the hero, who [what they want more than anything else in the world] but [allude to the main obstacle] and [tease with the ending].

Step Three – characters

So far you have a big pile of building materials (ideas) and a blueprint. But undertaking a huge project on your own is daunting. Characters are the people who will help you.

Get to know each of the characters helping you as if you were working on a long construction project. After all, you are going to get tired together, some of you may get injured, or damaged emotionally. Some of your team of characters may try to bully or cheat. You need to understand each character intimately, as you would if they were living in real life.

Get going on character research. Write those character essays. See if you can combine traits together to form one character – a fascinating and compelling character for the screen.

Character name

```

```

Traits

```

```

The plan

This section may look deceptively simple. And it isn't simple at all. If you figure this section out, you are pretty much finished. I have devised a few questions that, hopefully, will help you along your journey towards a character plan. Only use my ideas if they help.

What is your hero's goal?

```

```

Hint A goal is something that we can see when the hero succeeds or fails. A goal must be specific.

How does your hero plan to achieve the goal?

```

```

Hint A plan is not a goal. The plan is the method by which your hero believes he or she will achieve the goal.

How does the hero protect him/herself?

```
[                                                                    ]
```

How does the opponent counter the hero's plan?

```
[                                                                    ]
```

How does your hero protect him/herself?

```
[                                                                    ]
```

How does the opponent continue to counter the hero's plan?

```
[                                                                    ]
```

The plan is the set of guidelines the hero uses to overcome the opponent and win the goal. Since the opponent is the main obstacle to the hero's goal, we also need to know the opponents plan.

Next, try to list the reaction and action between the hero and opponent as each character tries to achieve their goal.

Copyright

The next chapter deals with copyright. In case copyright issues bore you, here are the main points.

1. You own the copyright to your screenplay as soon as it is created.

2. Copyright disputes are about whether or not you can prove that you created your screenplay.

3. Before you send your script out to any one, you must register a copy in order to get a birth certificate for your screenplay.

Step four – scene outline (structure)

Structure is a way your hero's plan unfolds. It is an organic process, and not one that easily fits into the traditional three-act paradigm.

Online Resources

You may find it helpful to use the nine-point paradigm I outlined on page 42. Only use a paradigm if you find it helpful.

Some writers use index cards and write their ideas for each scene on a card. Others elaborate this by using a variety of color-coded cards – blue for the opening (and emotionally less tense) and on through yellow and pink for the emotionally charged climax.

If you are writing on a script program like Final Draft, it will allow you to write the scenes on a computer then print them out as index cards, which you can then use to make notes, rearrange the order, etc.

figure 9.1
Index Card

Point of Scene	Scene No.	

Remember that you do not write dialogue at this point. If you think of a line of dialogue, write it on the back of the card so you can come back to it later. Try to keep your initial thoughts to a few words. Later, when you start writing the scene, you will find these words jog you back to the moment when you first thought of the scene.

Another advantage of writing cards is the ease with which you can reshuffle scenes.

Step five – scene writing

figure 9.2
Scene Writing Chart

Use a scene analysis sheet to plan each scene.

Scene no.	
Previous endpoint	
Cast members in scene	
Point of scene	
Goal of main character	
Endpoint	
Conflict	
Twist	

Write the scene, what happens, without dialogue

Using a visual organization tool may assist you in plotting your movie.

figure 9.3 Action Flow Chart

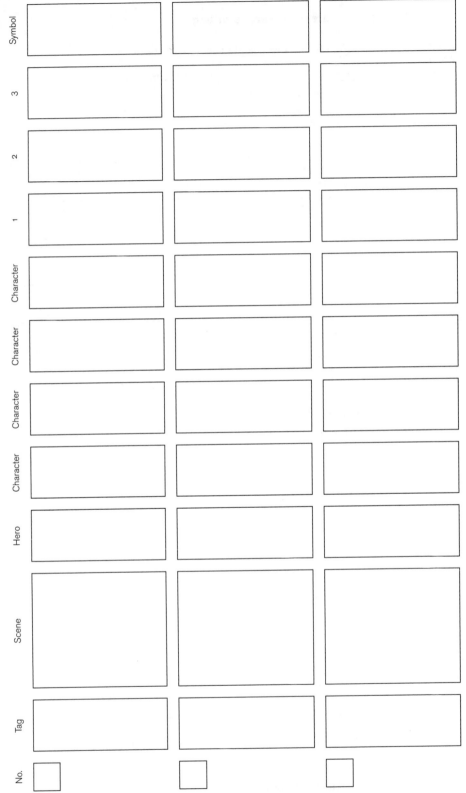

No-Budget Filmmaking

With your cards in order, you can now use the best no-budget filmmaking process in the world – your own inner projector. Simply get comfortable and look at each card, a scene at a time, and you will 'see' your movie. Be brutal. Edit and re-edit until your movie looks fantastic.

Step six – dialogue

Write three tracks of dialogue – story, moral argument, and key words. Then balance them. Do a table reading and rewrite.

When you have got your screenplay as good as you can, you are ready to market your script. But before you do that, who is going to try to rip you off, and how can you prevent it?

Step seven – troubleshooting

Chapter 17 is a useful troubleshooting guide which may assist you in analysing your script. When you look at this guide, try to see if anything leaps out as a possible problem with your script.

Most difficulties in the script can be found in the first few pages. If the movie starts at the right place, it usually flows from there.

To get the right start, go to the ending. How do you want your movie to end? Did she really die? Did he kill him? They robbed the bank and got away? Pick your ending, then go to the beginning. Then have a close look at Chapter 17.

This is also the day that you should start writing your next screenplay.

Summary

1. Know your basic premise inside out.

2. Know your characters inside out.

3. Play and replay your movie at the card stage, before you start writing. When you have your scenes and scene order completely firm, write the screenplay.

Who is going to try to rip you off, and how can you prevent it? Copyright is the next consideration.

10 Marketing Your Script

JUST AS WRITING your screenplay requires a method plus creative thought, so too does the task of marketing your screenplay. Try to market your screenplay without a plan, and plan to be confused. So see if you can follow the marketing plan.

Preparation

There are two things that writers hate – writers hate writing and writers really hate selling.

Unless you master the art of selling, you will never be a professional screenwriter – no one will pay you for your work. And selling your work need not be a painful and dreaded experience. In fact, it can be a lot of fun, if you have a plan of attack.

These next chapters are designed to help writers who hate selling, sell their script. But you have to follow my little system. Let's assume you have finished your script and are asking 'Now what?'

1. Let it rest

Put your screenplay aside for at least two weeks. I like to let mine rest for a month. You want to leave it long enough so you forget it – so it seems fresh when you see it again.

Perhaps you will start working on your next project, or simply try to catch up on seeing as many films as you can. This is a sweet moment. You have actually written your screenplay. You still don't want to show it to anyone, but at least you can announce that you are finished.

Leonardo da Vinci used to view his paintings through a mirror from a great distance in order to see the work in its entirety. He believed that weaknesses would be more obvious from a distance, and reversed through a mirror.

Time is your distance. When you return to your script, pick it up and read it for pleasure. You will find some gaping holes in your script so huge and obvious that you won't believe you didn't notice them before. Fix them!

You will also see some things you are really proud of. Congratulations. You will feel a warm wash of self-satisfaction sweep over you. You have succeeded, in part, in your quest to master the craft of screenwriting.

It might also be a good time to pull out the troubleshooting guide in Chapter 17 and have another look with fresh eyes.

Hint Rewriting is a crucial part of the writing process, but is often approached incorrectly.

The myth about rewriting is that it's a cure-all. Many writers think that they can fix their errors in subsequent drafts. They start the first draft before the planning process is complete and thereby create a draft that has fatal flaws.

If you have done your homework and made a detailed plan, your first draft will be built on a solid foundation. Then determine exactly what the theme of the piece is. Make sure all scenes focus toward the theme. Ask yourself if there is a bolder, fresher, quicker way to say the same thing. Cut, cut, cut. Fix the dialogue last.

2. Character rewrite

Go through the script with a fine tooth comb and set aside anything that does not directly pertain to the goal of the main character.

When you read the script again, you will be amazed at how much energy it has. Look at your script and see if there is anything new you can add to the script, or perhaps you can retrieve and recycle some of the material you set aside earlier. Maybe that scene you thought was a great set-up to the page forty-five scene would work better as the page seventy-five scene, and so on.

3. Table reading – the dialogue rewrite

When you have got the script as good as you can on your own, try a table reading.

A table reading with actors (from a local theatre group, or acting school) is a great way for your piece to come to life. Actors would not normally expect to be paid, although it is polite to offer some refreshments, or help with transportation costs.

Spend some time and cast the script as close to the characters you had in mind. Then gather everyone around a table and read the piece. You may have the actors read it as a stage play – dialogue only. Or you may have the actors alternate in reading the black stuff as well.

Tape-record the performance. Actors are trained to read dialogue. There may be phrases that just are hard for an actor to say, or others which do not make sense. Often the actors will make suggestions about the phrasing, or question the purpose of a particular line.

Writers experiencing a table reading of their work for the first time marvel at the experience. The sound of actors' voices helps them visualize their work for the first time, and gives them a huge boost of confidence. It is the first stage in making a screenplay become real.

Make the appropriate notes, and consider them in your next revision.

You are probably so tired of your script now that you might not be able to make it any better. There is probably a little voice inside you nagging away and what you really want to know is what someone else thinks about your script.

Now you are ready for feedback.

4. Your first reader

Who, exactly, do I send my screenplay to?

The first rule of marketing your screenplay is that you never ever send your script to someone unless they ask for it. Film companies are paranoid about litigation and will only accept submissions from people they know and trust – agents, established producers and entertainment solicitors. The trick is to get someone to ask for your script when you don't yet have an agent.

Make ten copies of your script and give it to nine acquaintances. Tell them to read the script and to scribble down any comments, observations, and even flattery, in the margins. Tell them you want their honest reaction. I always give the tenth script to my mother, because I know she won't lie.

Your first observation should be in noting how long it takes each person to read and return your screenplay. If they call you back the very next morning and say what a terrific screenplay you have – that is good. They have taken it home that evening, and opened the first page, started to read it and became so absorbed that they couldn't put it down. And they couldn't wait to tell you about it.

If you bump into them on the street a few days later and ask them 'How are you?' and they say 'Fine, oh yes, almost forgot to tell you – I started reading your screenplay last night and got about a quarter of the way through.' That is bad. They have started reading your script and you failed totally to grab their attention.

A good script is always a page-turner and will never take more than forty-five minutes to read.

Once all the scripts and comments are back, tabulate the results of the readers' comments and see if there are any worthwhile comments you can incorporate into your next revision. If everyone is saying 'I don't get it' – then you must have a fundamental flaw with the storyline. Fix it.

5. Professional reader's report

Certain individuals and organizations provide a script reading service. The quality of the reports vary, but at least you know that the person who has read your script has read quite a few, and their comments will be measured against other scripts currently in circulation.

Fees for this service are about £40 in the UK and $75 in the US. Expect to get four to five pages of written notes on plot, structure, characterization, dialogue, visual appeal and commercial viability.

Experts, such as Michael Hague, Syd Field and John Truby, charge up to $5000 to read your screenplay. You are buying their considerable experience when you pay this kind of money, and personally, knowing

Michael and John as I do, would save the cost of this level of critique for the production company to bear.

Again, incorporate the appropriate comments into your next revision.

At this point, when you feel you are satisfied with the script, you are ready to start the direct marketing of this script.

And don't forget! The day after you finish your first script is the day that you start working on your second. Your second script will be much easier, because you will have a system to follow. You are learning how to run your screenwriting business.

Curiously, an embittered screenwriter started a story circulating in London recently.

To prove that readers were incompetent of recognizing his great script, he rewrote Chinatown word for word, changing nothing but the characters' names and the title of the movie. Coverage returned to him used comments like 'shallow and superficial characterization', 'ruins the story' and so on.

Hint If you were a reader for Miramax and read my script and thought it was good, would you recommend it? What would make you recommend a script? If I were reading for Miramax, I would only recommend a script if I thought it made me look good – because I would be looking for a promotion. Thus I would never recommend a good script. I would only recommend a great screenplay – I want to be known as the reader who recommended the next Chinatown or the next Crying Game.

Professional readers are your first barrier into the film industry. But you need to understand the structure of how readers operate. Readers cannot approve or say yes to your script. What they do say is the word no.

Of the readers I know, about seventy-five per cent are female, ninety-five percent Caucasian. The one thing they share is that they are recent graduates of a recent university liberal arts programme. In other words, they are people on whose education their parents have wasted a huge amount of money. And they know absolutely nothing about the movies. Which is why they are hired.

There is a saying in Hollywood – 'If it ain't on the page, it ain't on the stage.' To get a job as a reader, the production company gives you a script that has already been assessed. You are asked to read it and comment on it. The company then reads your reviews to see if you picked up the same flaws as they did. Film producers value the opinion of the readers precisely because it is so neutral, and because they have no technical expertise. The minute a script reader becomes an expert, they are no longer useful as readers, although they have a valuable role as story consultants.

Hint Write for the reader. Make sure that your script can entertain at this level. After all, it is the entertainment industry.

---

6. Join a writers' group

Marketing a screenplay can be a lonely business. Joining a writers' group can help. Writers' groups are places where you can network, and get valuable feedback on your script. Look at the local library or call the nearest film organization to see if they can give you name of the nearest writers' group.

Each writers' group is organized differently. Some are intended as purely social occasions for the members. Others arrange screenings and talks by agents and producers, and others combine these activities by providing feedback on each other's work.

If you cannot find a writers' group near you, why not start one yourself? Consider the following tips:

Venue

Find a venue. It could be a church basement, an upstairs room in a pub, or someone's living room. It doesn't really matter where it is as long as you have a venue.

Advertise

Flyers or leaflets explaining what you are doing, along with the date, time and place of the first meeting, can be printed cheaply. Distribute the leaflets to film schools, libraries, actors' groups, theatres and art house cinemas. It is really helpful to have a telephone number on the leaflet so potential attendees can satisfy themselves that you are legitimate and not an axe murderer.

Refreshments

At the first meeting it's a good idea to appoint someone to be respon- sible for refreshments, and someone to volunteer to be the chairperson with the task of being on the telephone. This is useful for last minute changes to the schedule or for adding an event. These positions can also rotate. Meetings can be held weekly, or monthly – whatever seems right for your group.

Small is beautiful

If you have fifteen people respond to your advertising blitz, don't be sur- prised if only five or six become regulars. Don't allow the small number of writers in your group alarm you – small is beautiful, and you can get excellent feedback from half a dozen people, especially if you can share your common experiences as writers.

Minutes

One way to sustain interest is to write up simple minutes of each meeting. You can email, fax or post these to everyone. People who have missed a meeting will then feel a part of the group, and will feel free to contribute to the meeting they missed.

Longevity

Don't expect a writer's group to last forever. People change jobs, re-focus on their career perspectives and move. Creating pressure on participants to commit to a group forever and ever is really the kiss of death. Your writers' group will exist as long as it needs to help you!

7. Pedigree

This is the most important part of your marketing preparation: building pedigree for your script. A screenplay can command a very high price. A film production company, regardless of the size, considers the purchase of a script to be a significant investment. Before a company buys a screenplay, it has to be certain of its pedigree.

Usually, established writers sell their screenplays through literary agents, established producers or entertainment attorneys. Each of these people represents a filter that is trusted by a film production company, thereby enhancing the pedigree of the script. In your own life, you probably act in the same way. If a trusted friend calls you and says 'I have just heard a fantastic song by this new artist. You must get their CD.' The next time you are in a music store, you will probably search out this CD, perhaps even buy it.

However, it is very difficult for a new writer to attract the services of an agent, producer or entertainment attorney. So the Catch-22 is how to market your screenplay to a production company on your own.

Building the Pedigree for Your Screenplay

The receptionist theory

It costs money for a film company to accept delivery of your screenplay. Once it is inside their internal system, your screenplay has to be entered in the database, the actual script stored, possibly duplicated, and reader's fees and development executives' evaluation fees must be paid. To get a screenplay into a company, have it read once, a simple rejection letter typed and returned with your screenplay costs at least £200/$300.

Try to get someone in the industry, even a receptionist, to read your script. If they will write you a short letter telling you what they think, even better. You are really hoping that this lowly employee will brag about having read a really fantastic screenplay, and being overheard by one of the moguls next to the coffee machine. The receptionist theory is that this person can refer your script higher up the food chain. Make sure you say thank you properly to any receptionist that helps you.

Film organizations

Get someone from a film organization to read and recommend your screenplay. Organizations like the IFP in America and Raindance in the UK are respected by the industry. If you can get a letter of reference from an employee about your script, give yourself a treat. If you can persuade them to call up the head of development at a film company and recommend your screenplay – fantastic. If you succeed in this, the production company will read your script.

Some film production companies have close ties with organizations. In the UK, Working Title, FilmFour, BBC Films and Pathé are a few of the production companies with close links to Raindance. In America, Fine Line, NextWave and Sony Pictures Classics have ties with the IFP. A film organisation will only recommend your script if they really like it.

Stars

Get a star to read and recommend your script – even if they are unable or unwilling to play one of the parts. Another approach would be to persuade a star physically unsuitable for the part to read and recommend your script with the line 'if only I had stumbled across this screenplay in 1955 when I was younger – it would have been perfect'. Based on this recommendation, you search out a production company with access to an actor similar to the aged one.

Business or community leaders

Script competitions

You have now finished the preparation process for marketing your screenplay. In effect you have already started to market your script. Many of the people you are approaching could purchase your screenplay. By not asking them to buy your script, you are in effect taking the financial pressure off them and if your script is good enough, they will be happy to see you succeed and either recommend it to someone else, or they may buy the script themselves.

Do you think you could get Richard Branson or Bill Gates to read your script and like it? This would almost certainly guarantee a positive reaction from any number of film production companies. Which community or business leaders do you know? Perhaps your local car dealer, local councillor, pastor, sheik, bank manager, could read your script and write you a reference – remember that they really have to like your script. Film companies have a secret weapon on their desk that they use to suss out referees: it's called a telephone!

Producer

Find a producer who has made a film, even if it's not a very good one, and get them to read and comment on your script. They have already succeeded in financing one film and they know how the business works. If they read and like your script then people in the industry will take notice that your pedigree is just a little bit better than average.

Financiers

Any financier, but especially a film financier, has the potential to make your script have impeccable pedigree if they love your screenplay. So start bombarding your local credit controller with your screenplay. If you know anyone who works for one of the film financing banks, or the insurance bond guarantee companies, so much the better. If they read and love your script, and will agree to be quoted, your script starts to take on the pedigree of old leather top desks, waistcoats and Earl Grey tea. This helps make your script bankable.

Online Resources

Readers' reports

If you have had a professional reader's report (i.e. one that you have paid for) that is positive, either mention this in a covering letter, or include the report with your script. It shows that someone (albeit partial to you) had a positive reaction to your script. My experience is that a production company will often request a copy of your coverage, especially if your reader has pedigree. They will then assess the coverage, and make a decision as to whether or not they are interested.

The following chart will help you track the progress of your projects:

figure 10.1
Project Tracking Chart

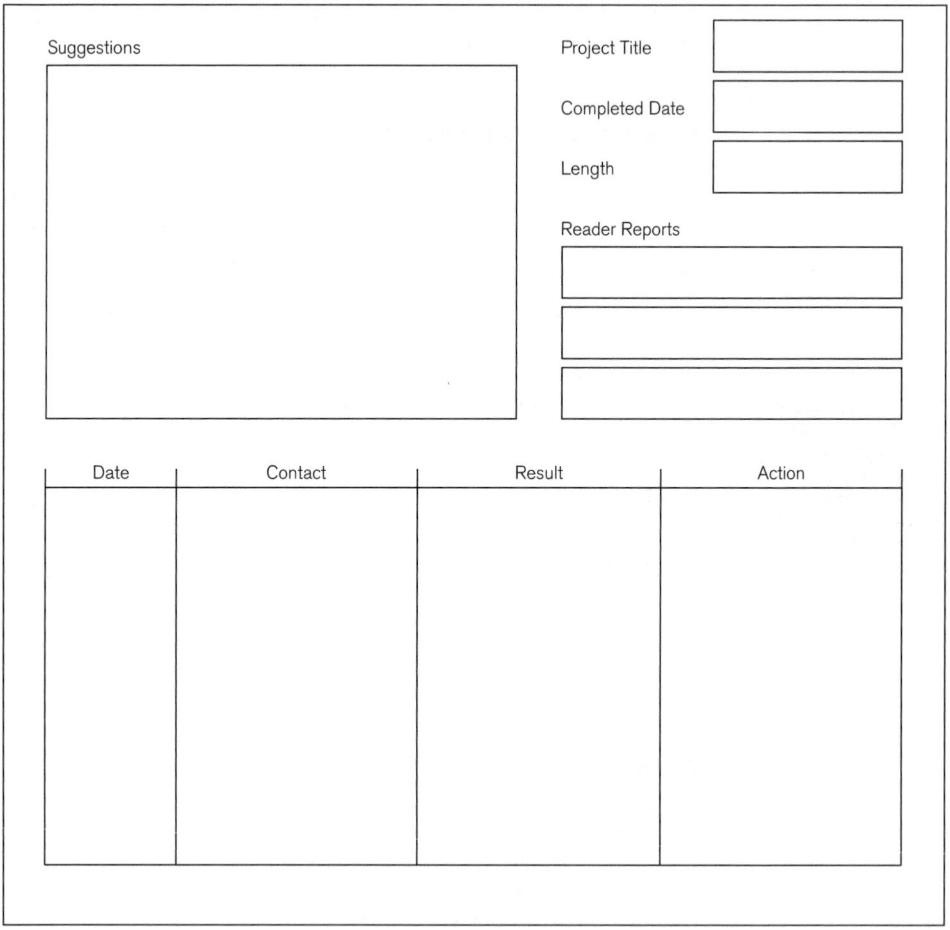

Suggestions			Project Title	
			Completed Date	
			Length	
			Reader Reports	

Date	Contact	Result	Action

Summary

1. Good feedback is bad feedback. The only good feedback is a cheque.

2. Scripts aren't written they are rewritten.

Next, we need to find out who is purchasing screenplays. And to do that, we have to play the movie game.

10 000 Monkeys – Copyright

COPYRIGHT LAW AROUND the world is based on a simple premise – surrounding the planet earth there is a cloud of creativity of ideas. Any two people at the same time can pull down the same idea. And ideas are free.

What is copyrightable is the expression of the idea, whether it be a poem, sculpture, libretto, novel or script. Sometimes, the difference between what is an expression of an idea and what is an idea can become complicated. Lawyers can get rich over this distinction.

Basically, two screenwriters could ostensibly come up with the same storyline for a movie. They write two very different screenplays, but the storyline idea (which cannot be copyright protected) cannot be disputed. You can only argue copyright on the expression of the idea.

I have taught enough screenwriters in enough countries to know that if you are reading this, you are getting pretty paranoid by now. Please force yourself to finish reading this chapter, so you can develop a positive mental attitude towards copyright.

Many writers and artists labour under the misconception that they must fill out an official form, and write the letter '©' in order to assert their claim for ownership of the copyright. In fact, all countries recognize that the artist owns copyright from the moment it is created.

The difficulty arises in proving that ownership in a court of law.

Protecting Your Screenplay

1. Protecting the idea

You cannot protect an idea. This is the whole point of copyright law. Your first task after coming up with a great idea for a movie is to write as detailed an account of your idea as possible. Generally, a page or two is not sufficient. A judge may be unable to distinguish your ideas from those of your competitors. Three pages are better, but I recommend ten. After all, you have an idea for a movie that will end up being ninety to a hundred-and-twenty pages long. Surely you can outline the key points in ten pages.

Hint Keep your idea strictly to yourself until you have written it down.

2. Ownership

If you have a great idea for a movie, you cannot tell anyone about it until you have registered the idea for copyright. Tell a shrewd producer that you have a great idea and he/she will ask you 'Have you written the script? A treatment?' If the answer is 'No' to either of these questions, you have just gifted them your idea. And there is nothing immoral, sleazy or dishonest about this. It is just the way that copyright works.

You own the copyright of your script or treatment the moment it is created. Suppose you are in your ivory tower, typing your hundred-page screenplay. You are on a complete roll, when suddenly, near the bottom of page ninety-nine, you hear the two most dreaded words a screenwriter will ever hear bouncing up the walls of your ivory tower – 'Honey! Dinner!'. You race down for dinner, storm through your food, and race back to your typewriter only to discover that a copyright thief has taken the ninety-nine page manuscript from you, typed a new page hundred, and is now claiming ownership of the script. In this example, the question of ownership would be won in court by you. You created the screenplay (minus page hundred) therefore you own the copyright. The only way that you lose the copyright is by assigning the title of the screenplay to someone else, presumably for a wad of cash. The difficulty is in proving that you own the copyright.

3. Creating the birth certificate

On completion of a script, screenwriters can apply to have it registered, in a similar way that parents apply for a birth certificate for their newborns. It is called a Certificate of Registration, and is available from the Writers' Guild of America at www.wga.org

At the time of writing, the fee is a modest $20. Send a copy of the final version of the screenplay. For your money, you will receive a letter with the date your script was received along with a serial number (to assist in file retrieval). Keep this number confidential.

Other writers register their scripts with the United States Copyright Office. You can check the current fees on www.loc.gov/copyright or call (202) 707 3000.

Other arts organizations in the UK, the trade union BECTU, and also Raindance provide the service free to its members.

Now you can promote and market you script to your heart's content knowing that you are able to prove the date of creation.

4. Proving ownership

There is however an additional administrative detail which you must attend to in order to back up the birth certificate. Should you ever go to court in a copyright dispute with another writer, or with a producer whom you suspect of using your script without permission, you need to prove that you are the one who registered the screenplay. In a real estate transaction, this is called chain of title, where your solicitor will look at the deeds of the house you are buying and trace all the previous owners back in time to make sure that the title is clean and has no unpaid mortgages, liens for city taxes and so forth. Screenplays are classed as intellectual property and the laws governing the trading of intellectual property are similar to those governing real estate transaction. So what you need to do is to keep a written record detailing everyone you tell about your screenplay.

Screenwriters also need to prove chain of title, although it is less formal than in property dealing. You have to keep a formal record of everyone you speak to about your screenplay.

Each time you meet someone and discuss your screenplay, make sure that you obtain their business card or contact details and send them the following letter:

The reason for explaining copyright is to demystify the question of who can rip you off. In order to sell your script you have to be able to tell everyone about your script. If you don't, nobody will know you have written it until after you're dead and gone.

Elliot Grove
Raindance
81 Berwick Street
London W1F 8TW

dd/mm/yy

Dear Elliot,

It was a pleasure meeting you at the cinema last night, and I enjoyed discussing with you my forthcoming screenplay 'Top Title'.

I look forward to working with you.

Yours sincerely,

Your name

Mail a copy to the person you met. S/he will probably toss your letter into the bin whilst muttering 'Nutbar! I never agreed to work with him.'

But what you have established is the start of a written contract with that person. By his silence, he has given tacit approval to your letter, and the start of a written contract is born. Later, if you discover that this person is making your movie without you, then you can get your attorney or solicitor to write him a letter stating in effect:

Elliot Grove
Raindance
81 Berwick Street
London W1F 8TW

dd/mm/yy

Dear Elliot,

After my client spoke to you on dd/mm/yy, I am surprised to hear that you are
making a film based on their idea without them

I look forward to hearing from you.

Yours sincerely,

Your attorney's name

A producer or director faced with a letter like this will immediately
have to deal with your claim to ownership or risk losing his investors,
frightened off by the threat of expensive litigation. Follow any court pro-
ceeding and you will get a sense of how expensive this can be.

Sometimes, in situations like this, you will get a response like: 'Isn't it
amazing that there is such a common currency of ideas in circulation?
Our idea is similar, but not identical to yours. Please go away.' or 'Pass!'.

Now you are getting totally paranoid. I know it! The person you have
just pitched claims to already know about your idea when you really think
they have somehow stolen your idea and are ripping you off before they
have seen your screenplay.

Writers must be prepared for this, and it is not as outlandish as it
seems. The film executive who tells you this has probably heard a thousand pitches. Even if he or she can't quite remember whether they have
heard your pitch before, they will pass even if they think it sounds like
another idea they have heard. They do this because they are very concerned about litigious writers pressing a claim for ownership. Life is too
short to contemplate litigation.

As I mentioned above, the entire world's copyright laws are based on
the concept that ideas are free and can be accessed by anyone. Indeed,
copyright law contemplates the likelihood that more than one person can
have the same idea at the same time.

5. Ten thousand monkeys

American scientists proved the theory of 'isn't it amazing that there is such a common currency of ideas in circulation' with an experiment in the South Pacific. There they found six islands on which lived a unique species of monkey, totalling ten thousand. Only five of the islands grew sweet potatoes – a very good food for monkeys – but none of the monkeys ate sweet potatoes. Approximately six hundred monkeys lived on the sixth island – the one without sweet potatoes. The scientists introduced sweet potatoes to the sixth island, trained a few monkeys to dig up the potatoes and to take them to the ocean and wash them, and then eat them. A very strange thing happened when approximately a hundred of the six hundred monkeys were digging up the sweet potatoes, taking them to the ocean, washing them, and eating them. Suddenly, the monkeys on the other islands started to dig up sweet potatoes, take them to the ocean, wash them, and eat them.

Isn't it amazing that there is such a common currency of ideas in circulation?

When I moved to London from Toronto in 1986, I was used to being a Lone Ranger. In Toronto, if I had an idea for literally anything, I would be isolated by all my acquaintances (I didn't really have 'friends') because they thought me, with my crazy ideas, quite weird. But when I moved to London, not fully appreciating the difference in size, and the broad depth of this cosmopolitan and multi-cultural city, I suddenly felt at one with a huge number of unseen friends. And whenever I have an idea I read about it in the newspaper the very next day – pretty scary for a writer.

Remember that whatever your idea for a movie, I can guarantee you that at least a dozen other people in the world right now have exactly the same idea. The only difference is that you are reading this book and attempting a better way to get it out onto paper. All ideas are basically sound. What makes an ordinary idea exciting is the way you bend, shape and state the idea. The expression of the idea is yours, and yours alone. The bolder and fresher you can be, the more valuable your idea will be in the market place.

Hint Don't let the common currency of ideas discourage you.

6. Misfortune

What if you have a great idea for a movie, register it for copyright, and voilà — someone else is making the movie? What do you do? Sue? Commit suicide? Give up writing?

Misfortune is a weird and dangerous thing. Consider this true story of a writing friend of mine in London. She came up with a concept for a television show based on the true-life experiences of people living alone, but sharing accommodation. In order to secure stories, she placed ads in London's famous Time Out magazine advertising for people to write in with their stories. She prepared a questionnaire for potential participants, which she returned to each person who responded to the ad. This process took place over an extensive period of time. Just as she was approaching her goal of getting the right mix of people for her series of shows, she was summoned to New York on an urgent family matter. While there she picked up a Village Voice, where to her amazement saw an ad that was worded identically to hers. She responded and received a questionnaire exactly like the one she had prepared in London, some eighteen months earlier. Back in London, she conferred with an entertainment attorney, another good friend of mine. He told her that she had a cases for copyright infringement, which he was willing to pursue for nothing, as a favour. Hard costs would be $5000 to $10 000. As she didn't happen to have that much cash lying around for a speculative enterprise as this, he advised her to pass. Even if she won her case she would still have to prove that she had suffered financial damages. As it was difficult to see how a classified ad in New York could possibly infringe on a television show destined for the United Kingdom, she decided to let go. A few months later, the trades announced the production start of a movie I cannot name for legal reasons, but roughly the story of single Caucasian females.

My friend had a great attitude to this misfortune. She shrugged her shoulders and simply said that it proved that her ideas were commercially viable, and she moved on.

Hint Misfortune happens. Don't take it personally. Learn to move on.

---

7. Waiver letters and submission release

Sometimes when you submit a script to a production company, they will send your script back with a letter that they want you to sign. The letter basically states that they want you to give up your legal right to sue them for copyright infringement if they ever make a film resembling in any way your screenplay.

My advice is simple. If you don't feel comfortable with the letter, don't sign it. The film company will not read your script. Go find someone else. Of course, I believe that astute writers understand that these letters are used by film companies, not to make it easier to plunder screenplays, but to defend themselves from dishonest screenwriters. Either way you look at it, don't do anything until you feel comfortable.

A submission release looks like this:

Person
Company
Town
Code

Re: [Title of material submitted], Number of pages

Dear Sir or Madam

Enclosed I am submitting to you literary works/screenplay [insert title] for
your consideration under the following express understanding and conditions.

1 I hereby confirm that I am submitting the enclosed material voluntarily.
I hereby agree that you are under no obligation to me regarding this material
unless you and I have signed a written agreement which will then become the
only contract between us.

2. I hereby confirm that any discussions, whether oral or written, between us
regarding the enclosed material shall not be construed to form an agreement
regarding the purchase of said material.

3. I hereby confirm that should the enclosed material not be new or original,
or if you have already received material similar to [insert title] from others,
or from your employees, then I agree that you will in no way be liable to me
for use of this material and I do not expect to be paid for such.

4. I hereby confirm that if you produce or distribute a television show(s) or
movie(s) based on the same general themes, ideas, situations, geographical
settings, period of history or characters as those presented to you today then
I agree that you will in no way be liable to me for use of this material and I do
not expect to be paid for such.

I hereby confirm that but for my agreement to the above terms and conditions,
you would not agree to accept and consider the material [insert title] submitted
to you today.

Yours faithfully,

[insert name and signature
of writer, date, address and
contact telephone]

---

8. Non-disclosure agreements

When you go to a pitch meeting with a film company, you may be asked
to pitch ideas to them. Of course, ideas are free and cannot be copy-
righted. Some writers know this beforehand, and only reveal ideas they
have already written down and have registered. Other writers feel con-
strained by this, and like to 'pitch from the hip' – firing off ideas that
pop into their heads. In order to protect yourself, it is wise to ask the

executives to read and sign a simple letter acknowledging that: A. you were present at their office on a specific date; B. that you pitched them several ideas; C. if they use any of the ideas you expect to be paid; and D. that all parties agree to enter into a formal agreement at a mutually agreed time in the near future.

This letter, when signed, affords the writer some protection against a shrewd but sly film producer, trying to wheedle an idea for the next Blair Witch Project out of you for nothing. If, on the other hand, you have a really hot script, then every producer you speak to will sign your agreement without hesitation.

Re: [Title of your project(s) or screenplay(s)]

Dear Sir or Madam,

This letter confirms that I am presenting to you ideas today, and delivering to you certain manuscripts, storyboards and documents for your consideration under the following terms and conditions:

1. Authorized use: The Prospective Purchaser may review the enclosed documents and the project to determine the suitability and desirability of entering into an agreement with [your name] and [company name]. Before Prospective Purchaser, an employee or any representative of the Prospective Purchaser shall view the Documents the Prospective Purchaser shall require each individual who will review the documents to read this agreement and sign an agreement identical to this.

2. The Prospective Purchaser agrees that no one shall receive copies of the documents, or shall be verbally told of the documents unless that person too signs this agreement.

3. Time limits: If the Prospective Purchaser decides not to enter into an agreement by [insert date], then the prospective purchaser agrees to return the enclosed documents and all copies made by registered express delivery to:[insert your name and address] within 24 hours

4. Damages: Since the concepts, characters and documents relating to the project are valuable to [insert your name and company] if the Prospective Purchaser discloses breaches this agreement then the Prospective Purchaser shall pay to [insert your name and company name] the amount of [insert the value of your project].

5. Should the Prospective Purchaser agree to proceed with a deal based on the Documents, then both parties agree to signing a long form contract at a time mutually convenient.

[Signature/Date/Witnessed by/Date]

---

9. Acquiring the rights to a true life story

Writers will often become aware of a true-life story based on a newspaper account or television news piece. These stories have become more and more in demand, especially with the advent of reality television shows. When you see an interesting news or magazine story, you still need to get the story rights from the individual mentioned. In order to acquire the screenplay rights to a person's true-life story, you need to approach the individual directly and secure his written permission to base a screenplay on his life. Usually the easiest way to source this person is through the journalist who originally created the story.

There are certain laws governing the stories of criminals. Most countries will not allow a criminal to profit from any story about his crime, through the American 'Son of Sam' laws or similar. If you are contacting a criminal, make sure you engage the service of an entertainment attorney who can offer expert advice.

Here is a sample letter you can use when contacting someone:

Person
Company

dd/mm/yy

Re: [Title of your project(s) or screenplay(s)]

Dear Sir or Madam,

I write to inquire whether the theatrical and film rights to your story are available.

I was able to get your contact details from [name of reporter or journalist].

Your powerful and unique story touched me greatly and I feel deeply that your story should be shared with others.

I would appreciate it if you could contact me at your earliest convenience at [telephone number]. Please feel free to reverse the charges.

Yours sincerely,

[Your name]

Summary

1. Take time to understand copyright.

2. Never tell anyone an idea until you have written it down as completely as possible and registered it.

3. Be professional. Keep track, by letter, of everyone with whom you have discussed your screenplay.

4. Make absolutely certain that you have the necessary permission before you start writing.

Now it's time to market your screenplay.

The Movie Game

IN ORDER TO illustrate the possibilities of potential sales for your script, it is useful to play the movie game – useful because it makes visual what is otherwise a complicated concept. It is a board game, and it has spaces that you can land on with your script, your playing piece.

figure 12.1
The Movie Game

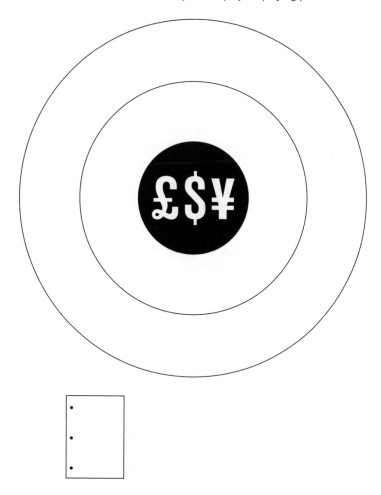

The second ring represents the areas inside the British film industry where screenplays can be sold, and the outer ring represents those areas outside the British film industry.

Hint The object of the game is to sell your screenplay (to get the deal) without any outside creative interference. As a writer, you do not ever want to hear the word 'rewrite'.

The Second Ring

The second ring can be subdivided into three areas:

1. BBC and FilmFour

These companies make films by first time filmmakers on a regular basis. In the case of the BBC and FilmFour, they usually rely on a writer's past performance as a writer of short films (Shane Meadows for example), or of radio drama (Richard Curtis) before snapping up a script for a feature film production.

Until recently, both FilmFour and the BBC accepted unsolicited scripts, but they no longer do so. In theory, you can submit your film to the channels and, if they like it, they will purchase the script and start pre-production. Reality dictates otherwise. It is very useful, when trying to sell your script, to put yourself behind the desk of the person you are targeting.

Hint The golden rule is that water runs downhill – make it easy for them to say 'Yes'. Don't expect water to run uphill.

The first task of FilmFour or, in fact, any production company in the world, is to find a director for that wonderful screenplay of yours that they have just purchased. Their second job is to find a producer. Then, of course, the casting process follows.

Make it easy.

Obviously, the more people you can convince to work with you on your script then the easier it will be to sell. The different people – actors, directors and producer(s) you convince are called 'elements'. The fact that they have agreed to work with you on your script is called 'attached'. For example, 'Michael Winterbottom is attached to the script' means that he has agreed in writing that he will direct your script.

This builds the pedigree of your script.

Probably the single most important person a writer needs to associate with is a producer – and a good producer is very difficult to find. In fact, it is much more difficult to find a good producer than it is to find an agent. A good producer is someone who is sensitive to your creative needs and vision but, at the same time savvy enough to be able to fight all the commercial battles needed to get your screenplay financed or sold.

A close friend of mine wrote an excellent screenplay and partnered with a producer. My friend was hired to direct his screenplay – for some, a dream come true. Unfortunately, this producer was a novice, and found himself being bullied by the financiers and senior creative staff on the picture to the point where he committed the writer/director's post-production budget to the scene builders instead. My friend realized that the soundtrack played an integral part in the picture – it was a horror picture – and without a music budget, his vision, his script, would flounder. It took an Oscar-winning showdown with my friend threatening to quit the picture and take the script with him that forced the producer to wake up. You don't want to have to resort to this to get your script made or sold.

figure 12.2
The Movie Game Played

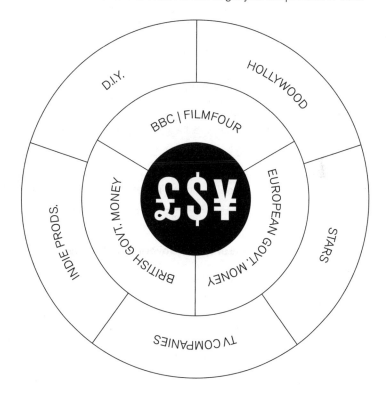

- ORIGINAL SCRIPT

- SCREENPLAY RIGHTS – NOVEL

- SCREENPLAY RIGHTS – TRUE LIFE STORY

If you ever find a producer who is part business head, part artist, and who is someone you like to work with, treat him or her like gold.

Hint Build your pedigree as much as possible by packaging the elements of our script together before you present your project.

How to find a producer
Let's be blunt about this. It is the film business, after all, right? You want to hang out with winners, I assume. So if you want a producer, you want someone who is already successful. Wouldn't it make sense to try to find someone who has already done it?

Shingling
In America they use the term 'shingling'. This refers to the shop signs, or shingles, that hung down Main Street. The theory behind this method is that you find a successful producer known to the main funding sources in your country, and ask him to present your script to the funders on your behalf. In exchange, you agree to pay a percentage, and do ninety-nine point nine per cent of the work.

Networking
It's a people business. It's not what you know, it's who you know. So just grab every single contact you have and see if you can find someone to produce, i.e. haggle, bargain and cajole on your behalf.

Hint Treat a producer like a star. A good producer is essential to your career. But never forget that the producer needs you too.

---

2. European Government Money

EMDA is based in London at 39c Highbury Place, London N5 1QP. Tel +44 20 7226 9903 or fax +44 20 7354 2706.

Through the auspice of an EEC programme called MEDIA, the European Community dispenses Euro tax money to filmmakers under nineteen different programmes. Each one is domiciled in a different European member state, and the one that directly relates to screenwriting is called the European Media Development Agency, or EMDA for short. Call and get the relevant literature and application forms if you feel that this particular programme is going to be of benefit to you. It's tangible.

3. British government money

The Film Council has been launched by the Labour government as a fuel-and-resource-efficient quango. Under the auspices of the Film Council will lie all of the government agencies which existed prior to 1999 including the British Film Institute, British Screen, the Arts Council (lottery funding) and the numerous regional arts boards and other national organizations such as the Scottish Film Council, the Glasgow Film Fund and so on. Look at their website, www.ukfilmcouncil.org.uk, and see what script development programmes exist. Request the relevant literature and application forms if you feel that a particular programme is of benefit.

The Outer Ring

Online Resources

The outer ring represents areas by category, where you can attempt to sell your screenplay outside the British film industry.

1. Hollywood

By Hollywood, of course, I mean the professional film and television community centred in Los Angeles. It is still the largest in the world. In fact, there are as many 35mm film crews and equipment available in LA as in all of Europe. Remember that there are many smaller companies in LA as well. Elisar Cabrerra went to Los Angeles with his script, determined to raise the finance so he could direct his screenplay. He came back to London with a cheque for $1500 and shot the film on video. The rushes were sent back to LA where the film was edited. So, by Hollywood, as I said in the introduction, I also mean the smaller companies around the world where films are made. London is now the second largest centre of English speaking production in the world, and there are many excellent companies operating in the UK who seek a variety of different types of scripts to satisfy their marketing policies.

Hint Knowledge is power. Research a variety of film companies and ascertain what types of films they make.

---

2. Stars

All stars share one thing in common: they have their own production company. They create a production company and hire a head of development to do one thing – find a script (starring vehicle) for the owner of the company.

It is possible that you will have a project which may interest a specific star. You might feel that you have the perfect vehicle/script for Hugh Grant. If you elicit the interest of the head of production at Bob Hoskins' production company and if Bob Hoskin likes it, they will purchase the screenplay from you.

Beware of what a star is. In the UK many writers feel they have a star interested in their script when in fact the 'star' is a cast member from daytime British television. This actor, away from this dull, damp, dark, island is totally unknown. A true star is recognized in every country in the world.

Hint If a star buys a script from you, he will usually sever all relations with you and hire his own writer, whom he knows and trusts, to rewrite the screenplay for him. This is an unpleasant fact. When you sell a script to a major star you will usually lose the writer's credit as well.

Here's what will happen when you submit your script to the production company of a star – or indeed to any production company. The only difference between a small and large company will be the number of layers your script will need to pass through.

figure 12.3
Film Production Company Structure

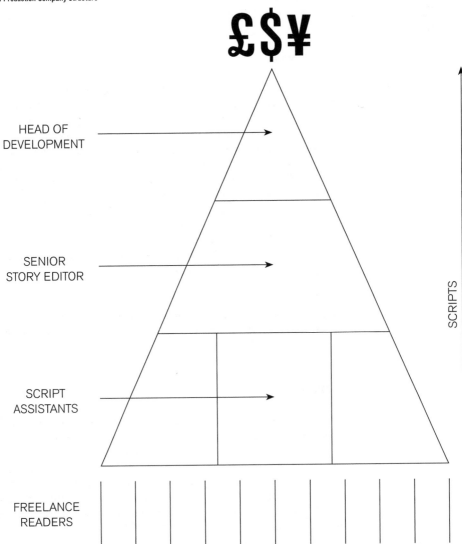

There are really only two types of screenplay. Firstly, there is the great script that is so good that the producer is ordering film stock and the director is lining up auditions. Secondly, there is the ghastly script. The great script, if it is a comedy, is so funny when you read it that, not only do you laugh out loud, but you pick up the nearest telephone and call your best friend in the world and say 'Can I tell you a joke?' If it is a horror script, you are afraid to turn the page. If it is a love story, the descriptive passages arouse you. These are signs of an excellent screenplay. Until you have a script that does this, you don't have a script.

What happens to your script when it gets to a production company?

First of all, let us consider a typical film production company. The personnel are arranged, pyramid style, with the final decision-maker at the top. In a company like FilmFour, the head of production is Tessa Ross. Her assistant, titled head of development, is Katherine Butler. Underneath are several assistant story editors. FilmFour receives between sixty and eighty submissions per week. It is physically impossible for these five or six people at FilmFour to read all of these scripts. So they don't read any. All of the new script submissions follow the reader route.

When your script arrives, the envelope is opened – usually by an intern – and the script's title is hand-written in magic marker on the spine or on the end of the script, depending which way the particular office's shelving is designed. Your script and your details are then logged onto a database and your script assigned to a reader. FilmFour currently employs about a dozen freelance readers. The readers are given between four and eight scripts per week, and paid between £25 ($50) and £40 ($80) for their reports on each script. For an unpublished manuscript of a novel, readers are paid as much as £85 ($170) per report.

The reader's report is called coverage. It is called coverage, because it is attached to the cover of the screenplay, making it easier to collate it with the appropriate script. All coverage is structured in the same way, although format varies from company to company. See figure 12.4 over the page, for an example of typical coverage.

Let's suppose that, in a typical week at FilmFour, ten readers each read five scripts and recommend one each. The ten scripts would pass up to the next level, where they would be read in-house. Let's say that of these ten scripts, three are recommended to Katherine Butler and, in turn, once a week she recommends one to Tessa Ross. The recommended scripts will then be read by the in-house team.

FilmFour produce twenty to twenty-five films per year, out of four to five thousand submissions. Inexperienced writers might be forgiven for thinking that this is a downer. In fact, it is amazing that FilmFour does twenty to twenty-five deals with feature film writers a year, many of whom are first time writers.

Hint Readers exist not because there are so many good scripts our there, but because there are so any terrible scripts in the system. Readers cannot say yes, but they can and will say no.

```
Title: OUT OF BOUNDS              Date: 6/9/08
Author: Tony Kayden             Form: Screenplay/119pp
Locale: New York, Los Angeles   Analyst:
Type: Action                    Source:
Date & Draft Number: 4/3/08     Revised First Draft
```

Theme: Alec Cage arrives in L.A. for a peaceful summer
vacation, but soon finds himself being chased by drug smugglers
and the police.

ALEC CAGE, 18, arrives in Los Angeles to spend the summer with
his Aunt and Uncle. At the airport baggage claim, he mistakenly
takes the wrong duffle bag. When he wakes up the next morning,
he discovers that the bag is filled with heroin. He goes
downstairs to notify his relatives and to his horror, finds
that they've been brutally shot to death. A neighbour enters
and assumes that Alec is the killer. When the neighbour lunges
at Alec, Alec accidentally shoots him. Startled and frightened,
Alec bolts from the house, fearing that the police will accuse
him of the murders.

Helpless and alone, Alec seeks refuge with the only person he
knows in LA, a girl he met on the plane named JAMIE. Jamie
helps Alec disguise his appearance; she dresses him up in chic
new wave clothing. Alec wants to find the owner of the heroin,
so Jamie takes him to the local drug hangouts, where they make
contact with all sorts of seedy drug types.

Meanwhile, GADDIS, the vicious killer and owner of the heroin,
is searching for Alec. Alec contacts the police to try to
straighten things out, but the police still think that Alec is
the real killer. Alec arranges a midnight rendezvous on an
abandoned shipping dock between himself, Gaddis and the police.
The rendezvous backfires; several officers are shot and Gaddis
gets away. Alec escapes with the police still thinking that
he's the guilty one.

Alec goes to Jamie's apartment to discover that it's been
ransacked by Gaddis. Jamie's pet bird and cat have been
brutally slaughtered. Fortunately, Jamie has escaped. Alec
finds her at a local hotel. With the cops hot on their tail,
they hide out in an abandoned building where they also make
love for the first time. Their brief respite is interrupted by
Gaddis, who grabs Jamie and holds her at gunpoint. Jamie and

Alec are saved by HURLEY and YOUNGBLOOD, two shadowy figures
who have been following them for a while. When Hurley and
Youngblood reveal themselves as federal narcs, Alec becomes
enraged. He is angry that he's been used as bait for Gaddis.
He refuses to cooperate and goes off to confront Gaddis on his
own. In a final showdown, Alec blows Gaddis away with a .357
Python.

Comments:

While the premise of this screenplay is potentially
interesting, it is executed in an unconvincing and
uninteresting manner. The first problem is that Alec's
character is not believable. He begins as a naive teenager
from White Plains, New York. But within a few days, he's
acting like Clint Eastwood — commandeering buses, careening
through roadblocks, kicking down doors with a .357 Python, and
delivering lines such as 'Out with your pieces!' and 'I'll give
his asshole a twin brother!' Quite simply, I never believe that
an 18 year old kid is capable of this behaviour. Because I
never believe in Alec's character, I don't care what happens to
him and I don't get caught up in the story.

Another major problem with the script is the excessive use
of violence, particularly on the part of Gaddis. Examples
of gratuitous violence include the skinned cat, the plucked
parrot, and the shooting of an innocent pawnshop owner. None of
these are necessary; we already know that Gaddis is evil and
vicious. It seems that the main function of the violence is to
titillate the audience.

This script has a lot of chase sequences and none of them are
especially original or interesting. Like all the other action
sequences in the script, they seem to have been distilled from
TV cop shows.

While the premise might have made for an interesting movie,
this script fails to engage the reader's interest.

NOT RECOMMENDED.

figure 12.4
Example of Coverage

Script reading is an entry-level job into the industry and is poorly paid.
Why does anyone do it? To try to get a permanent salaried job at the next
tier, it follows that the only way a reader will recommend a screenplay is
if it makes him look good. And how great is your script? If it is merely
good, the reader will pass, because his career will not be enhanced by his

The film industry is fiercely competitive. Reader's reports, like those at Scala Production, are created under adverse conditions, not out of lack of respect for your script, but out of sheer economic necessity. Imagine a hapless intern reading your script with the phone ringing off the hook. You want your script to be so engrossing that they don't hear the phone, even with someone screaming 'Get the phone'.

When that happens, the entire office knows they have found a hot script.

recommendation of your script. Everyone tries to move up the ladder.

Readers are the first barrier to your script. A reader, no matter how senior or respected, cannot approve the purchase of your screenplay. He can only 'recommend' it. Readers can and do say 'Pass' to scripts.

There is an old Hollywood maxim: If it ain't on the page, it ain't on the stage. And no movie can ever be made from a screenplay that the reader cannot see on the page.

Now go back to your descriptive passages. Do they really flow? Will they create visual images? Does your dialogue contain the three tracks? Is your script written in basic high school English essay style?

Hint Do not send out your screenplay until it is absolutely the very best you can get it. The readers will not read it a second time.

What happens when a reader gets your script?

Firstly, readers have guidelines on how to read the script. Guidelines vary from company to company. Some companies have a very pared down reader system. The legendary British producer Nik Powell has a unique strategy at his Scala Productions: interns form his reader base. They are asked to answer the telephone and read your screenplay at the same time. Their reader report consists of two numbers – the number of the page where they first got interested and a sentence explaining why, and the number of the page where they got bored, with another sentence explaining why.

Here are some guidelines that were handed out to script readers at a major Hollywood studio. It is somewhat scary that your script is read by someone with little or no script training who is asked to follow these guidelines while assessing your script.

figure 12.5
Instructions for Readers

```
Checklist For Reading And Evaluating Screenplays


CONCEPT/PLOT

1. High concept; big canvas for films; intimate drama for TV.

2. Imagine the trailer. Is the concept marketable?

3. Is it compelling? Screenplay should deal with the most
important event in these particular characters' lives.

4. What's at stake? Life and death situations are the most
dramatic. Potential for characters' lives to be changed.
```

5. Screenplay should create constant questions: Will he make it? Did he do it? Hook an audience with a 'need to know', and they will watch the rest of the film.

6. Original. Please, no more screenplays that start with a character waking up in the morning, so we can see what kind of person he is by the junk he has in his room and his walls. No more genre parodies.

7. Is there a goal? Is there pacing? Does it build?

8. Begin with a punch, end with a flurry.

9. What are the obstacles? Is there a challenge for the heroes?

10. What is the screenplay trying to say, and is it worth it?

11. Audience wants to see people who care, not two hours of gimmicks.

12. One scene where the emotional conflict of the main character comes to a crisis point.

13. Hero must have a choice, the ability to affect the outcome.

14. Non-predictable; reversals within major plot and within individual scenes.

15. Once reality parameters are built, do not violate. Limitations call for interesting solutions.

16. A decisive, inevitable, set-up ending that is completely unexpected. Best example, of course, is 'Body Heat.'

17. Action & comedy emanate from character, not from off stage.

18. Is it believable? Realistic?

19. Happy ending or at least a definite resolution.

20. Castable parts. Roles that stars want to play.

21. Young characters. Older audiences can relate to young people, because they were young once, and young audiences can relate too. But young audiences have trouble relating to older characters.

22. Heart. Good screenplays have strong emotions at their centre. An almost subliminal quality; need to read between the lines. Films with heart — 'The World According To Garp', 'Diner', 'Local Hero', 'American Graffiti', 'Terms Of Endearment', etc., and, of course, 'It's a Wonderful Life'. Heart can be negative emotions: 'Body Heat', 'Chinatown'. Avoid mean-spirited films.

TECHNICAL

1. Story construction and structure; three acts, two plot points.

2. No scenes off the spine of the story; no matter how good they are, they will simply die, and destroy the momentum of the film.

3. Screenplay should direct the reader's eye, not the camera.

4. Begin screenplay as far into the story as possible.

5. Begin a scene as late as possible, end it as early as possible.
A screenplay is like a piece of string that you can cut up and tie together — the trick is to tell the entire story using as little string as possible. No shots of cars driving up to houses, people getting out and walking to the door. Use cuts.

6. Visual, Aural, Verbal — in that order. The expression of someone who has just been shot is best; the sound of the gun going off is second best; the person saying 'I've been shot' is only third best.

7. The Hook; inciting incident. You've got ten pages (or ten minutes) to grab an audience.

8. Triple repetition of key points: get through the story as quickly as possible, but for the audience's sake, work on the essential points two or even three times.

9. Echoes. Audience looks for repetition. Useful for tagging characters: 'Annie Hall' ('La De Dah'); 'Indiana Jones' ('I hate snakes'); In 'Body Heat,' Lowenstein's dance steps. Dangerous element; if it's not done right, it looks real stupid.

10. Not all scenes have to run five pages of dialogue or action. In a good screenplay, there are lots of two-inch scenes.

11. Repetition of locale — mark of a well-structured screenplay. Helps atmosphere; allows audience to get comfortable. Saves money.

12. Small details add reality. Research.

13. No false plot points; no backtracking.

14. Silent solution; tell with pictures. Reference: the last seven seconds of 'North by Northwest'.

CHARACTERS

1. Character entrance should be indicative of character traits. First impression of people is most important. Great entrances: Rebecca De Mornay's character in 'Risky Business', strolling into the house, posing in front of the open window; Indiana Jones in 'Raiders', leading the way through the jungle, using his whip to snap the gun from a traitor's hand.

2. Root for characters; sympathetic. Recent example of this: Karen Allen's character in 'Starman'. Screenplay opens with her watching a home movie of her dead husband. From that point on, it is no contest; the audience is hopelessly sympathetic and on her side — all in less than a minute of screen time.

3. Dramatic need — what are the characters wants and needs? Should be strong, definite; clear to audience.

4. What does audience want for the characters? Are we for or against this character, or could we care less one way or the other?

5. Character action — what a person is is what he does, and not what he says.

6. Character faults; characters should be 'this but also that'; complex. No black and whites, please. Characters with doubts and faults are more believable.

7. Characters can be understood in terms of 'what is their

greatest fear?' Gittes, in 'Chinatown' was afraid of being played for the fool. In 'Splash', the Tom Hanks character was afraid he couldn't fall in love. In 'Body Heat' Racine was afraid he'd never make the big time.

8. Character traits independent of character role. A banker who fiddles with his gold watch is memorable, but clichéd; a banker who has a hacking cough and chainsmokes is still memorable, and more realistic.

9. Conflicts, both internal and external. Characters struggle with themselves, and with others.

10. Character 'points of view' distinctive within an individual screenplay. Characters should not all think the same. Each character needs to have a definite point of view, in order to act, and not just react.

11. Run each character through as many emotions as possible — love, hate, laugh, cry, revenge.

12. Characters must change.

When readers meet socially, they invariably ask each other if they have read anything good. More often that not, readers will say they haven't read a good script in weeks – and they mean it! Reading lousy script after lousy script can be very tiring. But when a reader reads a good script, he will usually say 'I had a very easy read'.

When a script reader opens your script to the first page and starts reading, he is really hoping to find the best screenplay ever written. Again, he wants to get noticed higher up the ladder. When script readers fail to get this feeling of anticipation as they start reading a script, they usually give up reading.

3. Television companies

TV companies in America started making cheaply produced films directly for TV to compete with the competition from Monday Night Football – a three hour programme.

Market researchers discovered during this period that American households typically have at least two televisions, and that men and women were two polarized groups during the football game. Furthermore, they noticed that men and women preferred different sorts of entertainment – men preferred sex and violence, women a story. In order to satisfy the demands of women, American TV companies began to develop stories about women for the female audience. Nicknamed Womijeps (Women in Jeopardy) films, or Movie of the Week (MOWs), these films were story-driven and usually starred a woman.

Later, presumably after running out of stories about women who hate men, or who have had terrible things happen to them, these television companies produced other stories: typically stories based on news items such as The Tonia Harding Story and Princess in Love (about Diana).

TV movies made from news-related articles and stories are created very quickly.

4. Independent producers (indie prods)

An independent producer is defined as a producer working on his or her own, seeking financing from inside and outside the film industry.

An independent producer is often the first source of financing or of a script sale. There are literally hundreds of indie prods working throughout the movie business.

The secret to a successful sale following this route is to ascertain which film, currently in production, most closely resembles your story. Contact the producer through his or her production company and see if you can get him to read your script.

An indie prod likes to have one film in production, a second out being sold, and a third in pre-production. Since the pre-production process is long, tangled and twisted, a good producer will have several scripts in pre-production, waiting to see which one gets financed first.

Independent producers can be sourced by reading the trade papers Screen International, Hollywood Reporter, Variety or by visiting the e-zines filmthreat.com and indiewire.com.

You could also source by capturing title credits from movies similar in style to your script, by word of mouth, and through networking at film-makers' groups like the IFP and NPA.

5. DIY

El Mariachi rekindled a trend to super-cheap moviemaking. In 1999 The Blair Witch Project demonstrated that it is possible to make and market a movie yourself.

The other encouraging development for filmmakers and screenwriters is the advent of new cheap technology which makes the cost-of-entry into filmmaking practically nothing.

Even if you, as a writer, have no intention of making the movie for no money, it is a useful exercise to film a few actors reading your scene in order to highlight successes and failures within the scene.

Writers should however be aware of the pitfalls of making their own script and launching their own career with what they hope will be the next Blair Witch Project. It may cause you to lose your sense of judgement about your screenplay. There is nothing worse than watching a film made with passion by a writer/filmmaker/director or producer, but which is based on a flawed script. It is embarrassing. I should know. I rushed the script of the movie I made, Table 5, and the film is so inept in places I can't even believe I shot it. The scary thing is that during the filmmaking process, I thought those bits were pretty good.

Playing Piece

The movie game is a board game. You can see by the layout of the board that there are hundreds of performers with their own production companies, perhaps twenty television companies making movies of the week, literally thousands of independent producers, and so on. The total number of squares you can land on to sell your script runs into the thousands in the movie game.

However, the movie game is a board game, and in order to play any board game, you need a playing piece. If you try to play the movie game without a playing piece, you are an onanist.

The playing piece is, of course, the script. There are three things that count as a screenplay:

1. An original screenplay

An original screenplay that you have created yourself, to which you own the copyright, and to which you can prove that you own the copyright.

2. The screenplay rights (in writing) to a novel or short story

The hot game in the late ninety's film industry was to travel to Central or Eastern Europe and acquire the screenplay rights to popular novels and short stories and resell them to Hollywood. The theory was that, if the story worked and was already commercially successful in another medium, then it was more likely to succeed as a movie.

To obtain the rights to make a movie from a novel or short story, use the following procedure:

The publisher is listed inside the front cover of the book. Contact him and ask who controls the screenplay rights for the particular title. He will give you the details of the party, be it the author, the author's estate (if deceased), or other company holding the screenplay rights. Simply contact that party and begin negotiations.

As always in the film industry, water runs downhill. Ask yourself what the author is going to be most concerned about. Is it not that you are actually capable of writing the screenplay to the book? And that you have the contacts to get it made by a reputable company with recognizable stars?

I can hardly imagine JK Rowling agreeing to let a little known short story she wrote before the Harry Potter craze be made by a group of students with a wind-up film camera. She did, however, assign the screenplay rights to her next four novels for the down payment on a modest cottage in 1995. Imagine if you had discovered her then.

The more you can bring to the table, the stronger is your position.

If the writer is little known, you should be able to form a partnership with them, with you contributing the screenplay, and the writer contribut-

Onanist and onanism are used in the context of self-gratification in the book.

Onanism is a term based on the second biblical reference that screenwriters need to be aware of. It refers to a terrible trap that writers can easily fall into:

'And it came to pass that Onan spilled his seed upon the ground. The thing which he did displeased the Lord; wherefore he slew him also.'
Genesis ch. 38, vs. 9 to 10.

Curiously, the Japanese language has the word onani, and French has onanisme. Both words refer to the practice of 'self-gratification'.

If you do source a hot manuscript and acquire the screenplay rights to it, producers, eager to buy out your position, will pursue you. Sadly they will have their own pet writers to complete the project. The trick in this sort of market is to try to get two or more producers bidding against each other in order to drive the price up.

In this sort of market, you as writer/talent scout become an entrepreneur – some would say a gold-digger. And this is not for everyone.

ing the source material. You would then need to attract the interest of a producer who is capable of raising the production budget of your film plus your writing fees.

3. The screen rights to a living person's true-life story

To acquire the rights to a person's true-life story, contact the person through directory enquiries, or through the newspapers, radio or television programme where you first heard the story. Again, the price you pay will depend on the publicity surrounding the case.

Another approach is to tell the true life story of someone who was involved with a major personality. Take, for example, Princess Diana , and tell her story through the eyes of a press officer, chauffer, chambermaid and so forth. Unfortunately many employees in this position are asked to sign a non-disclosure clause to protect their employers from this.

If you find a true-life story for a person now living, you must seek their written permission to create a script based on their life. If you are unable to get their permission, you can still write a script about their life if you base the script on the public record – radio and TV interviews or newspaper publications. If you want to use a biography, then you need to get the permission of the writer of the biography.

I once owned the screenplay rights to the life story of the notorious British gangster Mad Frankie Fraser. Reputed to have terminated the lives of over three dozen people with his bare hands, Frankie had just returned from Her Majesty's displeasure, having served over forty years for torture. He was eager to have his life story put on the silver screen.

Unfortunately, Frankie failed to develop a strong career arc in crime. Instead of committing one truly memorable crime, he had broken his career arc by committing dozens of lesser crimes and so no film company was interested. After interviewing him, I realized that the true story of Frankie was in the reasons he turned violent.

Born to a homeless street urchin before the Second World War, Frankie's early memories were of being led over Charing Cross Bridge to forage for food behind luxury hotels on the Strand and often returning hungry. When the war broke out, he was sent up north to a borstal for young boys. Because of the water shortage, he was forced to take a bath in an inch of water. After a few weeks he noticed that the prison governor was masturbating while the boys were bathing. One week, this man raped Frankie. Being small but extremely strong, Frankie nearly drowned the hapless paedophile in the bath and, for his efforts, was sent to prison. After the war, Frankie returned to London, where his career as the minder for gangsters like the Krays blossomed.

One Sunday he decided to look up his long-lost mother, whom he heard was living alone in London's docklands. He arrived to find the house empty. A few weeks later, he returned on one of the coldest days on record. He pushed open the door only to discover his mother dead from the cold, slumped in an armchair, holding his birth certificate. From then on, Frankie became extremely violent.

The Onanist's Rash

If you do not have a playing piece – a screenplay – then the players look-ing for scripts will class you as an onanist. And always remember that everybody in the film industry is very insecure. When you meet someone in the film world, it will take him about five seconds to ascertain that you do not have a screenplay. He won't be rude – he will say charming things to you like: 'Just send it in when it's finished and I'll look at it right away.'

In your naïveté, you will get home and announce to the people you share your life with that you have had a great meeting. What really hap-pened was that you were politely fobbed off, and what you didn't notice was the person's hand easing under his desk and itching over the 'eject' button. What is more, the minute you finally left his office, he clicked the page storing your personal details and deleted your contact details.

Worse yet, when you attempt to pitch the movie without a script, you will develop the 'onanist's rash' – a hideous facial deformity which is very difficult to eradicate. At the time of writing, this affliction had no cure. It is also very prevalent in cappuccino bars – particularly in Central London near my office.

It works like this: the onanist's rash is invisible to the victim. It is the result of the stress you feel when you lie. The rash itself is caused by a chemical reaction between the foam on cappuccino and exhaled breath. Recent experiments have shown that chemical changes in the body occur when people lie, altering the composition of the air we exhale.

Cappuccino bars are normally occupied by writers and film-makers sitting around, nursing cappuccinos and whining about their failed prospects. Whenever a producer asks a writer how his/her script is progressing, the writer raises a coffee to his lips and mumbles 'Great.' The lying air reacts with the foam and causes a rash to appear on the upper lip. The strange thing about this rash (it is an itchy rash) is that you can't see it. In fact, look in the mirror, especially after a meeting with a producer who sussed that you didn't have a script – the rash isn't visible at all. But you know you have it. And it really flares up when someone asks you about your script, and you raise the cappuccino to your lips, and try to hide the truth by covering your mouth and mumbling.

Summary

1. There are really only a few different areas you can sell your script to. But each area contains dozens of individuals who could buy your script.

2. Research your market place by reading the trades.

3. Build the pedigree of your script before you submit it.

How do you keep track of everybody? Create a power file.

13   **The Power File**

ACCUMULATING INFORMATION ABOUT potential buyers is one thing, organizing it into meaningful data is another. In this chapter you will learn how to create and use a power file.

figure 13.1
The Power File

First of all, construct a page in your notebook/computer like this:

Press		Name	
		Company	
		Address	
		Tel	
		Fax	
		Birthday	

Date	Purpose	Result	Action	Reward

Online Resources

Let us analyse this.

Note that the name of the person you are targeting appears in the top right-hand corner. Never put a company name there. The film industry is a people industry, and it is not what you know but who you know that counts. People in the industry often move jobs. Eighteen months is a very long time to be at the same job in the film industry. People move from company to company, and it is with the people that you build relationships. If it is a company you are tracking, for some reason, then you would need a new page for the company.

This isn't so different to when you move house within a city and keep the same doctor, dentist, decorator, and plumber.

On the left-hand side, under 'Press', list the press notices, radio and television appearances or interviews for the person you are targeting.

Another important source of information is the internet. Set up a key word search for the person you are pursuing, in order to get an email alert for each new web page that includes their name.

The next thing you should do is check the person's IMDB entry – in order to get an up-to-date snapshot of their career to date, and any new projects that they happen to be working on. All this provides useful gist to the mill when you are talking to them.

Under the person's name, list their contact details, including their birth date. You find out what their birth date is so that you can send them a birthday card. The film industry is fiercely competitive, and you want to do anything you can to distinguish yourself. If you send someone a birthday card, you are flattering him or her and are appealing to their ego.

Everyone in the film industry is very insecure. Anyone who has a successful niche or position in the industry knows that there are at least a hundred others waiting for them to fail or weaken in order to push them off their perch. They know that, because they know how they got to where they are.

How do you find out their birth date? Of course there are Who's Who websites and other directories. But what if you are really impatient? Wouldn't you just call up the person's office? And you know who answers the telephone at film companies all over the world? Interns!

Telephone reception is an entry-level position, but suddenly the person answering the telephone at the office of the person you are targeting becomes the single most important person in the world because they control direct personal access to the person you are pursuing. They decide whether or not you are going to be put through.

Back to the birthday card. If you live in the UK and are targeting someone in the UK, it is rather mundane to receive a card from someone in the UK. Isn't it more exciting to get a card from another country, especially an exotic one? How about Tibet, China or Kosovo? Maybe you have a friend or relative in such a far flung place. If you do, you can purchase an international postal order to the value of one air-stamp and mail it back to your home nation. Put the coupon into an envelope along with addressed birthday card and ask your friend or relative to post the envelope. Time the journey so the card arrives on the target's birthday and voilà! You will be noticed.

What do you write in the card? If you are pursuing Bob Hoskins, write:

> dd/mm/yy
>
> Dear Bob,
>
> While in Chechnya researching my latest movie, 'Top Title', I remembered it was your birthday. I'll look you up when I get back to London.
>
> Regards,
>
> Your name

I'll bet you're asking how to prevent Bob Hoskins from thinking you are a stalker? Remember, we are marketing your script. The person you are targeting has been selected because you think, as a result of your research, that he is likely to purchase your script. You don't have an agent, the film world is ruthlessly competitive, and you are starting a communication which you hope will result in a one-on-one meeting with this person. Modify your letter:

> dd/mm/yy
>
> Dear Bob,
>
> I met you at the Cannes Film Festival last year. While in Chechnya researching my latest movie, 'Top Title', I remembered it was your birthday. I'll look you up when I get back to London.
>
> Regards,
>
> Your name

All film people go to Cannes at least once in their careers. Some go every year, others go every other year.

When I go to Cannes, I go with business cards – it is the only way that you can get accreditation. Around thirty-five thousand people attend Cannes every year. Of those, there are about a thousand serious producers, sales agents and distributors trying to do business, about thirty thousand wannabes, and about four thousand tourists who stumble into town during the most exciting week in the film industry calendar.

Every time you meet someone at Cannes, you have a brief conversation and exchange business cards. When the person turns and leaves, you jot on the back of the person's business card one of two things – 'Nutbar', or 'Call when I get back home'. Later in the hotel room, you empty your pockets onto the bed and sort through the business cards. I always have to buy a new bag to carry home all of the business cards, free magazines and flyers.

It is very likely that the person you are targeting will have been to Cannes recently, and will have met many people to whom they made promises but can't exactly place.

If you can't obtain their birth date, or feel it is too tacky to use it, then you can dream up an excuse from another moment in their career. The first time they appeared in, directed, or produced a film that opened in Leicester Square, or Times Square, the anniversary of their first Oscar nomination, and so on.

Your next job is to use the power file regularly.

Suppose you have written a script that you feel is suitable for Clint Eastwood. You discover that his production company is called Malpaso Productions (from noting the credits in the cinema or on TV). You can get this telephone number by dialling directory information. You can get contact details for directors from the Directors' Guild of America (or in Great Britain, the Directors' Guild of Great Britain), and for actors from the Screen Actors' Guild in New York or Los Angeles (for an American actor), Equity for a British actor. The guild will give you the telephone number of the agent or personal manager for the person that you are targeting, and from that person you can get the address of the production company.

The first person you will deal with is the gatekeeper. The gatekeeper should get their own page in your power file. If you call Malpaso Productions at midnight on a Sunday to sell your script to Clint Eastwood (purpose), you will get the answering machine (result), and an instruction to call back when the company is open 10 to 5 pm Pacific Coastal Time Monday to Friday (action). But give yourself a reward. Get a box of little gold stars and paste one in.

Selling your screenplay is a very lonely business and, a few days or even weeks later, when you are skimming through your power file, that little gold star will give you a reminder of the burst of positive action you made, and it will cheer you up.

Everytime you start writing a script, start thinking about potential purchasers. By maintaining a record of who these potential clients are, and by making note of their names, you create useful marketing data.

The gatekeeper theory

The first person you speak to in any company in the world is the gatekeeper – a lowly paid person or intern who also has their own career aspirations.

Treat this person as you would a god, for they control direct personal access to the person that you are targeting.

If you want to see how serious you are about writing and selling a script, you can do your own private onanism test in the privacy of your own home. If, six months after reading this page, you do **not** have at least a hundred names in your power file, then it's official: you are an onanist with no intention of writing or selling your script.

Adding to the Power File

Here are some ideas as to how to fill your power file to overflowing:

1. Read the trades

The American trades are Hollywood Reporter and Variety; the British trades are Screen International, The Business of Film, and Screen Finance. In Canada there is Playback; and in France there are Film Français and Ecran Totale.

Buy a copy of a trade magazine. You will find that they are organized like this:
- Front-page story to remind you what is currently the hot topic
- Inside front three to five pages there are production notes from around the world about films in production. Here you would note any projects either similar to the one you are working on or would like to start working on
- The centre of the trade magazine generally covers topics of interest to filmmakers, exhibitors, distributors and other executives – for example a focus on Icelandic cinema
- The end pages have a production survey where all of the films from around the world are listed and tracked through the production process. The first time they appear in the trades, they have a complete cast and crew list, the name of the writer and producer, contact details, and a synopsis of the film which can either be short, like 'Thriller', or long (three to eight words) like 'Three school boys chase the same girl.' Again, note any projects that might be of interest to you and make a note of the producer and/or writer, or any other relevant people from the production listing that you think might be useful to you
- All trade papers publish the box office charts and this is another source of data that can be useful. The box office charts will give you an idea of what is commercially successful and the decay rate of films once they have been released. For example, a horror film opens strongly, and curves down after about two weeks. Comedies build for several weeks before peaking and tapering off

2. Read the product guides

There are three film markets during the year and they are attended by most of the filmmakers, film sellers and film buyers. It is obvious that this is a tremendous resource to a writer in order to ascertain the types of genre or story that are currently easiest to sell.

The three film trade markets occur mid February in Los Angeles at the American Film Market (AFM); the Marché du Cannes during the Cannes Film Festival in May; and the MIFED market in Milan in October. There are also several television markets during the year. For each market, the major trades publish a thick product guide with all of the films (product) on sale, as well as the film buyers attending.

It is a good idea to attend as many markets as you can. The one easiest to access is the Marché du Cannes in France. Because it runs simultaneously during the Cannes Film Festival, attendees are spoilt for choices for parties, networking, screenings, free magazines and so on. Cannes is also near some spectacular countryside which makes a great diversion for a day or two when you tire of the hustling of the market.

The trade papers publish a product guide prior to each market. Listed in the product guide are key market players – buyers of films and sellers. Pages from product guides list the home address of the company, along with the names and titles of executives attending.

Product available at the market is listed in one of three categories:

– Completed, or screening now, or DVD available. This means that the film is completed and the representative of the film is eagerly seeking a sale of the film to the territory represented by the buyer

– In production, or 'Delivery scheduled for…' (date three to ten months in the future) means that the representative of the film is attempting to create a buzz about the film prior to completion, or the production company is suffering from a cash flow crisis and is attempting to sell the film rights to a territory to raise the completion budget

– The film is listed as in pre-production. At this stage, the production company is attempting to raise the production budget of the film by selling the rights to the film at a discount over what the film would command in their territory when completed. This is called a pre-sales agreement. The producer will then take the contract back to his home nation and give it to a film financing bank which will assess the creditworthiness of the buyers, and then use the agreement as collateral against a loan to the production company to enable the film to be made

This is a golden opportunity for writers to sell their scripts but, to pull this off, a great deal of pre-planning is necessary. By preparing your power file, ascertaining the different film companies attending, and ascertaining the different types of product which they purchase, you will eliminate irrelevant companies and make sure that you shoot with a rifle and not with a shotgun, and have a better chance of hitting the target.

3. Promote Yourself

Every time you meet anyone, tell him or her about your movie and ask him if he knows anyone who would be interested in the script. Everyone wants to be in the movies and, even if they aren't personable, interested in or able to advance your project, in this way you at least expand your circle of influence.

You are also using the 'six degrees of separation' rule – that you are only ever six contacts away from anyone else in the world. Guy Ritchie may have married Madonna. Even without her contacts, he is considered to be one of the best-connected people in the UK.

Packaging Your Screenplay

Packaging is the process whereby you add talent or expertise to your screenplay. The more you add to your screenplay, the easier it is for a production company to say 'Yes' to your script.

1. Find a producer

This is the hardest task a writer has to do. The wrong producer will leave you in a pile of jangled nerves and so bitter and twisted that you will probably abandon a career as a screenwriter.

The right producer is a joy to work with, someone you can bounce ideas off, and who helps pick you up when you are down.

To go to a film market as a writer, your goal is to raise money for the production of the film. The right producer will assist you in closing the deals necessary to get your film into production. Within that budget will be an amount for your screenplay.

2. Marketing tools

The most successful sales at the film market have resulted from some cheap printed marketing materials. In the same way that you would not market your home without a sheet of details and a floor plan or photo or, even worse, attempt to get a job without a one-sheet (CV), so too, it is pertinent to create a one-sheet for your movie.

When your script is sold to a producer, financed, shot and edited, the producer creates a one-sheet to give to the agent responsible for selling the film. It is on the basis of this one-sheet that initial interest is gauged, and the similarities between using a property one-sheet when selling a house, and a film one-sheet for selling a film, are obvious.

Why not try some test marketing on your script before it is written?

Hire a graphic designer and give him the pitch, or allow him to read the screenplay. It is instructive to see what the designer comes up with. Does he or does he not 'get' it? If he doesn't, perhaps your screenplay is not clear enough.

Roger Corman has used this approach successfully for decades. Much of his inspiration comes from juxtaposing newspaper headlines. If he comes up with a title, for example Teenage Werewolf in Paris, he creates a one-sheet and takes it to the film markets. If the poster arouses enough interest, he returns to LA, hires a screenwriter to create a script that represents the poster, and then shoots the movie.

A one-sheet is a cost-effective way to test your market idea.

If it is easy to go and pitch and sell your film or script at a film market, why isn't everyone doing it?

The answer, as with most things in the film industry, boils down to money. It costs approximately $20 000 to join each market, plus the cost of a stand, staff, travel and advertising will set back a company at least $50 000. Most writers cannot afford that.

Because most writers cannot afford to attend film markets, a new breed of industry professional was born: the sales agent – someone with the financial ability to set up at a film market and who is able to amortize the cost of attending the market over several projects, some completed, some in post-production, and some – like yours – in development, or pre-production.

A sales agent will charge the producer of a film a commission for any pre-sales agreement achieved during a market. Armed with your one-sheet, try to get a sales agent to represent you at film markets.

This doesn't prevent you from sitting around in the lobby of the Majestic Hotel, one-sheet in hand, ready to pounce on a celebrity, financier or producer when they walk through! Indeed, film lore is rife with the tales of success from the lobby of the Majestic! A word of caution: don't ever pay an advance to someone purporting to be able to sell your script.

Let's deconstruct the one-sheet shown in figures 13.2 and 13.3

Title

Two or three words which start to sell the story. Commercially successful films have titles that sum up the entire movie in two or three words. Meet the Parents, Castaway, Traffic, Airplane, Analyze This all sum up the story of the movie. Choose words that make your film resonate with emotion and action.

Log line

The log line is an expansion of the title of the movie – usually no more than eight words. Although filmmakers often look to the writer for ideas for the log line, it usually is the marketing department of the distributors who come up with the log lines. Be prepared to wince.

Visual image

A strong visual image that represents the movie, or scenes from the movie if shot. Whatever the image, it should fire the imagination. As you preview the artists' ideas, you will start to see the first visual images of your script.

Credits

These are usually placed at the bottom of the page. Here you would add any people that you have committed to the project. Don't worry if you don't have anyone signed up yet. Just make it look strong and confident. Make certain that you place your contact details in legible type.

The back of the poster contains the following:

Top paragraph

Here's an application for the basic premise that has been driving you crazy: those twenty-five words or less which sum up the movie.

figure 13.2
Sample One-Sheet (Front)

figure 13.3
Sample One-Sheet (Reverse)

More images

How well did your screenplay inspire the graphic artist?

Naked self-promotion

Finish off with a well-written paragraph or two explaining why your script is this year's hot topic. You are the writer. You are the genius. Stop blushing and market yourself (this is blatant self-aggrandizement).

Other Ways to Add to Your Power File

Your power file is only as good as the information you put into it. And the more information you put into it, the better chance you have of developing a truly good power file. Successful writers are always adding to their power file.

Hint The film industry is a people business – it's not what you know, it's who you know

---

1. Start with people you know

Call up every single person you know. Tell them you have finished your script. They will already know what it is about, because you will have been talking to them so much about it. Ask them if they know anyone who could buy your script, or would know anyone who might know someone who would be interested in buying your script. Even if they do not know anyone they probably will know someone who does know someone. Apply the 'six degrees of separation' rule and expand your circle of influence.

I found out yesterday that I am one person away from Bono, Woody Allen, and the editor of Wallpaper. Of course I'm still debating which script to send to whom!

2. Watch movies

This is the fun part. See every single movie that you can. If possible try to see films in a cinema – it is useful to see films as they were intended to be shown, it gives you an opportunity to gauge the audience's reaction, and is generally a more pleasurable experience than seeing everything at home on the television.

Every time you see a movie similar to the type of film you want to write, or have written, capture the production company details (they are always in the credits). Note everyone in the production that might be interested in working with you – the writer, the director, the producer. Maybe you can get in touch with the script editor.

If you want to get in touch with a star, a director, a writer, there is a secret telephone number that you, as an aspiring writer, can use. It is 411 (in North America), and 118118 in the UK. Directory Information, or look at www.whorepresents.com

How you make this call is important. The Guilds are extremely busy and understaffed. Limit your request to three names per telephone call. The telephone numbers they supply will not be the personal home telephone numbers of the stars that you are pursuing. You will get their agent's telephone number. Call the agent and try to ascertain whether or not the person you are pursuing has a production company (if you can't find out any other way) or ask him for the production company telephone number (if you can't find out any other way).

3. Read magazines

In addition to the filmzines and fanzines, you should subscribe to the excellent newswire services. In the UK there is 6degrees.co.uk and in the USA indiewire.com which provide quick, reliable information about what is happening in film. And they are free.

More fun work. Reading magazines on a regular basis, however, can be gruelling. Nonetheless you must keep abreast of developments in the industry. Trade magazines like Variety publish invaluable information on what is happening at the moment and who is looking for what.

Magazines can also offer information on who is doing well, and who is heading for their next session in rehab. This information may not have a direct use, but it helps make you industry-smart and savvy.

4. Surf the net

The internet offers unparalleled opportunities to research films and film-makers. Don't ignore this amazing tool.

Summary

1. Try to relax as you suck in all of the information from the various trades and markets. There is no science as to what works best – you just sort of get a feel for it.

2. Try to get a feel for the business side of the industry as you build up your power file.

You've got your power file in shape and someone calls you up and asks you to come into a meeting. You're ready to pitch.

14 Pitching

WHEN SOMEONE ASKS you what your screenplay is about, and you tell them, you are verbally pitching your script to them. If they ask you for a written summation – a treatment – you are submitting a written pitch.

The word 'pitching' is really a misnomer as it conjures up visions of a snake-oil salesman peddling questionable wares to an unsuspecting public. But if you took pitching out of the film business, the entire industry would collapse. Every movie ever made was made as a result of pitching. And the film industry is a people business, which means that your communication skills are very important.

In the film industry, pitching is the process which you as a writer, director or producer, use in order to impart your passion for your project to others – cast, crew or financiers. British filmmakers' pitching skills are very primitive compared to those of their American counterparts. While some British producers like Nik Powell and Steve Wooley are legendary in their pitching abilities, most British filmmakers do not pay enough attention to this very valuable and necessary skill.

Pitching is the fundamental foundation of the film business, and if you took pitching away from writers, directors, and producers, you would not have any film industry. If you are unable to pitch properly and effectively you are doomed as a writer of screenplays (unless you can align yourself with a director who can pitch for you).

Pitching is the process whereby you convey your passion for your project to potential financiers, to talent and to the crew.

Hint Pitching is the single most important skill anyone, including writers, should acquire in order to succeed in the film industry. The skill is to express your story in clear concise terms that create visual images in the mind of the listener.

In our everyday life, we pitch all the time. When your best friend or dearest relative calls up, they will ask you 'What's new?' You will then pitch them either a problem at work (to elicit sympathy) or prospects in love or work (to gain support or admiration). People who can't succeed at this elemental task are often referred to as 'cold' or 'loners'.

The Structure of a Pitch Meeting

In order to pitch properly it is important to understand the structure of a pitch meeting and the various signs, cues and clues of the meeting, how to read them, and how to capitalize on them.

Any pitch meeting has three parts (just like your screenplay): Beginning, Middle and End. Here, the elements of a pitch meeting are broken down, along with a list of the goals you must achieve, in order to sell your screenplay. I also list some tools you can use in order to help you achieve your goals:

Beginning

Most pitch meetings are fifteen to twenty minutes long, and the first part can take anywhere from twenty-five to fifty per cent of the time, depending on variables beyond your control.

Your task in the first part of the pitch meeting is to schmooze with the person you are seeing so that they can get to know you, and so that you can get to know them. Remember that the person you are meeting is nervous too.

We do the same thing in our everyday life — when we see a friend in the street we say 'How are you? What's new? How did the job interview go?' and in the UK we usually comment on the weather. At the start of a pitch meeting, both sides are trying to figure each other out, and both parties are nervous. The only difference is that the person to whom you are pitching is usually more experienced at pitch meetings and therefore better able to cover up his or her anxiety.

If you have been able to do some proper research, then you might start off by commenting on their recent television interview, the news article on a current project or the success of one of their projects which is similar to your own.

Your first goal in a pitch meeting is to see whether you are pitching to a left brain or a right brain person.

Our minds are divided into two. The left side controls rational thought, the right side controls the subconscious and the emotions. While you are schmoozing, cast a glance around the office to see if you can ascertain clues about the type of person you are meeting. Do they have wall charts with circled deadline dates hanging next to profit and loss statements (left brain — number man)?

No one is totally left or right brain, but most people lean one way.

A good tool for determining whether or not you have a right brain or a left brain person is to place two items on their desk a few minutes after you start the meeting — a neatly typed one page synopsis of your script and an object from the script, maybe the revolver, a photograph, or a map of the enchanted island. Observe which one the person picks up. A left-brainer, who favours logical analytical thought, will probably pick up the typed sheet, while a right-brainer, who thinks more creatively, aesthetically and intuitively, will most likely be drawn to the object or image. It is useful to know what sort of thinker you are dealing with as this will influence the way you pitch and improve your chances of success.

Author, producer, and publisher Michael Wiese, while working at Viacom, had the good fortune to stumble across the home video rights to boxing fights in the forties and fifties. His innovative approach to this worn material was to edit out the knockout rounds from the films and edit them together for home video and call it 'Boxing's Greatest Hits'. In order to enhance the value of the product, he decided that an image of Don King would make a great cover jacket.

Through his observation and networking, Michael ascertained that Don King was a right brain person and was therefore easily carried away with the emotion of an event. A video jacket with Don King's face was prepared in advance of the initial pitch meeting. Michael went with an assistant who was told that, when cued (approximately half way through the start of the meeting), he should place the box upon the desk where Don King could see it, leave it there for exactly five minutes, then remove it, but he was to count the number of times Don King made direct eye contact with the image of himself for a period longer than three seconds. King did this an incredible thirty-seven times during the meeting. Needless to say, he did the deal.

You will know when you are at the end of the first part of the meeting when the person you are pitching says 'How can I help you?' or 'What do you have?'. You are now in the second part of the meeting.

Middle

Start with your basic premise, the so-called 'twenty-five words or less'. Do not read from notes. Reading from notes is the kiss of death at any pitch meeting. You want to establish direct eye contact with the person you are pitching. If you read from notes it will appear that you do not feel totally comfortable with your material, or that you are not passionate about your project.

See if you can gauge the person's interest. If his head is going 'Yes, yes, yes' then you have time to give an expanded, more detailed pitch.

You are waiting for him to say 'Could you have your agent or representative contact our head of business and legal affairs?' Kerching! You have done the deal.

Often, however, after you have finished your short introductory pitch, you will hear instead 'No thank you.' Your task now is to discover why. Is it because you are pitching to the wrong person? Maybe the circumstances of the company's finances have changed drastically since your appointment was made. Maybe they just didn't like your idea.

Whatever the reason, you then reach back into your quiver, select another arrow, and fire it off. It is a good idea to take at least three fully developed pitches to a meeting. Maybe you start with a pitch other than the one you were asked to bring, just to warm up. Do whatever makes you feel comfortable.

Often too, after your initial twenty-five words, you will hear 'No' expressed in a different phrase – a phrase that will strike terror into your heart: 'Stop, please, we have something exactly like that.' More commonplace is something like 'Isn't it amazing that there is such a common currency of ideas in circulation?'

If that happens to you, make a positive choice. Yes, it is a shame that the company you are pitching to already has something similar to your idea. But hey, at least you have proven that your ideas are commercially viable! It is extremely rare that film companies steal ideas from writers. What does happen, however, to beleaguered story development executives is that they think that they have heard something similar to your idea from someone else. Development executives can hear dozens of story pitches in a week and it is likely that they have heard something similar to yours in the last month, or in the last one hundred pitches.

So move on.

Reach into your quiver and pull out another arrow – another of the three fully prepared pitches you have brought to your meeting. It would be a shame to go to a one-on-one meeting, considering all the time and effort that it takes to set one up, with just one pitch. Be prepared.

Hint Development people are nervous about meeting you and hearing your pitch too. They just have more experience than you do. So relax.

The End

You will know when you are in the third part of the meeting when you either hear 'No thanks' or what you are dying to hear: 'Could you have your agent or representative contact our head of business and legal affairs?' Kerching!

However you arrive at the third part of the pitch meeting, your task is to leave as quickly as possible. Do not make small talk, do not comment on the weather, the news, or the jukebox in the corner. Just leave. If you linger you overstay your welcome and the minute you leave will be the minute that your contact details are destroyed.

Film people are notoriously insecure – so insecure in fact that they seem over-polite. If you make small talk in the third part of the meeting, don't mistake the person's interest as anything other than a polite attempt to disguise his efforts to lean over and push the eject button.

Three Golden Rules of Salesmanship

These rules work for a pitch meeting for a screenplay, or just about any situation where you are trying to get the deal, film industry or not.

1. Never say a number

He or she who says the first number loses. Think back to the times that you had to negotiate payment for a job. Do you remember having to answer the request 'Make me an offer'?

For research and a laugh, walk into any car salesroom anywhere in the world. Car salesmen are trained to get you to say a number. And they are not beyond lying to get that number out of you. A car salesman always asks you what your budget is — what you want to spend. If you resist naming a price, the salesman will badger you until you say a number, using phrases like 'We'll work with you/Let me paper you into this deal/ I'll speak to the manager, but you have to give me something to work with'. Before you know it you are saying something like $200 per month.

The minute you say a number, you lose. If you say a hundred to a hundred-a-fifty a month — do you think for a minute that the salesmen heard the number one hundred? The irony is that the car salesman should be at a disadvantage because the cars all have huge sale stickers on them.

Similarly, in a pitch meeting, the person you are meeting, whether he is a producer, agent, or story executive will often ask you what you are looking for as payment for your script. Never say a number. You may over-price or under-price yourself. Always make it very clear that the person that they need to speak to regarding money, or price, will contact them later. You will make yourself look more professional, and can limit the content of future meetings to the creative issues involving them and you. If you don't have an agent or representative, now is the best time to get one. Other alternatives are to use a friend, or a solicitor.

At the time of re-writing this book, I have been working simultaneously on a novel to be illustrated by a world-famous artist. As a result of his attachment to the project, and a few contacts in the film industry, it was relatively easy for me to get an agent based on the prospect of immediate publication. I found myself sitting in the editor's office of a British publisher known for publishing a series of the most successful children's books of all time, all of which had been made into blockbusters. Sniffing, I suppose, my great talent and the prospect of duplicating this huge money machine, she leaned over and said 'How much do you want?'. I had been forewarned by my agent and responded 'What is the retail price?'. She said 'Between $12 to $30, depending on whether or not you actually get this artist to illustrate', 'Oh,' I said, 'And how many copies are you planning to print?'. 'Two hundred thousand', she said. 'World-wide, or just Europe?' I said. 'We'll have to see how it goes', she said.

Can you see how we were kicking around the price, without actually saying a number? Author royalties are ten per cent of wholesale, and wholesale is thirty-five to forty per cent of retail. I guess it's a good thing to brush off your mental arithmetic skills.

Hint Never talk money with a producer. Not only will you come out short-changed, but you could scuttle the deal.

---

2. Never go to money

By this I mean you should try to get the person who you are pursuing with your script to come to your place of work. If they never come to you, you are dealing with an onanist. The theory is that, if the person will not leave their yacht, penthouse, or mansion to come to visit you, then they will never take you seriously. Getting potential investors or script buyers to take you seriously is part of the challenge.

This rule definitely applies to producers attempting to raise money, but, as a writer, it is always more difficult to get a story development person out of their office – they are simply too busy. Try, however, to get them out onto neutral territory: a coffee shop, or park bench.

Never suggest lunch. A lunch meeting can take an hour or more. If you have not met this person before and he doesn't take to you, or if your pitch is wrong, he will feel totally trapped by you.

Hint When they start calling you, when they start trying to hang out with you, then you know you are getting hot.

---

3. You don't ask, you don't get

If you are ever in the second part of a meeting and you notice that the person you are meeting glances at his watch and you have yet to ask for the deal, you are automatically in the third part of the meeting.

You must ask for the deal the minute you are in the second part of the meeting. Of course you don't blatantly ask if they want to buy your script – that would be tacky and an ineffective marketing approach. However, you can say: 'I hear you are looking for a thriller' or 'Since your most recent project was a hit, isn't it true you are entertaining romantic comedies like the one I have?'

You basically try to build accord with the person you are selling to. If they say 'No' then it is your job to discover what kind of 'No' it is, for, in my experience, there are three different kinds of 'No'.

Believe it or not, when I was really broke, I became a professional debt collector. My job was to call up corner store owners who had defaulted on their extortionate loans for wet/dry vacuum cleaners. Some of you will recall such machines in many corner stores in the mid-nineties. My job was to get them to settle their debts, either by rescheduling their payments at a better interest rate, or by repossessing the vacuum cleaners. It was on this job that I learned the three kinds of 'No'.

'No' number one means: 'The house is on fire. Emergency! No! I can't speak to you for another second.' Fair enough. They're busy. Maybe you can call back later. When you are pitching a script the equivalent might be that the company has just been bought-out, and no one knows what the new owners want to fund. Put the contact to one side for a few weeks and call back later.

The second type of 'No', the 'No' I hate, is the 'maybe No' and sounds like this: 'Can you put some details in the post and we'll review your material and get back to you (if we are interested)?'. No way. You bet. Sure thing. That's the huge pile of stuff beside the desk that nobody looks at. I got so many actual 'No's' that I didn't even bother sending stuff out to the 'maybe No's' – they just never responded and I, as a commissioned salesman, was charged for postage. I'd just pass the file over to the student lawyer who would start court proceedings.

I used to think there were only two kinds of 'No' until one day I had a revelation: these people didn't really mean 'No' – they just needed more information. They were frightened to get a telephone call from a debt collector and they were fearful about the consequences. I changed my tack with comments like: 'Let me explain why I think we can sort this problem out right now. It will only take a few minutes'. Of course my success rate rocketed.

The third kind of 'No' was the 'No with reservations'. This became a joy to my ears because it meant that they wanted more information. It meant you had a chance to close. The way to handle this situation was to learn to recognize objections and then offer alternative information to make them feel comfortable with the transaction.

Trial closings

The final aspect of 'If you don't ask, you don't get' is the trial closing. You have to ask for the deal. You say things like: 'I understand you are looking for a thriller,' if that is what you have. Or, 'How would you feel if Kiera Knightley was playing the lead?', if you want to evoke an image of the lead female role. If you haven't asked by the time they sneak a sideways glance at the LCD clock in the upper corner of their computer screen, you are automatically out of there – you have struck out and you are in the third part of the meeting.

Can you remember talking to someone who is really boring when you have an important meeting to go to? Remember how you go into all sorts of convoluted gestures in order to see what time it is without this boring unfortunate recognizing what you are doing?

In your pitch meeting you have to start asking for the deal as soon as you are in the second part of the meeting: 'Is this the type of thing you are looking for?' or 'Did you find it scary?'. And so forth.

Pitching Tools

The trick with pitching is to evoke a visual image in the recipient's mind. There are several tools you can use to accomplish this. Practise them until you get comfortable with each one. Stand in front of the mirror. Practise on your friends. Keep working on your pitch until you know excatly how to frame your story. Then you will be able to use the tools appropriate for the person you are pitching.

The first few seconds of your pitch are really important. It is in these vital few seconds that you set up your pitch and engage the listener. Then you move them towards the last few seconds – the ending.

1. The camera angle

'We see the park. It's autumn. There's a park bench. It's cold. Leaves are falling. And over there is the body. Oh no. Both eyes have been gouged out. Is this what you have been looking for?'

In this pitch we start with a wide shot, and then zoom into the eyes of the victim. By using the camera angle, we involve the person in the first few frames of your movie. Of course this takes a few seconds of time, but you also sneak in a rather ambiguous trial closing.

2. What if?

'What if everything you have heard about extra terrestrials is true and you find out that your husband/wife is from outer space?'

The advantage of the 'what if' is that it allows you to condense your premise into a few lines and test it out. If at the end of your 'what if' you can't get any reaction from your target, then you are in trouble. Get ready for another line of attack.

3. The movie cross

Comparing your movie to one or two other movies is called a movie cross – 'My story is a cross between Shawn of the Dead and Bee Movie.'

The advantage of this technique is that your target immediately gets a feel for the movie's style. The disadvantages may be too risky to justify the use of this technique. If your target has not seen one of the movies you mention, then the movie cross is meaningless, and your target is flustered. Or your target may not agree that your movie has anything to do with the movies it has been compared to. Be careful with this one.

Perhaps a better strategy is to compare your movie to a movie of the same genre. Aliens was successfully pitched as 'Jaws in space".

4. Pop a question

When you ask a direct personal question of your target at the start of a pitch, you immediately focus the target's attention on you and your story. And it becomes intensely personal. But you have to be careful not to make it too personal, like this opening sprung on me and on a hundred other people at one of the Raindance Film Festival's pitching events called Live!Ammunition!.

'Have you heard of Death Watch? You haven't? Well, that's a shame, because it's watching you.'

This was just a little too dark, the delivery was flat, and didn't get people's attention – they just squirmed, thinking to themselves 'Shut up.'

Better perhaps, was this one:

'Did you know there was, in fact, a fifth member of the British Royal Family? This is the story of Norma who has been forced to work as a lowly toilet attendant at a luxury hotel in London. From there, she is planning her revenge on the House of Windsor.'

This approach uses the question in a less direct or personal way. It still personalizes the story to the target, but in a less intense way. It also tries to portray the main character in a visual way.

5. The elevator pitch

Can you hook your entire story into a couple of lines and grab the attention of a producer or story executive you just happen to share an elevator with for a few floors?

'It's a rom-com, but also a God-com. Steve Guttenberg plays Jesus. Naomi Watts plays a nun. It's sort of The Passion of the Christ for girls.'

They pause with their finger hovering over the open door button and you slide in with another line and, if you are really good, they are intrigued and beckon you on over to their office, and sign you up for a deal.

Tips For Pitching

1. Reading notes

The sure-fire way to bomb in a pitch meeting. Don't read, ever. You cannot look passionate if you are reading from notes. Refer to a few notes made on an index card if you are worried about freezing in your pitch. But I know you won't freeze, because you know your story inside out, backwards and forwards and are passionate about your story.

2. Be brief

Time is money. And you won't have much time if you ramble on and on. Get straight to the point. Don't waste time. Remember that lengthy introductions are either sophisticated excuses or the sign of a frustrated amateur lacking confidence.

3. Be entertaining

Nik Powell is one of the world's most successful practitioners of the art of the pitch. Having produced the Monty Python films, Mona Lisa and The Crying Game, Nik has had a hand in the launch of many new writers and directors in the British film scene. I asked him how many times he had pitched Back Beat – the story of the fifth Beatle – before he got the money. He said about four thousand times. I asked him if he could give me a sample pitch. He said he couldn't because it was different every time. He tailored each pitch in order to entertain the person he was pitching to. Like being the best joke at the pub.

4. Sell the sizzle not the steak

Your pitch should describe the elements of the story with salesmanship in mind. When you call up a travel agent for details of a tropical holiday – what do they send you? The plumbing, wiring and electrical diagrams of the hotel they want you to stay in (the steak) – or the glossy photo of the hotel with the artist's impression of the pool – yet to be built (the sizzle)?

The common error many writers make is that they pitch their story as 'this happens, then this happens, and then that happens' – a guaranteed snore.

Summary

1. Passion is everything when you are pitching.

2. Be persuasive.

3. Be clear and concise.

How can you get a film company to consider your script when you don't have an agent? Write the eight-line letter.

Eight-Line Letter

ASK AND YE shall receive. Well, maybe not every time.

But ask in the correct manner, and your chances of success start to soar, whether it be a request for funding, for a favourable equipment rental deal, or for interest in your screenplay.

The first rule of successful begging is to ascertain exactly what it is you require. Then it is necessary to quantify the need in simple straightforward sentences that are clear and yet entertaining to read.

If the first item on the agenda is film stock, find out where there are advertising production companies and word your request as follows:

'We are attempting to create the world's first 35mm feature film (ninety minutes long) with a budget of absolutely zero. We wonder if you have any redundant film stock that you would allow us to utilize in exchange for a credit on the film.'

Let us analyse this simple paragraph: Notice how often the key words such as '35mm' and 'feature film' are repeated, emphasizing the precise goal we were trying to achieve. Nobody would mistake our request for a donation to the local sports centre.

The choice of words is also important. For example, we asked to 'utilize' film stock. I discovered early on that I had a very negative response to the term 'give us'. And if you think about it, once a roll of film stock is utilized, it is pretty much utilized.

The next task is to ascertain the identity of the target person in the company. Simply ring up the company and ask, for instance, for the person responsible for script development – if you are trying to sell a script. If you were seeking financing, you would ask for the person responsible for client's discretionary income (within an accountancy firm). Of course, you could ask for the person responsible for redundant film stock, if you are blagging film stuff, and so on. Once you have this person's name, you are nearly ready to go into battle.

The last piece of information you need to provide is a simple paragraph describing yourself. Try to do this in an interesting way, even if you have a boring day job – 'I am a singing bus conductor who writes screenplays in my spare time.'

Film people are paranoid that they will miss the low-key individual that really has talent, and they also know that many successful filmmakers started as very shy individuals.

You now have a choice. You have to target names. Why not first try a cold call telephone pitch? Try to get the target on the telephone and persuade him with your charm that you are worth helping or worth meeting.

If it fails, or if a film company tells you that, as a screenwriter, they will only speak to you through an agent, you can try the eight-line letter.

Often, the only way to present your script to a production company is through an agent or entertainment attorney known to the company. Here's how you can get that elusive company to call you.

The secret is to compose a well-written letter, exactly eight lines long. Send it by post, or by fax, or e-mail to an actual human being at the production company. Target the person whom your research has shown to be the person responsible for deciding whether or not their company should purchase your screenplay, or whether someone from their company should meet with you for a one-on-one pitch meeting.

The reason that your letter must only be eight lines long is because you want that person to read it. When you write a letter you must understand that the person to whom you are writing is most likely to be extremely busy. An eight-line letter, which is a clear and concise, stands a far better chance of being read.

If the letter is ten lines long, or, heaven forbid, twenty lines long, your letter will require too much of that person's time. And since the person does not know you, your letter will probably be consigned to the same paper shredder as your script was.

If you haplessly send a letter to a film company marked 'To the person in charge of script acquisition', your letter will also go straight into the rubbish bin. If you, as screenwriter, are too lazy to call and discover the appropriate person in the company to send a letter to, they are justified in assuming that you paid as little attention to your script. You, as a writer, will be attempting to approach the head of story development, sometimes called head of acquisitions. If you are writing to the local firm of accountants seeking an introduction to the most wealthy clients in their office block, then somehow you want to find out if that firm has a person employed who is responsible for client's discretionary investments.

Elements of an Eight-Line Letter

1. A good visual style

The paper does not need to be expensive, but should be crisp and clean. Avoid the use of fancy colours. Plain white is difficult to beat.

You should design a logo or graphic image, along with the name of your company. The image should say, very simply, why you are hot, or why you are going places.

Next, try to invent a company name for yourself, but don't get silly with names like '20th Century United Artists'. Rip-off names like these garner little respect, especially if an aged relative of yours answers the telephone when your target calls you.

And this brings me to a related point on professionalism: make sure that you have a reliable answering machine service. It is also advisable to get a second dedicated fax line. If you cannot get one, try to find a friend who has a fax machine that you can use. If you have a second dedicated fax line, you are one big step away from rank amateur first timer: 'tel/fax number' on your letter just doesn't carry a sense of success to it.

The company name should be fresh and simple and, above all, shouldn't sound pretentious. You can register a company and become a limited company, either by buying an off-the-shelf company (£100 to £125) or by setting one up yourself. The fee is a mere £20.00. The drawback of registering a limited company is that you have to keep the records and file annual tax returns. Failure to do this can get you in all sorts of problems with the authorities. If you anticipate that your trading is going to start on a more limited basis, then consider starting a proprietorship – a company under your own name. For example, Joe Bloggs trading as Hot Shots. You can get a bank account in the name of your company and type the company name on you letterhead.

If you are pursuing a company in America, put in these two words somewhere in your letterhead – Thatched and Royal. North Americans are very impressed with low-budget films like The Crying Game, Four Weddings and a Funeral, Full Monty, and Sliding Doors that have come out of the UK, and, in this fiercely competitive business, you must learn to take advantage of every situation.

2. The text of the letter

In the first three lines describe yourself, and what you do as your day job, even if it is boring. It is here in the first few lines that you must grab the attention of the reader. It is also an opportunity to bend the realities of your life. You should exaggerate when you are talking about yourself.

If, for instance, you are a butcher, then state 'I am a butcher, recently made redundant by the BSE crisis, who writes scripts in my spare time'.

The point is to grab the reader's attention. A film development executive will be just as intrigued with your ability to write a screenplay if you are a disgruntled housewife, as he would be if you were a style-setter.

3. Twenty-five words or less

Next, you should outline your screenplay in twenty-five words or less. Many new writers get this wrong, and you will find this to be the most difficult thing in the world to do. You must sell the story, not tell the story.

Try to imagine yourself as the proud owner of a chalet in the south of France. If you got a request for information about renting your chalet for the summer, what would you send? The blueprints and heating plans of the building, along with the surveyor's report? Or would you send the most flattering photo you could take?

```
                                          Logo and address

Mr Bigshot
Film Producer
Address


dd/mm/yy


Dear Sir or Madam,

The first three lines are when you describe yourself, your day job
and what you do for your day job, even if it is boring. It is also your
chance to create a mystique about yourself.

The next three lines are the basic twenty-five word pitch for your
project. Try to recreate the little paragraph on the back of the video
jacket, and remember, you only want them to call you for more details!

I would like to submit my project to your company for consideration.
I look forward to hearing from you.


Yours faithfully,




Your name
```

The twenty-five words should read as follows:

'My first [second, forty-third, etc.] feature script is the story about [here you describe your hero – young man, beautiful girl, depressed athlete] who [put in what they want most in the world] but [here you describe their worst nightmare, or allude to the opponent who will prevent them from getting their goal] and [give us the outcome screenplay to your company for consideration. I look forward to hearing from you.'

Sign your name.

Remember that the sole task of this letter is to get this person to call you. Put the letter in the mail, or for some real added zing, fax it. The novelty of getting a fax in the current business environment is certain to get you noticed. And it is a lot cheaper than sending the entire script.

A good practise would be to try the letter out on friends and family before you send it. Remember how close you are to the project, and how easily you can forget the magic of clarity.

What Happens to Your Letter?

Let us look at what physically happens to your letter once it reaches the office of any kind of film production company in the world. Travel with your letter, leapfrog the receptionist, and sit on the other side of the table.

Whether it arrives by fax or post, the development executive's assistant will place your letter in a tray along with the rest of the correspondence of the day. People in the film industry work notoriously long hours and, at the end of the day, there is an unwritten rule that all calls and letters must be responded to.

It is a long-standing joke in the film industry that calls are returned at the end of each day. They call late and try to get your answering machine. In that way they can say that they tried to get back to you, but hey! It wasn't their fault you were out. This is called telephone tag. As they are returning calls (many film people process in excess of a hundred calls per day), they start going through the mail with a Dictaphone so that they can record their written instructions to their assistant.

When they come to a fourteen-line letter it gets immediately placed into the nutbar category. They don't have time to read it and, besides, their date is waiting at the bus stop, and it's now 7:15 p.m., and they're annoyed and very late. Perhaps their date has threatened them with divorce if they are late one more time.

Next is your letter. It's short and concise. If you write a good first few lines, and especially if you make them respond, wince or smile – you are seventy-five per cent home. Then it's down to those twenty-five words or less. How good are they? How original are they? It's really up to you to figure that out. But I do know this: if you send your letter to the right company and it is well written, they will call you. And that is what it is all about.

I know the eight-line letter works. We always use this form of a letter when we want to set up a meeting for sponsorship, or to get a celebrity to attend one of our events at the film festival.

I met a former student of mine on the street a few months ago and she told me that the eight-line letter didn't work at all. She showed me the letter, and it looked pretty good. In order to sell her screenplay, she needed to find a production company in the southeast part of the United States. She did her homework and discovered thirty-eight companies that were just the right size to produce her film. She told me that she had sent her eight-line letter to all of them, and but had received only four requests for her script. I had always thought that a success rate of one in ten was pretty good! The day I met her she was returning from the post office where she had mailed her scripts to America. I haven't seen her since, but I am certain that she was successful.

A screenwriter friend of mine in Glasgow used this technique to market his script directly to Oliver Stone. Oliver Stone' production company called within three days and gave their Fedex account. In other words, they paid to have it couriered to Los Angeles.

Writing a good query letter is one of the easiest and most effective ways to get the script buyer in your world to call you.

Summary

1. Make your eight-line letter entertaining.

2. If the letter isn't working, rewrite it and make it better.

3. Don't expect every letter to work.

Now let's talk about the deal.

16 The Deal

The laws covering the sale of screenplays are strikingly similar to the laws covering the sale of property.

THERE ARE ONLY three ways that screenplays are bought and sold: outright purchase, option deal and step deal.

Outright Purchase

Online Resources

A producer who reads your script may want to purchase your script outright. He/she will negotiate with you, or your agent, and agree a cash price for your screenplay. You then get a cheque. The copyright for the screenplay passes to the producer, and the deal is done.

Within the body of the contract, you may have certain rights and privileges directly expressed. A simple one might be that you are reimbursed for any travel expenses to meetings, or a salary might be included to cover the cost of your time for any rewrites or polishes that the producer may want you to do.

When the demands of a writer become too harsh or onerous for a producer to bear, or if the writer is unwilling to compromise, it is referred to as 'holding your script hostage'.

The theory is that if the producer wants your script so badly (because it's hot) then he/she will be a much easier target from whom to extract concessions. Writers who want to direct their own script most frequently use this tactic: 'I will only allow you to purchase my script if I can direct'.

This is a perfectly legitimate marketing ploy, but you should understand that the chances of selling your script decrease the greater the number of encumbrances you attach to the sale.

Option Deal

Sometimes a producer will want to buy your script and, after agreeing a purchase price, will offer to option the script from you. By making a down-payment (usually ten per cent), the producer effectively rents the copyright from you for the agreed period of time (usually twelve months). This allows the producer to complete the financing, casting, and other pre-production details, and conserves his cash flow. By signing an option contract, you agree not to show the script to any other party. The producer can represent to his investors that he owns the copyright.

The balance of the purchase price is due and payable either on the anniversary of the option contract or on the first day of principal photography – whichever comes first.

Option strategy

You can continue to market your screenplay after you have signed an option agreement, but you must inform the producer with whom you signed the option, of each person to whom you have marketed (or intend to market) your screenplay.

Understandably producers take a dim view of this practice, and may attempt to get you to sign a clause in the option agreement that prevents you from doing this.

If in doubt, consult the Writers' Guild of America or the Writers' Guild of Great Britain for advice.

At the end of the option period, one of three things may happen. Firstly, you may receive a cheque for the balance. Secondly, the producer may say he/she is no longer interested in which case you keep the deposit, and the copyright reverts back to you. Thirdly, the producer may feel that he needs more time to complete the financing. In that case he will offer you an additional deposit in return for an extension of the option for an agreed time. This additional deposit may or may not be applied to the purchase price, depending on the terms of the agreement.

These points are usually made at the opening negotiations. In other words you may be asked to sell your script on a one-year option, with a ten per cent down payment, with the right of two further twelve-month extensions, each with a pre-agreed payment.

The terms of an option agreement are all negotiable. I have known options to be as short as three months with payments as high as fifty per cent (for a hot script).

Option payments can also be considered a useful revenue source. Even if your script is not produced, you can represent that it has been sold. This elevates your stature to a writer with a script in pre-production. If the copyright reverts back to you, then you can re-market the script, knowing that it has already gathered serious attention.

Sometimes a producer will ignore step and option deals and try to persuade you to let him 'try to stir up some interest' on your behalf. When you agree, the producer picks up the telephone and verbally itches it, and is effectively using your script without the legal right to do so. Worse, later on, when the producer has tired of your project, and you then attempt to call someone, they tell you that your project has already been submitted and rejected, leaving you in a no-man's land.

A producer can ruin the sale prospects of a script in an afternoon.

A good producer will pay you for the script, either as a purchase or as an option, and then develop a marketing strategy for the screenplay. To attempt to sell a script without a marketing strategy is career suicide.

The Writers' Guild of America prohibits shopping in its agreement with producers, and producers who ignore this are subject to heavy fines. Unfortunately however this practice continues to be widespread.

Here is an example of a deal memo letter between a writer and a producer that I have used. All people and titles are fictitious.

This sample agreement is provided for educational and informational purposes only. To protect your own interests I highly recommend that you use the services of a qualified entertainment attorney who will advise you on the specific terms and conditions in your contract that will meet your particular requirements.

Entertainment attorneys

When you sell a script, or are hired to write one, there will be deal points to negotiate and contracts to sign. An entertainment attorney is your employee who is trained specially to anticipate your problems and cover you with a warm layer of protective language.

Entertainment attorneys are well-connected players who are totally consumed by the movie business. A good one will know all of the latest gossip, will know to the penny who is getting paid for what and, ultimately, if he/she likes your script, will be able to push it in the right directions for you.

When you are ready for a lawyer, make certain that you obtain the services of an entertainment attorney. Someone who specializes in property conveyancing or divorce law will be worthless to you as lawyer.

Good entertainment attorneys are hard to find and are elusive – like top agents. The best way to get to one is by personal recommendation. Try to find someone in the industry who can put you in touch.

Lawyers' fees are not cheap: from £100 ($150) per hour to £300 ($500) per hour. Sometimes a lawyer will agree to defer their fees against a percentage of your future earnings. The usual rate is five per cent – half of what an agent will charge.

Mr Bigshot
Film Producer
Address

dd/mm/yy

Re *Table 5* by Elliot Grove

Dear Sir or Madam,

This letter shall confirm the agreement between AEC Ltd (Purchaser) and Elliot Grove (Author) for Producer to acquire certain motion picture, television and allied rights in and to the screenplay titled *Table 5* (Property) for the purpose of producing a theatrical motion picture, a television motion picture or mini-series (Picture).

I understand the terms of the agreement are as follows:

1. Option

A. Commencing on May 1, 2001 the Purchaser shall have an exclusive and irrevocable six month option to acquire certain motion picture, television and allied rights in and to the Property. As consideration for such option, Purchaser shall pay Author £1000 immediately. The foregoing option shall be applied against and in reduction of the purchase price.

B. Purchaser shall have the right to extend the option for a further six-month period by giving written notice and paying the Author a further payment of £1000 on or before the initial six month option expires. Said payment will not be applied against a reduction to the purchase price.

2. Cash purchase price

If Purchaser exercises the option to exploit the Property as a television movie or mini-series, then the purchase price shall be £15 000 (less option monies paid to the Author pursuant to Paragraph 1A).

If Purchaser exercises the option to exploit the property as a theatrical motion picture, the purchase price shall be: £30 000 if the total budget of the film is less than £2 000 000, or £40 000 if the total budget of the film is greater than £2 000 000.

Payment will be made to the Author in full on the earlier:

A. Exercise of the option on or before the end of the option period; or

B. The first day of principal photography.

3. Contingent compensation

If the Author shall have sole screenplay or teleplay credit then the Author shall receive 5% of 100% of the net profits from the picture and all elements thereof, from all sources and all media. If Author receives no credit or shared credit, Author shall receive 2.5% of 100% of the net profits.

Net profits shall be calculated and defined per Purchaser's standard definition of net profits, subject to good faith negotiation within standard industry practices.

4. Television mini-series

Purchaser shall not have the right to exploit the property as a television mini-series without first negotiating per episode royalty and other payments as may be feasible.

5. Credit

Author shall receive credit on all Pictures produced from said Property, as opening title single card credit and in paid ads under the Purchaser's control, included in any otherwise excluded ads if the director receives credit.

A. Subject to arbitration the credit shall read 'Screenplay by Elliot Grove'.

B. Author to receive credits on all other versions, DVD, VHS, remakes, sequels, Internet broadcasts, etc.

6. Theatrical release

If the Purchaser exploits the Property as a television movie and there is a UK theatrical release for the picture or any portion of it before the television release, then the Author shall receive full payment as per Paragraphs 2 and 3.

If there is a subsequent theatrical release in other territories then the Author shall receive 50% of the compensation paid in Paragraphs 2 and 3 per territory released. These additional monies will be paid to the Author upon the date of release in said territory.

7. Sequels and remakes

The Author shall receive 50% of compensation payable in Paragraphs 2 and 3 for each sequel, and 33.3% for each remake of the Picture. These additional monies to be paid to the Author upon the first day of principal photography.

8. Reserved rights

All rights not granted to the Purchaser are reserved to the Author. The author reserves the following rights, without limitation: live stage Author written sequels and prequels, audio cassettes, live television, live dramatic tape, radio and all publication rights, and all digital Internet transmission rights.

The Purchaser shall be entitled to publish summaries and synopses of the Property not attributable to the Author, not exceeding 7500 words. Purchaser shall not be allowed to publish a novelization or photo-novelization without Purchaser and Author negotiating the terms thereof in good faith.

9. Miscellaneous

A. The parties shall negotiate in good faith the compensation for the Author for any other exploitation of the Property. The Author shall also receive a free video cassette of each programme based on the property, and further agrees to sign a customary letter prohibiting duplication.

B. The Purchaser shall name the Author as an additional insured on the errors and omissions policy for the Picture.

C. There shall be no relief of the purchaser's obligations under this agreement should the Purchaser assign its rights and interest in the property.

D. Should the Purchaser enter into an involuntary arrangement with its creditors, or become bankrupt, then all rights under this agreement shall revert directly to the Author.

E. The Purchaser shall pay all pre-approved personal travel expenses in connection with the Author's services.

F. The Author represents that he has the sole right and authority to negotiate and enter into this agreement and is able to convey the rights expressed herein without restriction or limitation.

G. All payments and notices from the Purchaser are to be made to:

Elliot Grove c/o Raindance
81 Berwick Street
London W1F 8TW

The Writers' Guild of America has a Minimum Basic Agreement (MBA) which covers basic rights for writers. The following is a list of additional rights a writer may want to add to the MBA. Producers will fight and fight against these deal points but, if you can, try to get them:

1. Sale/Option – the writer should be given the first reasonable opportunity to rewrite a script. If a new element (i.e. director/actor) has been added to the package within three years of the sale/option then the original writer should have right of first refusal to rewrite/revise the script.

2. Step deal – where a writer is hired to write a treatment or script and the purchaser contemplates replacing the writer, then ample time and opportunity should be made available for all parties to meet and discuss the continued services of the writer.

3. The writer should have an opportunity to view the director's cut of the film in time to allow suggestions by the writer to be incorporated into the film.

4. The writer should be included personally in any press junkets, press kits, premieres, previews, trips to festivals or award shows.

5. Screen credit, if due, to be included on all posters, film titles, press kits, all advertisements for the film, regardless of medium, in a size and placement no less than that of the director.

---

10. Other terms

Other terms and conditions incorporated by reference in this letter herein are those that are customary in agreements of this type in the United Kingdom television and motion picture industries, subject to good faith negotiation within customary industry parameters. The parties intend to enter into a formal long form agreement incorporating the terms and conditions herein.

Please contact me immediately if the above is in any way inconsistent with your understanding of the agreement.

Otherwise this letter shall constitute a firm and binding agreement until such time, if any, as a more formal document is executed by all parties. If all is in order, please sign this original and the enclosed copy and return them to me.

Yours sincerely,

Elliot Grove _____ Date _____

Agreed and accepted by _____ Date _____

Mr Producer, Any Entertainment Company (AEC) Ltd

For documents signed in the UK add the following:

In the presence of _____ Date _____

Name
Occupation
Address

Step Deal

Far more common than an outright purchase is the step deal. A producer will read your writing sample script and call you in for a meeting where he will tell you that, as much as he loves your descriptive writing and the way you handle dialogue, he does not want to make your script. Instead you will be required to write his story. The writing process is divided into a number of steps – thus step deal.

Producer/Writer Agreement

The following sets forth the principal terms of the agreement between

Producer _____

and

Writer _____

in connection with the project currently titled [insert name of screenplay]

ι The Producer hereby engages the Writer to write a first draft screenplay and a first set of revisions (the Work) of the project currently titled [insert name of screenplay] intended as a theatrical motion picture (the Picture). The Work shall be based upon the story and ideas agreed between the Producer and the Writer.

2. The first draft shall be delivered no later than [insert date]. The Producer shall thereafter have a four week reading period. The first set of revisions shall be returned no later than [insert date].

3. In consideration for the services of the Writer, the Producer shall pay the Writer a guaranteed sum of [insert fee] payable as follows:

A. The sum of _____ upon the execution of this agreement.

B. The sum of _____ upon delivery of the first draft.

C. The sum of _____ upon commencement of the first revision.

D. The sum of _____ upon delivery of the first revision.

4. The Producer shall have exclusive rights to present this Work to any studio or third party financiers as seen fit subject to the following terms and conditions:

A. The terms of any third party option and acquisition shall be negotiated between the Writer's representative and third party in good faith.

B. The Writer shall be entitled to the same conditions of employment with a third party as offered to the Producer.

C. Terms and conditions to be negotiated include an optional rewrite and polish, sole and shared credit bonus, passive payments for sequels, remakes and TV productions, a first opportunity to write subsequent productions, representations and warranties, credit, anti-injunctive relief, notice, suspension,default and termination.

5. The Writer agrees to execute a certificate of Authorship as well as all other documents reasonably necessary to effectuate the purposes of this agreement.

6. The Writer shall give the Producer the first negotiation right in connection with [insert name of project]. If and when the Writer is prepared to exploit said project the Writer shall first offer the Producer the right to produce the picture on terms then to be negotiated in good faith. If terms cannot be agreed within fifteen days then the Writer shall have no further obligation to the Producer for [insert name of script].

7. If the Producer has not financed the Picture within twenty four months after the Writer delivers the first set of revisions, then the Writer shall have a non-exclusive right to attempt to finance the Picture without the assistance or involvement of the Producer provided that:

In the event that the Writer succeeds in financing the Picture, then the Producer shall be

A. Reimbursed the monies advanced to the writer plus interest, plus a bonus of [insert figure] per cent.

B. Pay to the Producer an amount of 5% of 100% of the net profits of the first motion picture which net profits shall be defined, computed, accounted for and paid to the Producer in the same manner as they are to the Writer.

This agreement shall be covered by and construed under the laws of [state or country suited for you].

```
┌─────────────────────────────────────────────────────────────────┐
│                                                                   │
│   Writer                      _____   Date  _____  │
│                                                                   │
│   Agreed and accepted by      _____   Date  _____  │
│                                                                   │
│   Mr Producer, Any Entertainment Company (AEC) Ltd                │
│                                                                   │
│   For documents signed in the UK add the following:               │
│                                                                   │
│   In the presence of          _____   Date  _____  │
│                                                                   │
│                                                                   │
│   Name                                                            │
│   Occupation                                                      │
│   Address                                                         │
│                                                                   │
└─────────────────────────────────────────────────────────────────┘
```

Upon contract, you will be paid a fee for the completed script. The fee will be broken into several performance-related steps.

The first step is the treatment. You will attend a meeting where the story will be outlined. You will then have a deadline – usually three weeks – to write a treatment and, when you deliver it, a second payment will be made, according to the payment schedule in the contract. Then follows a cooling-off period where the producer may decide that your services are not required. In which case you keep the money, and the producer keeps copyright of the treatment. You will be unable to market the treatment, because you will not own the copyright. You cannot own the copyright because you are a writer for hire.

Or they may like your treatment, call you in for notes, and send you off to write the first draft. The minute you are commissioned to write a first draft, another payment is due. Like the treatment stage, there is a contractual deadline and, upon completion, the next payment is due. There then follows another cooling-off period, when the producer may decide not to continue with you (you have effectively been fired, but in the nicest possible way), followed by the second draft and polish steps. The payments, in total, represent the total amount of money you agreed in the opening stage of the negotiations. The Writers' Guild of Great Britain and the Writers' Guild of America both have recommended mini-mum amounts which production companies, who are signatories, have agreed to pay.

Writing a Treatment

There are two types of treatments: The first is a step outline, which writ-ers often prepare for their own use. It is simply a 'This happens, this happens, and then this' outline of the entire story. A treatment that you write as part of a step deal or as a tease for your own screenplay is structured differently. Essentially you are writing a sales tool for your idea. A Hollywood phrase is 'Sell the sizzle, not the steak' or 'tell me your idea in twenty-five words'. By that, your challenge is to distill your idea into a tightly knit essay, which may or may not be in the chronological order of the actual finished screenplay. Imagine yourself as the owner of a chateau in the South of France which you want to rent out to holiday-makers for the summer. A request from a jaded northerner, or a curious North American comes in. What do you send to the prospective client? The plumbing and wiring diagrams? Or the glossy brochure with the artist's rendering of the swimming pool, yet to be finished?

Hint Writers are exploited – 'Write me a treatment for a script/star that I have interested' says the producer. He hopes you'll effectively partner with him but in reality is using you to jumpstart his producing career!

Reality Check: Negotiating the Sale of Your Script

The prices mentioned opposite are the going rate for established writers with opening title single card credits as screenwriters.

And the Writers' Guild of Great Britain mentions the words 'Suggested Minimum'. Can you imagine how I feel about the word 'suggested' when I am producing?

Producers working with unproduced writers will try to get the lowest possible price for a screenplay. In the UK it is about a thousand pounds. Roger Corman told me in 1996 that he pays on average $15 000 to $25 000 for screenplays, even though the WGA minimums start at about $35 000.

Has the writer been exploited? It really is up to you to answer this.

If you feel uncomfortable with any deal, you should walk away.

On the other hand, if your film can be made and if the producer you are negotiating with has the ability to make your film, and make it well, then your will enhance your marketability on your next film.

Many writers have sold their scripts cheaply in order to get a screenplay credit. Future scripts are then marketed on the basis that the writer achieved one screenplay credit, and therefore the subsequent screenplays are more valuable.

Is it possible to get a percentage of the profits? Never. It only happens for a handful of movie personalities such as Harrison Ford and Jack Nicolson. When a producer convinces you to accept a percentage of profit in lieu of payment, they are fairly certain they can reduce your payments to next to nothing using creative accounting. This is not to say that you shouldn't form a partnership with a producer in order to get your film made. This deal requires that you vend your script into the company for a percentage of the shares, effectively making you a partner with the producer. These deals typically have a time bomb guaranteeing the return of the copyright should the production of the film hit certain milestones relating to financing, casting and production. Neil Jordan and Steve Wooley operate their production company along these lines.

Writers' Guild of Great Britain Film Rates

Please note that these fees are not buyouts. There are considerable additional use payments. For full details, buy the PACT/WGGB Agreement at £10 from the Guild office.

	Features Budgeted at £2 Mill +	Features Budgeted £750K to £2 Mill +	Features Budgeted at under £750K
Treatment			
Commencement Payment	£3375	£1350	£1350
Acceptance Payment	£2025	£1350	£1350
First draft			
Commencement Payment	£6480	£4725	£4725
Delivery Payment	£6480	£4725	£4725
Second draft			
Commencement Payment	£3240	£1620	£1620
Delivery Payment	£3240	£1620	£1620
Principal photography payment	£6480	£3510	£3510
Total minimum payment	£31 320	£18 900	£18 900
Additional use pre-payment	£10 800	£6750	*
Total guaranteed payment	£42 120	£25 650	£18 900

*The terms for films in this category to be exactly the same as for films budgeted at £750 000 and up to £2 million, except that the producer is not required to make the £5000 advance payment against additional uses. The Total Guaranteed Payment is therefore the same as the Total Minimum Payment of £14 000, for the fee the Producer opts, before the first day of principal photography, to take either worldwide theatrical rights or two UK network television transmissions.

Writers' Guild of America Film Rates – Theatrical Compensation

		Period effective 11/01/06 to 10/31/07	
		Low	High
A.	**Original Screenplay, inc. Treatment**	$49 439	$91 940
	Installments:		
	Delivery of Original Treatment	$20 614	$34 134
	Delivery of First Draft Screenplay	$17 916	$34 134
	Delivery of Final Draft Screenplay	$6960	$17 062
B.	**Non-Original Screenplay, inc. Treatment**	$39 822	$74 035
	Installments:		
	Delivery of Treatment	$14 928	$22 758
	Delivery of First Draft Screenplay	$17 916	$34 134
	Delivery of Final Draft Screenplay	$6968	$17 143
C.	**Original Screenplay, exc. Treatment or Sale of Original Screenplay**	$30 893	$63 577
	Installments for Employment:		
	Delivery of First Draft Screenplay	$23 608	$45 511
	Delivery of Final Draft Screenplay	$6962	$17 060
D.	**Non-Original Screenplay, exc. Treatment or Sale of Non-Original Screenplay**	$24 877	$51 195
	Installments for Employment:		
	Delivery of First Draft Screenplay	$17 916	$34 134
	Delivery of Final Draft Screenplay	$6961	$17 061
E.	**Additional Compensation for Story inc. in Screenplay**	$5692	$11 377
F.	**Story or Treatment**	$18 538	$28 261
G.	**Original Story or Treatment**	$25 599	$28 261
H.	**First Draft Screenplay with or without Option for Final Draft Screenplay (Non-Original)**		
	First Draft Screenplay	$22 249	$42 391
	Final Draft Screenplay	$14 828	$28 261
I.	**Rewrite of Screenplay**	$18 538	$28 261
J.	**Polish of Screenplay**	$9274	$14 130

Again, choosing the right producer is difficult and a writer should always ask whether a producer is capable of getting the project off the ground and completed. After all, getting that first elusive credit as a screenwriter will enhance your career, and increase your value in the marketplace.

What if you want to direct as well?

In the film industry a writer who declines an offer of purchase for their script unless they are allowed to direct is considered an egomaniac with delusions of grandeur.

Not only does the industry recognize the mental and physical stamina required to direct a movie (did you know that directors must pass a physical test conducted by the financier's physicians?), but writing a screenplay is very difficult.

A writer who 'holds their script hostage' is announcing to the world that he is taking two of the most difficult and demanding jobs in the film industry and combining them into one – the writer/director.

True, this is certainly the most glamorous job in the film industry but, as a writer, you must recognize that your script is much more difficult to sell or finance when you encumber the deal with the fact that you want to direct.

Again the low-budget independent filmmaking route beckons aspiring writer/directors. Remember to get a professional outside opinion on the merits of your script before you start filming. Otherwise you stand the chance of leading a host of private investors off the cliff with you. This basic reality is one of the few advantages of seeking traditional industry financing for your project.

More Reality Checks

This is where we go into downer in a serious way. Let's do a reality check on the deals and monies that screenwriters are paid. In order to do that I need to put my producer's hat on.

1. Outright purchase

I'm a producer. You are a screenwriter? As a producer, do I love the word 'suggested'? How many times was the word 'suggested' used in the section above? How many opening title credits as 'screenwriter' do you have on a feature length movie that got theatrical distribution in more than one cinema and not at a film festival? None? I thought so. Do you want an opening title credit? And do you want to be paid? I'm going to suggest you take $1000 for your screenplay. As producer, I'm going to turn your screenplay into a movie in the best way possible, not give you a penny of the profits, but you will have that elusive first opening title credit. In other words, you will only be paid $1000 for your script.

UK producer Paul Brooks, now living in LA, once told me that he had never paid more than one thousand pounds for a script – and he had produced six UK features at this point. Each of the writers he has worked with has gone on to bigger things, notably Vadim Jean and Gary Sinyor whose film Leon The Pig Farmer launched the British film revival in the early 1990s

If you take this deal have you been exploited?

Firstly, you don't need to take this deal and you should never take any deal that you are not totally comfortable with.

Secondly, if you seriously consider a low money deal, you should ask yourself if you are likely to get any other offers, and then weigh up the probability that this producer will make your script into a great movie. You are in effect partnering with this producer – who is likely to be starting out as well.

You will need to make certain that you are willing to enter into an intense business arrangement with the producer for a deal like this to work.

Remeber that payment of box office royalties is always subject to the creative accounting procedures Hollywood uses. You won't see a dime in a scenario such as this.

Hint Always ask yourself who is likely to make the best movie of your screenplay. This is the producer you should sell your screenplay to.

---

2. Option deals

A producer will attempt to option your screenplay from you for a very modest sum against a low purchase price (or even against a 'suggested' price in this depressingly common scenario). What you are really doing in this case is becoming a business partner with the producer. In certain situations you may know the producer very well and this type of partnership can work. But, like any personal relationship, two people can very easily fall out under the stress and strain of a business deal.

Producers used to attempt an option payment for as little as $1. Cases like this are less common because of recent commercial litigation. In several cases, producers took writers to court because the writer had signed a $1 option with them and then sold the screenplay to someone else. In all cases the producers lost because they were unable to prove the payment or 'consideration' needed to solidify the transaction. Not many writers I know would bank a cheque for a dollar or a pound. Now producers offer a payment for as little as they can. Fifty to a hundred dollars or pounds seems to be the going rate.

Again, you are forming a business relationship with the producer. Make sure you are comfortable with this indivdual before you agree. Making a film is a long and emotionally charged project which could well take several years. Sometimes however, it is a wise decision, especially because as one of the producers, you should be able to exercise more control.

Hint Use this deal to bolster your CV – 'I have sold my first script. Here is my second'.

---

3. Step deals

Everything is negotiable. A step deal I did in London several years ago was with a single Australian mother of three children. Because she was on the dole, I couldn't pay her any money. I met her every Friday afternoon at a supermarket, where she would give me the sides she had written that week, and I would give her two bags of shopping worth no more than £40 ($60).

After a few months she fell in love with her ex-lover and moved to New Zealand. I now have sixty-seven pages of a script that I don't know how to finish, but I use page thirty-seven as the script format guide which can be found at the end of this book.

Everything is negotiable.

Hint Never sign any deal that you don't feel comfortable with.

---

4. Playing God

Lawrence Bender optioned the screenplay Reservoir Dogs from Quentin Tarantino for a small sum and got the budget together. It was their first picture, and they both launched brilliant careers from the success of that film.

Games they play in the movie business – suppose your agent calls with a 'good news, bad news' call. Which would you like to hear first? The bad news? It's an option deal. And the good news is that your screenplay has been sold for $75 000. This means, under the standard deal, your agent will receive a total of $7500, deduct their ten per cent and remit to you the balance, $6750 (minus any expenses).

This is actually a good deal for you. Although your movie may not get made for a long while, you have actually earned some money, and what is more, if you get a second script written and optioned, you are earning about twenty per cent of what you would earn if you sold one.

I know several writers who make a good living from their option fees. Whenever I see them, I ask them about such-and-such a script and they respond by saying 'I've just got that one back, and my agent thinks someone else is interested'.

But back to the deal your agent has done for you. What you don't know, and what your agent didn't know, was who was really interested in you script. It was optioned by an independent producer in LA, priding themselves at being a creative producer and an expert in doing lunch.

Have you been exploited? Or do you feel cheated? Why didn't you, or your agent, approach the star directly. Now stop crying, and remember that your marketability has been greatly enhanced by this transaction.

Let's suppose that the producer who bought your screenplay had a direct contact to the company like Icon Entertainment (Mel Gibson's company) and knew exactly what sort of product this company was looking for as the next Mel Gibson vehicle. Your script fits the bill exactly. But major stars don't star in scripts by first-timers, and they especially don't pay minimum rates for them.

What this producer did was sell the company an option for $750 000, and accept a down-payment of $75 000 from which your payment of $7500 was made. The way you find this out is not from your agent, but from a telephone call from your best friend with a copy of Variety in front of them. All of your friends are delighted. They now know someone who has sold a script for $750 000 to the company of a major Hollywood star. What they don't understand is why you are not out at the pub buying everyone drinks. You can't. You only have a cheque for $6750.

Hollywood is full of producers who make a specialty of 'doing lunch' and trying to find material for studios and production companies. Often the producer will have multiple deals and yet not have these scripts produced due to the vagaries of the movie business. However they earn a good living. Understand that they have costs too, and often underwrite the costs of rewriting the script themselves, trying to get the right vehicle for the company or star they are pursuing.

What usually happens near the end of the option period is that the copyright reverts back to you. The star loses interest. You wouldn't tell anyone would you? Your agent would quietly sell your script elsewhere.

5. Sharks

Sometimes you will run across a producer who will option your script under the standard option deal, and then manage to get the film into production. You are expecting your cheque on the first day of principal photography but, in the excitement of production, the cheque is not forthcoming. Perhaps you lack the confidence to make sure the money is paid, or are unaware that your cheque was due on this deadline. As a first-time writer you are further disadvantaged by your ignorance.

Typically, the producer may fob you off with various promises, until at some point you lose patience and bring up the grubby issue of money. The producer will tell you to sue, knowing that the cost is prohibitive.

Instigating a court action for payment involves a lawyer – who will demand a hefty deposit for legal fees. It also involves waiting months and years for a court date. Even if the producer loses, he/she could still appeal the decision, adding another lengthy delay with more legal fees. After a time, the producer hopes you will become so weary of the litigation process that you will abandon your court action.

Sharks are not that common, but are known within the industry. It is a good defensive action to enquire about the credibility of any producer who purchases your script. Network with other writers and filmmakers. The film industry is quite small, and if a producer has treated other writers badly, his reputation will follow him.

If you discover that you are dealing with a shark, you have two options: either abandon the deal and hope for another purchaser; or, deal with the shark, knowing you will not be paid but safe in the knowledge that your script will get made and win you the elusive opening title credit.

6. Shopping

Some producers will offer to take on your script for a short period of time while they pitch it to companies all over the globe. If they fail to sell your script, you will find a 'reject' mark next to your script making it impossible for you to present your script back to the company, unless you re-submit the script to the company under a new title. Make sure the producer tells you in advance who they are approaching and insist that any additional companies are cleared ahead of time, by you, and in writing.

7. Finder's fees

Occasionally you will run into a producer who will offer to take your script to specific people in exchange for a fee.

You will be looking for a producer who is well-connected with the type of production companies that will be interested in the type of story you have written. You also want to be aligned with a producer who has a good working relationship with these various companies.

Certain producers are expert at presenting scripts, and they earn their money from you, the writer, and often are also paid by the company to whom they sell your script. As producers they have little inclination or aptitude for the actual production process.

Be wary that they are not shopping your script, and ask them to sign an agreement like this one:

Finder's fee agreement

As an inducement to [name of person or company name] for presenting [name of story, book, manuscript or screenplay], [your name or company name] agrees to pay the sum total of [x per cent] of any or all monies or other consideration earned or received by [your name or company name] at any time in connection with the name of story, book, manuscript or screenplay, if [name of person or company name] delivers one or all of the following:

A. If the material is optioned in any form and/or

B. If [your name or company name] is hired on a development deal.

This fee is to be paid in less than fourteen days from the date the monies are received by [your name or company name].

I, [your name or company name] and [name of person or company name] agree that if any legal action takes place because of a violation of the terms of this agreement then the prevailing party shall be entitled to full recovery of legal and court fees.

This agreement shall be covered by and construed under the laws of [state or country suited for you].

Writer _____ Date _____

Agreed and accepted by _____ Date _____

Mr Producer, Any Entertainment Company (AEC) Ltd

For documents signed in the UK add the following:

In the presence of _____ Date _____

Name
Occupation
Address

Summary

1. Credit = credibility = power = career = money.

2. Writers say: 'If we work as writers for hire (for money) we are hacks, if we work for nothing we are chumps.'

Next we discuss the Life of a Screenwriter.

The Life of a Screenwriter

WRITING A SCREENPLAY is very hard. Writing a good screenplay involves a certain amount of good fortune and a strong belief in the first biblical reference. But, like everything else, I believe that there can be a plan. And with a good plan you stand a better chance of succeeding. The key to being a successful screenwriter is really very simple: think up great ideas, write them down in a distinct personal style, circulate each finished script in the film community and, as soon as one script is finished, start the next.

If it is so simple, why isn't everyone doing it? Because writing a screenplay is difficult. Writing a truly great screenplay is very, very difficult.

My first suggestion is not to try to write the world's greatest screenplay every time. Write according to the structural details I have outlined. Write stories from the heart. Write stories that you are familiar with and which appeal to you. Make sure the characters are well developed and that you really know them. Write the screenplay knowing that it is a screenplay. A saleable screenplay in fact. But not your best work. Every couple of years, try to write the world's best screenplay. Write it in a timeframe that you believe is reasonable. If you feel yourself getting writer's block (lack of confidence) then you know it's time to set it aside for a while and get on with the journeyman pieces that might be able to help you pay the rent. If, in the writing of this great screenplay, you solve one of your inner problems and truly become a better person, then I believe that the very act of writing that screenplay, regardless of the success of the screenplay, has in itself already been worthwhile to you.

Understanding Genre

Genre is really the key to a successful career. Choose a specific genre and study it inside out. Then learn another. Writers should specialize in two or three genres and become skilled at blending them. Become known as the expert in the genre blends that you have chosen to major in. Hollywood prefers genre mixes, like romantic comedy, sci-fi horror and thriller love.

The Screenwriter and Creativity

Have you ever walked down the street and had a great idea for a movie? Have you ever noticed how these great ideas seem to pop into your head as you are doing something mundane? As a writer you need to understand the greatest tool you have: your mind. Knowing how your mind operates will give you the knowledge to utilize your mind even further.

Our minds are divided into two parts. The left side and the right side. The left side controls rational thought and motor control of our muscles. It is this side that keeps our hearts beating, allows us to do repetitious work like walking, without having to think about it, and is the side that calculates our bank balance. The right side of the brain controls emotion – the panic if the bank balance is too low, the bursts of sadness or happiness when you see the news. It also controls the subconscious.

When you are doing something boring, like walking or vacuuming, the left side of your brain is occupied, freeing the right side of the brain. That's why all of those wonderful ideas for a movie come bubbling up.

But notice how quickly they vanish. If the telephone rings and you walk over to answer it, within seconds that wonderful idea has vanished. When you finish the telephone call, you remember you had a great idea, and spend the next hour or two in agony trying to pull it back.

Much has been made of the great artists of the last century. Picasso and John Lennon, to name but two. I do not believe that any artist was more talented than any other mortal on this planet. They are simply better at accessing the ideas that come to them in alpha state.

But how do you capture those great ideas?

Alpha State

Capturing ideas in alpha state is easy and fun. But, like a muscle, it improves with practice.

Identifying alpha state

The moment you do any physical movement you will be in alpha state. You may not realize it. Tasks like walking, driving, cycling, ironing and cleaning send me into alpha state in seconds. Here is a simple exercise that you can perform to put yourself into alpha state:

Close your eyes and roll them upward until you feel your eyelids flutter. The effort of keeping your eyelids fluttering will put you in alpha state. If you want to take this exercise a step further, close your eyes, roll them upwards for exactly a minute. Can you see the first minute of your movie? Are you aware of a color? An image? An emotion? If yes, perhaps these ideas can give you an idea for your movie. If not – perhaps this is just too crazy for you, or you were distracted by a noise.

Capturing the Moment

The only way to capture those wonderful alpha state ideas is to jot them down as they happen. How you jot them down is important. You should carry a small pad and pencil with you at all times. If you are a frequent driver, perhaps a Dictaphone is a safer idea. When you have an idea, whip out your pad and jot down a couple of words that will jog your memory when you are back at your computer. I never write down more than eight words. The words you should write should be just enough to jog your memory and allow you to return to the moment that you had the idea. You will then be able to finish off your alpha state daydream and experiment with different possibilities.

I discovered alpha state by accident.

I live with a dog, and walking the dog every morning is my responsibility. It is a task that takes twenty minutes, rain or shine. I used to hate taking the dog out, until I discovered alpha state. Now I look forward to those precious twenty minutes at the start of each day where I can see what the solutions are to the problem at hand.

Leonardo da Vinci was a great walker and filled hundreds of notebooks with thousands of drawings, poems and ideas while he was walking.

I can't assign tasks like 'I'm two hundred short for the rent today – what am I going to do?' to the alpha state. But solutions to the problem and opportunities in my life get answered every single morning. I just don't know which ones – which is why I carry a notebook.

Hint If you utilize alpha state while writing your movie, make sure you really get to know your characters inside out. If you do they will actually talk to you during your alpha state moments.

While I was writing Table 5, I was struggling with the relationships between the girl and her ex. I had a scene that just wasn't working. One morning, while walking the dog, I realized I had rewritten this scene at least a dozen times. At that moment I thought I felt a hand on my shoulder. I turned around, and heard Ramona's voice saying 'Elliot, I wouldn't ever say that.' 'What would you say instead?' I asked. And she spoke the lines. I scribbled down a few key words, raced back to my desk and finished the scene in under an hour.

Alpha state will work for you like this as long as you don't ask it to solve mechanical problems like your overdraft.

Getting an Agent

Having an agent is wonderful. A good agent offers moral support, handles all your professional correspondence, gives you feedback on your work, and drums up new business. For this an agent will charge ten per cent of the money you make – a very reasonable deal. But finding an agent who is able to satisfy your requirements is very difficult. Any good agent will have a client list packed with screenwriters, and will be reluctant to take on a new writer – especially if existing clients are selling well.

It makes sense that the best time to get an agent is when you have someone interested in your screenplay. By using your power file and writing the eight-line letter, you can get serious interest in your screenplay. Then contact an agent and see if they will represent you and close the deal. For this you will pay them ten per cent.

It is a popular misconception that agents will continue to market your work. Marketing yourself and your screenplay is your responsibility. It is a certainty that an agent will sell your script if they see a buyer for it. But with dozens of other writers on their books, they cannot be expected to think solely of you. So keep selling yourself and your scripts. But conduct all the business to and refer all the leads to your agent. This will make you look professional to both the script buyers and the agents. But what if you haven't got a deal? How else can you get an agent?

Hint Having an agent is desirable and preferable. But it is not absolutely necessary to have one. Do not let the lack of an agent encumber your marketing programme.

The Four Routes to Getting an Agent

1. Make friends with someone in the agency

Get your script to that person and ask him or her to read it. If he likes your screenplay he will recommend it to someone else. The theory of this technique is that this employee wants to move up the ladder and will use your screenplay as a demonstration of his or her ability to discover hidden talent, and to expand the revenue of the agency.

2. Research existing agencies

See if they are looking for new writers. Find an agency that is willing to consider new writers and submit three screenplays: a half-hour script for episodic TV for an existing show; a ninety page suitable for a low-budget production; and a two hour script where you really let loose.

A reality check, please. Put yourself in the shoes of an agent. You are very busy. You don't have time to read scripts at the office, so you bring them home. Despite your intention to read them during the week at night, you haven't. Now it is Saturday morning. You have three scripts to read from an unknown writer, plus a new script by an existing client. The existing client's previous script sold for three times the Writers' Guild minimum, earning you a hefty commission. Which script would you read first? And one more thing – you have to get ready to go to a family wedding in a few hours.

The film industry is fiercely competitive.

Back to your three scripts. Suppose the agent has time to devote to you. The three scripts are lying in a pile, next to the wedding clothes he has to put on. Which script would he read first? He would read the short script, of course. And if it were great he would read the ninety-pager. And if it were fantastic, he would probably read the two-hour script in the back of the taxi on the way to the wedding. Any agent in the world would want to work with you. You are prolific and versatile, and the agent can see that he can get you work (and earn money) from your television and film scripts.

If the first script the agent reads is boring, if it has clumsy descriptive passages or dialogue without moral argument, do you think he will bother with your second script? Of course not.

Hint Never send a script out until it is a good as you can get it.

---

3. Specialize in other areas

Many screenwriters start in dramatic radio, especially in Britain where the BBC produces about 1000 hours of drama a year. Radio doesn't pay as well, but it does pay. Once you have been produced, you can add that to your CV when you approach agents who would like to represent you.

Another route is theatre. This is accessible to anyone with a stage play. Simply hire a room and put on your show. Invite agents to your show so that they can look for the spark of talent there that they can sell. If you write a stage play that is produced by an established company, then you will almost certainly get an agent on the strength of that.

4. Start your own agency

I don't recommend this route but I know several people who have started their own agencies. In the UK you can start an employment agency by paying a £50 ($75) fee to the local municipal government office. You get a licence to run an employment agency – in this case for screenwriters. The theory of this route is that the agency will allow you to get around the barriers put up by film companies who will only accept screenplays from agents. The difficulty is that your agency is still unproven. A tactic to combat this is to get someone already in the industry to be a patron – someone who will allow you to put their name on your letterhead but who has no legal or financial responsibility for your company.

Another tack is to team up with other writers, directors, and actors and form a co-operative agency. The drawback here is that, as the company grows in size, someone has to raise operating capital to pay for an administrator, computers, office rent and so on. But it is still an interesting proposal. Why not start the next United Artists?

Researching the Marketplace

You need to keep abreast of your industry. The more you know about current trends, the better able you will be to see the future. Reading the trades, networking at film festivals and industry events, and keeping up to date with various film magazines and e-letters all takes time. But it can be fun. Learn to enjoy. And remember to devise a filing system that will allow you to retrieve easily the information you put into it.

1. Story ideas

Discovering commercially successful story ideas is the mother-lode for a screenwriter. But writing for the market is risky and dangerous. It takes two to three years for a screenplay to go through the writing, production and marketing process. To guess at public taste two or three years from the time you sit down at your computer is impossible. The first source of your story must come from your own life and, if you write about what you know, you are more likely to write with passion. And it is the passion which will appeal to your audience even three years from now.

2. Cannes, festivals and markets

The Cannes Film Festival is the largest film festival in the world. It is also free to enter as a filmmaker, writer or director. Every year, thirty-five thousand people descend on the sleepy town of Cannes to attend the festival. Of these, about a thousand are film sellers, three or four thousand are film buyers. The rest are cinema fanatics, wannabes and tourists.

By tracking films at the Cannes Film Market, which runs parallel to the film festival, you will be able to see what sorts of films sell. Attending Cannes is also advantageous for the networking opportunities, and, after one pays for the airfare to Nice, can be very inexpensive. While in Cannes, you can arrange to meet sales agents, directors and producers from around the world. I go to Cannes each year for a few days and discover that I end up forming alliances with people that I use for the coming year.

Attending other festivals which are smaller than Cannes has the advantage of intimacy. You will be able to get relatively close to the festival programmers and filmmakers which will enable you to see what sort of films work in the film festival. If you have a feature or a short in a smaller festival, it will be very easy for you to gauge the audience reaction. Probably the quickest way to learn how to write is to sit in a non-partisan audience and note how your script is received. Learning first hand whether or not the laughs are in the right places is a harrowing experience.

3. Book fairs

Book fairs are a great place to see what is going to be commercially successful. At book fairs books are sold from anything including galley proofs and posters. In fact my publisher first touted this book at the Hamburg Book Fair in October 2000. She attended with a mock-up of the jacket and a two-paragraph synopsis. When she got back to London, she was able to tell me that the book had a favourable response from book buyers and started to say the word 'deadline' to me. Book fairs are the sharp commercial end of the marketplace.

4. Style magazines

Being a writer is fun. You can always justify the expense of some beautifully produced glossy style magazines as your contribution to keeping in touch. Here you will read stories planted by PR companies and journalists, all vying to identify the next trend. But why not? It is showbiz after all. Perhaps you can get a feel for what trends are developing and use this instinct to help plot the content of your next script.

5. Do you have to live in Hollywood?

No, but it helps to live there if you're dealing with a company based in Los Angeles. If you don't live in LA, but want to deal with an LA company, you could treat your out-of-town address as exotic. Everyone I have met in LA is desperate to leave.

When you sign a deal with a major Hollywood company, don't be surprised if a condition of the deal is that you physically relocate to LA for the duration of the project.

And despite what many LA executives might tell you, there are many film companies in cities other than LA.

Map of the Film Industry

Yes, it's true. There is a blueprint of the film industry building – a giant warehouse in a secret location. I can't tell you where it is, or show you the blueprint, but I can tell you about it. I hope that you will be able to use this information to get through one of the many doors in the film industry and sell your screenplay.

From the front, the film industry building is vast. It is one of those massive Victorian buildings built at the turn of the last century, and it has large pillars with a long flight of steps in front of it. In front of the film industry building is a very busy road. Directly in front of the entrance there is a loading bay and a bus stop. Across from the road there is a train station. Every morning at 9 a.m. dozens of workers alight at the bus stop and train station and race up the steps to go to work. A little later, you might see a limousine pull up and disgorge some bodyguards and a star who also run up the steps and into the film industry building. Everyone seems very busy. Oddly enough, most days you can see several hundred people waiting on the steps of the film industry building. When a star comes out, these paparazzi snap away like mad and hound them for autographs.

If you spent a complete twenty-four hours there, you would be amazed at how late some people leave, and how early some people arrive. The film industry is noted for the long hard hours people work.

Turning to look at the front of the building, the first thing that springs to mind is the fact that there is no threshold guardian. No one is checking the credentials of people scurrying into the film industry building. Unlike the medical industry building, or the aerospace building or the legal building where the threshold guardians closely check documentation, it would appear that anyone can enter the film industry building.

Moving up the steps and through the front doors, the first thing you notice is the size of the place. The corridors stretch ahead of you as far as you can see. Doors line both sides of the hallway. And, unlike the medical industry building, each door is unique. In the medical industry building, there are only a few doors: general practitioner, paediatrician, surgeon, dentist, holistic medicine, and gynaecologist. But every single door in the film industry is totally different.

The first door on the right is covered in cobwebs and there is a huge padlock on the lock. At first glance, it would appear that the doorway hasn't been used for years. Closer inspection reveals a fresh nick in the keyhole. Hammer Films, one of the great names in British filmmaking, which has lain dormant since 1981, has just been taken over and the new owners are planning to go into production.

If you look up the hallway you see hordes of people walking up and down. Some are hurrying to the doorways, pulling out a set of keys, and letting themselves in. Others stop at high-security doors, press a PIN number into the lock and get zapped inside. That's something we must do – get the right set of keys or figure out which buttons open which doors.

Of course if you spend more than a few hours in the hell, you will see lots of people suffering from the dreaded onanist's rash walking aim-

I came back today from a meeting with the new owners of Hammer Films. Despite a media blitz when they brought the back catalogue to the company in Britain and America, they received a princely total of six speculative scripts.

The new CEO had even cleared several bookshelves to accommodate the rush of the scripts! And they had let it be known that they were looking for another Hammer House of Horror film.

But before you get your screenplays and stamps out, remember, by the time you read it in this book, it's too late. I am sure they have enough scripts by now to last them a lifetime.

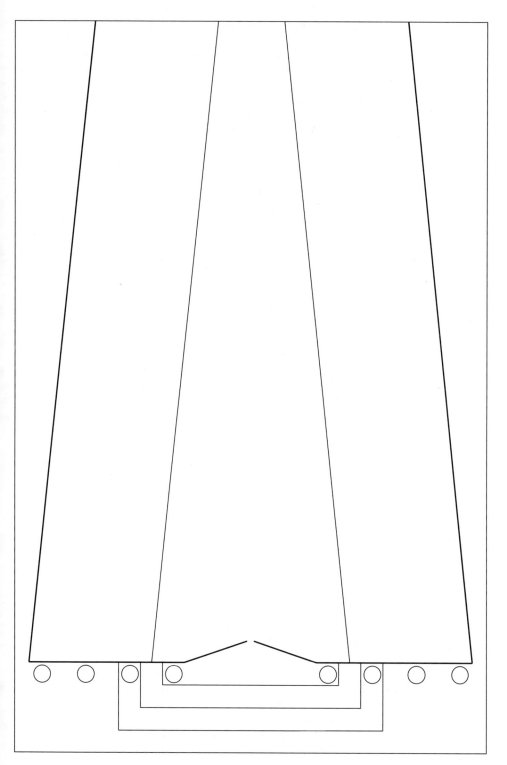

figure 17.1
The Map of the Film Industry

lessly up and down the hallway. They rarely get into a doorway, unless it's like the one over there. Here there is actually an open doorway, with an attractive shrub in a pot outside. In this office there is a comfortable couch, a coffee table with free magazines, an urn with free coffee and a government agency or film society dispensing free information. These doorways are nice on a day when you have suffered a lot of rejection.

Maybe you are walking up the hallway and you see one of the doorways that is guarded by security guards and infrared light beams. Standing there you notice that the doorway is made of stainless steel, like a bank vault. To the right hand side there is a keypad where one enters a secret code. As you are peering at it, trying to figure out the combination, the security men (who are dressed in black – naturally) toss you rudely aside. You look up as a group of people scurry in and you think you recognize a star. Not just any star, but the star that would be perfect for your script. You leap to your feet and race to get inside, but the door clangs shut in your face. So you are back in the corridor.

Hint Your job is to get out of the hallway and into the rooms. Keep your power file up to date and never stop networking. Find out where the keys to the doors you want to go through are kept.

You see that another door is ajar. You peek in and see that they are looking for screenplays. You walk in and observe the plush trimmings and the telephone bench with not two, but three telephone receptionists. You befriend one of them and discover that the person you need to see with your screenplay works in the office directly behind you. Hell, she even gets her to read your screenplay. And you have an appointment a week later, Thursday at 4 p.m. That is a glorious week. Every time you pass an onanist in the corridor you can brag about your meeting.

You arrive fashionably early on the day, are greeted by your friend on the switchboard, and are invited to sit on the white leather couch. A telephone with free outgoing calls sits temptingly beside you, but you resist. An hour passes. Your friend keeps gesturing reassurance to you. Another hour. 6:15. Still no meeting. Your friend comes over to you and apologetically tells you that your appointment has been cancelled due to an unexpected but lengthy transatlantic conference call that is still in progress. Of course you reschedule for a week Tuesday.

This is the story of Miramax in the early years. Rumour was that you wouldn't get a meeting with one of the brothers until you had been cancelled, without notice, ten times. Not very funny, if you have saved up your last penny to get a cheap ticket to New York from London. Apparently this is the way they tested one's passion.

The same thing happens again and again. You finally get into the room and meet the big cheese. You pitch your guts out, she is nodding 'Aha, Aha, tell me more' when suddenly it hits you: this isn't the big cheese; this is the threshold guarding for the real big cheese in the next room.

Back in the corridor. Walking a little further along you come to another door with a simple letterbox. Feeling suicidal after your rash of cancellations and other nobler forms of rejection, you take the plunge, form a good solid knuckle and rap on the door for what might be your last sales pitch ever. To your amazement, someone says 'Come in!'. You push open the door cautiously, and there, in a small room lit by no more than a naked light bulb, sits an independent producer. Surrounded by scripts, red-letter notices, a fax machine, and a worn out photocopier is, quite possibly, the best chance you have to get your first script made. Don't overlook this option. But don't be bullied by a producer. You will know when you meet the right one. It will leap out at you.

Allow me the indulgence of telling you a true story about a particular adventure in the film industry building.

In 1998 I had the idea of creating a film award show to honor British filmmakers, writers and actors. We called it the British Independent Film Awards. In the second year Diana Ross actually showed up and we got miles of coverage. Coming up to year three I asked the William Morris Agency to represent the awards in order to get a television deal.

We arranged for a meeting at the prospective broadcasters and I attended with my assistant, Fred Hodge, and our agent. We arrived, were given a choice of expensive drinks, were ushered straight into the Big Cheese's Office, from where we were taken into the Super Big Cheese's Office. The room was a classic British library room with wooden floors and expensive tapestries and hunting prints on the walls. The window overlooked Green Park and, in the distance, Buckingham Palace. Facing the window was a floor-to-ceiling wall of expensive original edition books.

The Super Big Cheese sat at a desk with his back to the window. On the desk were copies of the contract, bound with red legal ribbon in the quaint British tradition. Our agent reached to pick one up, but the Super Big Cheese reached out and said 'Let's wait for a minute. We like to keep things professional.'

The three of us retreated to our leather wing chairs in front of the bookcase. We ran through the main points of the contract and were in total agreement. As we were about to get up and sign — I even had my pen out — the Super Big Cheese's assistant, Big Cheese, came in and said 'Excuse me, sorry to interrupt, but Harrison Ford is on the line'. Naturally we shrugged as if a call from Harrison Ford was totally routine for us.

I am not sure if the call from Harrison Ford was authentic or not. I suspect it was. My fantasy is that Harrison Ford was in on it too. What I do know is that, as Big Cheese nodded to get our consent to take the call, he turned towards the window. And what I hadn't noticed then, but remember now with painfully accurate recollection, is that at our feet was a semicircular groove around our chairs and our bookshelves. And as Super Big Cheese turned to talk to Harrison Ford, he reached under his desk and pushed a button. Suddenly the whole bookshelf started to revolve and we were spun out of the office and into the corridor. It was so sudden. And we were back in the corridor.

The deal, so tantalizingly close, vanished before our eyes without a single explanation. The only thing I can say is that my last glimpse of the office was of Big Cheese mouthing the word onanist at us as we were turned out of the office. And it all happened so fast. That took a few days to get over, let me tell you. My agent said that these things happen sometimes, and to get on with the next deal.

Hint Never take anything personally. Of course it is almost impossible not to take it personally. But try not to.

Summary

1. Remember that you are a professional. Act like a professional and you will be treated like a professional.

2. Be creative in the way that you approach your career.

Next, how you present your script to the industry is an important part of looking professional.

18   Script Format and Style Guide

Online Resources

SCREENWRITERS HAVE AN ideal entrepreneurial opportunity if they think of themselves as the manufacturer of a product: take a ream of paper, available from any stationers, and turn it into a screenplay worth thousands by using just a few pennies' worth of ink, your time, and your mind.

If you treat your writing like a business, then it follows that you are a professional, and certain rules apply to your profession as they do to any other profession. What follows is both a format and style guide which attempts to give you an idea of the different choices and strategies involved in the craft of screenwriting.

Screenplays must be submitted in the correct format or the industry personnel you are pursuing will ignore them. If you do not pay attention to the simple formatting rules your script will look amateurish.

The film industry has become institutionalized to the point where scripts follow one set of rules for screenplay and another for television. This chapter explains the basic rules for screenplay.

Basic Principles

1. Twelve-point Courier typeface

Screenplays and teleplays are written in 12 point Courier typeface, which is a legacy of the old manual typewriter's typeface. One page of a script set in 12 point Courier, properly formatted, will roughly equal a minute of screen time. A similar script set in a more pleasing font like Helvetica will confuse the reader as he will not know how long the screenplay is. Use A4 paper or, in the US, use 8½" by 11" white 3-hole paper.

2. Don't write camera directions

Scriptwriters should not use camera directions in their scripts – this is the job of the director. Unfortunately, beginning writers often see produced film scripts with camera angles and scene numbers, and assume that this is how a script should look.

It is important to understand that the author's script is the beginning of a creative process, and that a produced script goes through many different stages of appearance, with the input of producers, directors, and technicians, all of whom mark the script with scene numbers and camera angles as an organizational tool. Writing a presentation script for a sale should not include scene numbers and camera angles.

The best way to avoid writing in camera directions in your script is to write in a way which is sufficiently visual that the camera angles are implied. This strategy also works to make the script more readable, since camera descriptions are often clumsy and break up the flow of the script. Consider, for example, the following extract from The Shawshank Redemption by Frank Darabont:

```
He reaches for the glove compartment, opens it,
pulls out an object wrapped in a rag. He lays it
in his lap and unwraps it carefully --

-- revealing a .38 revolver, oily black, evil.

He grabs a box of bullets. Spills them every-
where, all over the seats and floor. Clumsy. He
picks bullets off his lap, loading them into the
gun, one by one, methodical and grim. Six in the
chamber. His gaze goes back to the bungalow.
```

3. Don't break scenes up into shots

In your script use only master scenes which describe the whole action in one setting. Remember that the person reading your script for the first time must be able to understand what is going on – clearly.

4. Don't number your scenes

Scripts are only given scene numbers when they are budgeted and scheduled to be shot. An author's version of a script (presentation script) should never have scene numbers.

5. Length

Each script page is generally considered a minute of screen time. In order to appear professional, it is important that your script be of a proper length. Feature film scripts have some flexibility, but they should generally be within the 100 to 120 page range. Television programmes are necessarily more precise, with shows varying to some degree in how they divide up the commercial time, with teasers at the beginning and short epilogues or tags at the end. For a writer looking to write a spec script (speculative, without pay) for an established show, it is strongly advised that you watch the show carefully and, if possible, obtain 'the bible' for the show – the document which details the characteristics of the main roles.

You can make a script of 122 pages appear to be 120 by simply calling three pages within the script 62a, 76a etc. The final page count will then number 119 or 120.

6. One-camera film format vs. three-camera tape format

One-camera feature films are filmed television shows which have a different format from taped, three-camera television shows. TV shows with a great deal of action or exterior scenes tend to be filmed. Sitcoms, variety shows, game shows and talk shows are mainly shot in a video studio using a three-camera script format. The feature film script uses single spacing for both the dialogue and scene description. In the three-camera format, both the dialogue and scene direction are double-spaced.

7. Acts

Feature films are not formally broken down into acts. The creation of acts comes from theatre where the curtain would fall after each act. Cinema is a much more fluid medium and there is no curtain.

Television scripts, with the blocks of time set for commercials, are structured into distinct acts. Movies-for-television are generally broken into seven acts, sitcoms into two acts, and one-hour programmes into four acts. Again, television programmes vary with the use of introductory teaser scenes and short epilogues.

8. Make it perfect

Although it may sound trivial, correct spelling and grammar are a must. Good grammar and spelling won't sell your script, but you don't want to give potential buyers another reason for rejection. The finished product should be clean and neat. Make certain that the final spell check is done manually to eliminate the errors of a computerized spell-check.

The Screenplay

1. Covers and binding

Stay away from the green neon metal flake covers. The last thing that a writer wants is for his script to look like a vanity press publication.

Screenplays are bound with beige, white or grey card.

The title page should contain nothing more than the title and the author's name. The title should be typed in upper and lower case. If you type your name in caps, you say to any industry person who picks up your script that you are a megalomaniac. See figure 18.1 opposite.

Include nothing within the covers other than the title page and the screenplay itself – no cast of characters, casting suggestions, related articles, previous correspondence, autobiography or illustrations. In America, the traditional binding for scripts is three-hole punch on the left side with brass brads in the top and bottom hole (to facilitate copying). In Europe, A4 with a wire clip through two holes is adequate. In America, double-sided copying is acceptable – and greener.

2. Title page – drafts, dates, WGA registration

Conventional wisdom varies on this point but, for a beginning writer, it is generally best not to number drafts or type the date of completion. This information is only important once the script is purchased and it goes through a series of rewrites. It is not necessary for you to mark your script with the WGA registration number in order for it to be protected, and many people view this practice as amateurish – it is common for beginning writers to be overly concerned about the possibility of their ideas being stolen. The title page should have nothing more than the writer's name, address, phone number, and the title of the script.

3. First page

The first page is not numbered. Centre the title in caps and quotes. For television shows broken down into acts, type in the act, centered, in caps and underlined, three spaces down from the title. Four spaces down, all scripts begin with **FADE IN:**

4. Scene Headings

Scene headings, or slug lines, indicate whether the location is an interior (**INT.**) or exterior (**EXT.**), the location, and whether it is day or night.

Occasionally, a scene is both interior and exterior, as in a doorway or at a window, and this is expressed as **INT./EXT.**

INT./EXT. APARTMENT WINDOW – NIGHT

If the location encompasses a large area, such as a football field, the writer needs to specify a certain area, such as **ON THE BENCH** or **AT FIFTY YARD LINE**. The time has to be either day or night, not morning, dusk, or twilight. The day or night designation is for shot scheduling

figure 18.1
Incorrect Script Title Page

AIRPLANE THAT LANDS SAFELY

By

Budding Author

© 4th Draft, 17th Revision

Lawyer	Budding Author
Address	Address
Home	Home
Office	Mobile
Fax	Office
Email	Email
	Website

figure 18.2
Correct Script Title Page

LAST BUCK

By

ELLIOT GROVE

Copyright Control
Raindance Ltd
81 Berwick Street
London
W1F 8TW

purposes and needs to be straightforward. Subtler distinctions in time should be indicated in the text of the scene description.

Sometimes extra information must be included in the scene heading such as the season or year. Put this in parentheses after the location.

```
EXT.  LOS ANGELES (1939) — DAY
```

When scenes continue to another page, you can type (CONTINUED) in parentheses at both the bottom right margin of the first page and without parentheses and a colon at the top left margin of the second page. But this practice is really for scene numbering, which comes later when the script is broken down for production, and isn't really necessary. Some writers use CONTINUED, others don't.

5. Scene endings

Scene endings are always in caps at the far right tab with a colon. **FADE OUT** is followed by a period, ending the act or the entire script. It is not necessary to put a scene ending at the conclusion of each scene.

6. 'Cut to:'

Some writers never use CUT TO: arguing that moving from one scene to another implies the transition. Other writers use CUT TO: after almost every scene, liking the way it sounds when read aloud. Still other writers reserve CUT TO: for sudden changes in location, or for cutting back and forth from different locations during an action sequence. I prefer the latter.

7. 'Dissolve To:' and 'Fade To:'

These endings have become less and less popular in filmmaking with the emphasis on hard cuts. In addition, the photographic look of scene transitions is really a choice for the director to make.

8. Fade out

Used to end all scripts.

9. Scene description

Always double-spaced down from the scene heading, the scene description or direction indicates in the most economical terms what the setting is, who the characters are, and what action is taking place.

10. Paragraphing techniques

The greatest flexibility in format for the screenwriter is in the style used in scene description. The particular form that a writer uses to describe the setting and the action in a scene has a great impact on the way it reads. Some writers format scene description in paragraphs like one would see in a novel, one sentence after another in long blocks.

Other screenwriters break their scene description into short one- and two-sentence paragraphs. Whichever paragraphing form you use, it is important to develop a strong individual writing style that is clear, concise and visual.

Here are some examples:

```
Racine tries the door. It's locked. Racine shakes
it hard, but it's solid. Racine looks to his
left. There's a window down the wall there. He
moves to it. It goes into the dining room. Matte
watches him from the same spot, through the
dining room door. Racine pushes up on the
window. It won't budge. Racine moves to his
right, past the front door, to the large
window off the living room. He pushes at it as
his eyes lock with Matte, who watches from the
hall. The window won't move. Racine spins and
picks the nearest object, a wooden rocking chair.
He lifts it, turns and smashes the big window.
Glass showers into the living room.
```

(Lawrence Kasdan, Body Heat.)

```
NICOLI staggers down the street, unarmed.

DOYLE is waiting at the foot of the stairs.

NICOLI sees him, turns in desperation to run back.

DOYLE has his .38 drawn. He fires three shots
into NICOLI's back.

NICOLI stiffens and falls backward at DOYLE's
feet. DOYLE collapses next to him.
```

(Ernest Tidyman & William Friedkin, The French Connection.)

This technique has the advantage of isolating separate actions and images. It also tends to prevent the reader from missing the key story information, which can get buried in a long paragraph.

A third method, which is becoming increasingly popular, is to set key images in short sentence fragments, capitalized, on a single line.

GITTES' HEAD SLOWLY CLEARS THE SOFA TOP

and he looks.

GREEN SMOKE CURLS

up lazily from his desk drawer.

REACTION GITTES

sees he's been had.

(Robert Towne, The Two Jakes.)

Used properly, this style is very visual, economical, and readable.

Many writers use a combination of these three paragraphing styles for various effects at different moments in their stories. Developing an understanding of the particular effect of each of these styles is an important part of the craft of screenwriting.

11. Capitalization

When characters are first introduced, their names need to be capitalized. Thereafter, in the descriptive passages, their names appear in upper and lower case. This serves as an organizational device to assist casting directors, script supervisors and performers and tells them the size of their parts.

When sound cues are used, the first word in the cue needs to be capitalized to alert the sound technician skimming the script that his expertise is going to be needed here.

If a scene is to be shot mute, the proper abbreviation is $M.O.S.$ This confusing looking stage direction comes from the early days of sound picture when a German director bellowed through a megaphone: 'Mit Out Sound'.

Camera cues are to be avoided like the plague, but if an occasional camera direction is used it should be capitalized (ANGLE WIDENS, CAMERA DOLLYS, IN CLOSEUP). Even better, if the writer can use a term which implies a camera angle (SEE, FOLLOW, AND LOOK), then it too must be capitalized.

There are three camera directions that are commonly abbreviated — foreground is $f.g.$, background is $b.g.$, and off screen is $o.s.$ When these abbreviations begin a sentence the first letter is capitalized.

12. Character cues

The character cue is simply the name given to the character that speaks the line of dialogue that follows. Always capitalize character cues. The abbreviations for **VOICE OVER (V.O.)** and **OFF SCREEN (O.S.)** are used with the character cues to denote two different things.

VOICE OVER is used when dialogue is put over a scene, either through narration, a character thinking out loud, or when a tape recording is played in a scene.

OFF SCREEN is used when a character is heard but not seen, as when a character talks from another room in a house, or is simply out of the camera frame.

Both **(V.O.)** and **(O.S.)** appear abbreviated, capitalized, and in parentheses directly after the character cue.

Characters with small roles are sometimes given numbers such as **FAN No 1** and **FAN No 2**. Or the role that a certain character plays is sometimes put in parentheses next to the character cue as in **JOSEPH (CARPENTER)**. Some writers feel that one should try to give every character in the script a name in order to help define the character. Others think that since the viewer often has no occasion to learn a minor character's name, there is no point in mentioning it in the script.

13. Character direction (parentheticals)

Character directions are special instructions to the actor, pertaining to the specific dialogue that follows. Generally, the use of these parentheticals should be avoided. Character directions in a script can seem to be an attempt by the writer to tell the actor how to act. Actors generally will strike the parentheticals from a script.

In most cases, the tone should be clear from the dialogue.

Some writers use character directions to pace the dialogue by using the term 'beat', meaning a pause.

```
                    DENYS
          There's a woman there, Tania.
          He's been with her some years now.
          (beat)
          She's Somali.
          (beat)
          The comfort you'd bring is less
          than his pain if you knew. You
          mustn't go.
```

(Kurt Luedtke, Out of Africa.)

Occasionally, a writer might use dialogue in an ironic or comic way, going against the expectations of the situation, and the character direction then becomes necessary. Some writers also use parentheticals for directing the movements of a character during a particular passage. But for the most part, this is best left in the scene description.

Another use of a character direction is to make it clear to the reader that three people are involved in a conversation:

                              JOANNE
                    (to Ben)
                    How old is Elliot? I'll bet he's...

                              BERNICE
                    ...thirty-six.

14. Format

Personal direction always appears under the character cue in parentheses. If the dialogue of a single character is broken up by scene
description, when the dialogue resumes a parenthetical is used with the
word continuing.

                              HACKETT
                    (continuing)
                    I suppose we'll have to kill him.

Another long contemplative silence.

                              HACKETT
                    (continuing)
                    I don't suppose you have any ideas
                    on that, Diana.

                                          (Paddy Chayefsky)

15. Dialogue

Unlike in plays and novels, dialogue in the screenplay is as short and
economical as possible. Many screenwriters see dialogue as another
form of action, putting characters at odds, driving the plotline.

A helpful tip is to consider a two-character scene as one where character A asks something of character B, who misunderstands the question
(or maybe ignores it), and answers another question. When done skilfully,
this type of dialogue can be followed by the audience and creates the
'reading between the lines' that is considered 'sub-text' in many screenwriting manuals.

A large part of rewriting a screenplay, especially for beginning writers,
tends to consist in large measure of simply cutting down unnecessary
lines and fragments of dialogue.

16. Dialogue format

– Spell out two digit numbers, personal titles, and indications of time
– Do not hyphenate words, breaking them from one line to the next

3"

COREY   (cont'd)
one suitcase. That leaves you out
of it. I'm going to shoot Blazers'
mouth shut.

She fondles an ashtray

EXT. JERSEY STREET - DAWN

But Blazer isn't available right now,
because he's rollerblading towards the
flapping door of a circus tent.

                              CUT TO:

INT. TENT - DAY

1½"   1"

Blazer glides into the tent and comes
to a perfect stop right under the nose
of PHIL,the Balloon King. It's taken
the FAT LADY about two seconds to
realize where she's seen his face before.

                4"
                    PHIL
          What do you want?

His voice breaks out in an audible sweat.

               BLAZER
I'm looking for a couple of high wire
boys - Elliot Groveski and his mate.

The swinging overhead light shatters into
a million pieces.

               BLAZER
    3½"   (continuing)
I want to show them new ways to fly.

figure 18.3
Script Format Guide

- Never break sentences from one page to the next
- When a long passage of dialogue needs to be continued onto another page type **(MORE)** at the character cue tab and then **(cont'd)** after the character cue on the following page
- Omit these shooting script devices: scene numbers, capitalized sound effects, the word 'continued' at the bottom of each page whenever a scene extends to the next page; numbers or dates of successive drafts, or any other indications of rewritten or revised material
- Type a character name all in caps when that character is first introduced into the screenplay. Do this is in the action/description paragraph, never the dialogue
- All scenes begin with a new scene heading, followed by an action/description paragraph. Never begin a scene with dialogue
- In a new scene, mention character names before giving dialogue

New writers that I work with love to debate the finer points of script format. I believe that it is such a popular topic because it prolongs the moment until they actually have to touch a computer.

And if you are typing a fantastic screenplay, does anyone actually care whether or not the word 'gunshot' is all upper case, underlined, or not?

Summary

1. Take the time to format your script properly.

2. Don't be intimidated by the formatting rules — it will just make you delay the writing process.

Are you ready for the moment of truth? Try my troubleshooting guide.

19

Troubleshooting Guide

THIS USEFUL GUIDE should be referred to whenever you get stuck. Ask yourself the following questions, and see if you can unlock your story, and discover the fractures in your story.

Premise

☐ the premise is fractured
☐ the premise is not spoken to in enough scenes
☐ the premise doesn't speak to a larger theme
☐ the premise is not commercial

Hint Is your film high concept or low concept?

Action

☐ the action is not integrated to the story
☐ the action is contrived
☐ there is no action

Hint A well-written script should be composed of visual stimulation.

Ghost

☐ the story has no ghost
☐ the ghost is not painful to the hero
☐ the hero overcomes the ghost too quickly

Hint Examine your ghost for the unique characteristics of each genre.

Hero

- ☐ the hero is too passive
- ☐ the hero is too reactive
- ☐ the hero is cold (audience cannot sympathize or empathize with hero)

Hint Review your character essays until you know each one intimately.

Hero's goal

- ☐ there is more than one goal (the story is fragmented)
- ☐ the goal arc begins too late
- ☐ the goal arc is not specific
- ☐ the goal arc does not build in intensity or importance
- ☐ the goal is unimportant
- ☐ the goal arc is reactive/too negative

Hint Most stories fail because the hero does not have clearly defined goals and needs.

Hero's Needs

- ☐ there is no psychological weakness
- ☐ the psychological weakness is not painful to the hero
- ☐ the moral need is vague
- ☐ the moral need doesn't affect/hurt other characters
- ☐ the hero has no moral need

Hint A good hero has two problems to solve – an outer problem (goal) and an inner problem (need). There are two types of inner problems – psychological (personal weaknesses) and moral weakness (how your hero reacts with other characters).

Backstory

- ☐ the backstory is redundant or starts too soon
- ☐ the backstory relies on hackneyed devices like flashback
- ☐ more of the action should be included in backstory

Hint Most scripts start the story too early.

Opponent

- [ ] there is no main opponent in the story
- [ ] the choice of main opponent is wrong
- [ ] the story lacks conflict
- [ ] the main opponent is internal
- [ ] the main opponent is an organization
- [ ] the opponent is flat or one-dimensional

Hint The development of the opponent character is the most important in your screenplay.

Scene writing

- [ ] the scene has no climax
- [ ] the scene has no conflict
- [ ] there is no point to the scene
- [ ] the scene does not move the story

Hint Scenes contain their own structure – a beginning, a middle and an end.

Descriptive passages

- [ ] the descriptive passages are overwritten
- [ ] the descriptive passages are too static
- [ ] the descriptive passages are not visual
- [ ] the descriptive passages do not contain movement

Hint Great descriptive passages describe people and objects moving with emotion.

Dialogue

- [ ] does not sound like different people talking
- [ ] is on the nose
- [ ] is overwritten

Hint A picture is worth a thousand words. Show your characters doing things as much as possible.

Setting

☐ the social stage is not appropriate to the story
☐ the choice of social stage is unclear
☐ there is no social stage

Hint The choice of setting (social stage) will predetermine the qualities of the hero.

Summary

1. The more time spent planning your script at the first draft stage, the fewer flaws your script will have.

2. Remember that you are an intuitive storyteller, and this troubleshooting guide may not apply to your story.

To be a successful writer, you must follow the three golden rules of screen writing.

20

Three Golden Rules

Syd Field taught me the real meaning of downloading. It was so refreshing to talk to an amazing writer like Syd and hear him say that he didn't write. He spent half his time each day downloading the alpha state ideas he had from the previous day, and then spent the rest of his daily writing time evaluating and polishing the ideas he wrote down from the day before. Syd says that he 'throws his ideas onto paper' and then worries about whether or not they are any good.

BECOMING A SUCCESSFUL screenwriter means following a few simple rules. Of course the usual mental and physical health rules apply. The biblical golden rule – Do unto others as you would have them do unto you – is also a pretty good rule to follow. A successful screenwriter needs, I feel, a few more specific rules that outline a plan of attack to the specific problems that a screenwriter faces.

Rule Number One: Quantity, Not Quality

Just throw it down on a piece of paper. Every day. Write for half an hour. Don't worry if it's any good. Just throw it down and determine at a later date whether what you have written is any good.

Ernest Hemingway used to say that you must relax. And write down everything that you have damned up in your alpha state. Throw it down. You can always polish it later.

Hint Chances are that ninety-nine per cent of what you write is rubbish. The important thing is not what you write, but that you do write.

Rule Number Two: Discipline

Thinkers think, joggers jog, writers write. If you can get paid for thinking or jogging, fantastic. But writers write. They move their fingers for about three hours a day.

I know, discipline is a nasty word. It implies a degree of physical pain and mental anguish in order to get your screenplay written. But rather than overlook this second golden rule of screenwriting, let's try and make the very thought of discipline palatable.

First of all, you must write every single day.

But rather than start with an eight-hour bash on your Saturday off, why not try a half hour a day, five days a week? The half-hour works like this: the first half (about fifteen minutes) is spent downloading from the alpha state. The second half is spent polishing what you have written down the day before.

After four weeks of this, see if you can gently raise your writing time to forty-five minutes, then to an hour. Professional writers I know rarely work more than three hours per day unless they are on a deadline. Then it is the long eighteen hour days.

If you plan to write Monday to Friday, then you must pick a time of day when you know you can write every single day. If you plan to write at night and are used to spending Wednesday nights out, then you have to compensate by writing on a Saturday or Sunday for a half-hour.

The important thing is that you write for the same length of time every single day. You will be amazed at how prolific you will be by writing for just a half-hour a day. And by spreading your writing times out by twenty-four hour intervals and utilizing the alpha state opportunities that you may have travelling or walking the dog, your work will have a freshness and vitality that will distinguish it.

A friend of mine has been commissioned to write a how-to filmmaking book for Focal Press. He works on this book in three four-week spurts, burning the candle at both ends and leaving himself in a state of physical and emotional exhaustion. Following these workathons, he does nothing for months on end, suffering increasing tension from pent-up guilt and frustration. This attacks his confidence to the point where he is seriously contemplating abandoning his excellent project after spending hundreds of hours on it. His (and my) poor editor is reeling from the dozens of missed deadlines to the point where it appeared that the book would be abandoned.

When I saw him recently, I asked him how much longer his book would be, and he estimated three to four months of 'round the clock' work. I convinced him to try an hour a night, and he suddenly realized that three to four months of sixty minutes a day would probably suffice to get the book delivered.

We all live very different lives from each other. But no matter what kind of life we lead, we all have a rhythm, or a routine to our daily existences. Programming oneself to write for a set time each day is just another one of these habits that we must form if we want to work as a writer.

Perhaps you will find after writing every day that writing doesn't suit you. This is fine. There are many other jobs in the film industry that might suit your temperament better.

Hint If you find yourself avoiding the discipline of writing, stop 'writing' and try downloading from the alpha state. You will soon have so much raw material that you will suddenly feel the urge to write. Alpha state is the hidden resource of writers.

Rule Number Three: Reject Rejection

Writing is a lonely business. Filmmaking is a crazy business. Putting the two together means that you are faced with heaps and heaps of rejection. Nothing is more competitive than the film business. You will face untold amounts of rejection and, unless you develop a plan to deal with rejection, you will never make it as a screenwriter. And rejection will get you down to the point at which it affects all areas of your life – if you do not learn to follow the third golden rule of screenwriting. There are three types of rejection.

1. Physical rejection

Three years after I started Raindance, I suffered both physical and moral rejection to the point where I couldn't imagine continuing. I packed up all the files, gave notice to the landlord, and called the telephone company to disconnect the telephone. A good friend of mine called me, listened to my sorry state of woe and said – 'Quitters never win, and winners never quit'. I sat on the packing boxes for an hour, and unpacked them. That was twelve years ago.

Announcing your ambition to write a screenplay, and then announcing that you will actually start to write a screenplay, have the same effect on your personal life as announcing a marriage, or divorce. It is cataclysmic and, unless handled properly, will totally ruin your writing career.

When you first announce your ambition to write a movie, you will be swept away by a rip-tide of enthusiasm and approval for your chosen goal. There is, after all, nothing like a glamorous daydream.

However, fail to deliver an Oscar-winning script on your first foray into the movies, and your friends will desert you. 'Why don't you get a real job, a real hobby, why are you always dreaming?' will be the chorus that rings in your ears at every social gathering, or stabs you in the back every time you leave the room.

Worse yet will be the words from your loved ones who will try to get you to abandon your screenwriting career because of all the rejection you will suffer. They are just trying to help, and again, if not dealt with in a loving and caring way, will destroy your writing and, if you are not careful, your relationships as well. I don't have a solution for this, but I do know lots of people with the rash who fall at this hurdle.

And the reason you will give up writing at this stage is because you will lack confidence in yourself and will not be able to maintain belief in the biblical quote 'in the beginning was the word…' Which will mean you will not be able to take the screenwriter's leap of faith, and which means you will see your whole dream, your goal, as a worthless pursuit. Which would be a pity since you have talent.

2. Moral rejection

You will beat yourself up if you are not aware of the destructive power of moral rejection. Sometimes you will read the facts in such a way that you will be unable to continue. Discouragement will reign supreme.

You might start looking at statistics of the film industry. Reading the trade papers, you will be horrified that 40 000 screenplays are registered every year for a copyright, yet only a few hundred are actually produced.

If you aren't careful, this statistic will send you seeking the solace of the tallest rooftop in your neighbourhood.

Hint Reject rejection means being true to your goal. Follow golden rules one and two and they will make rejection much easier to handle.

Before you give up, I implore you to perform a simple exercise: Look in your correspondence file. Find out how many letters of rejection you have. If you have none, it means you haven't been trying to sell your screenplay. If you have dozens, have you exploited them properly? Have you found out why they said 'No'? Have they said 'no' because the office was on fire and they had to leave in time to save themselves? Have they said 'no' because they are out of the business? Have they said 'no' because they want you to sell them more? Is there any useful advice they can give you regarding your story concept, characterization, scene description and dialogue? Always try to find out why someone says 'no'.

You have to remember that statistics can be bent to suit any political voice. It is better to analyse the meaning behind the statistics. Of all the scripts registered at the Writers' Guild, it isn't the ratio that counts, it is the percentage of great scripts to clankers. It is also true that the Writers' Guild admits 500 new writers per annum. The only way you can join the Writers' Guild is if you have sold a screenplay to a company that the guild officially recognizes. In other words, to reframe the statistic, why not say that despite the number of screenplays sent to the Writers' Guild every year, an average of over one writer a day sells a screenplay under WGA terms and conditions.

Hint Reframe the statistics. This will breed confidence.

---

3. Psychological rejection

Sometimes you will suffer such a humiliating amount of rejection that you will feel like giving up. You will enter your own page seventy-five, your personal Big Gloom. You are beating yourself up. You have lost the light at the end of the tunnel.

There is nothing I can say to you except that at this point you are probably suffering from the one disease which no doctor can cure – self-pity. There is only one person who can help you and that is you.

In closing, let me tell you a true story: After high school, I went to art school in Toronto. In order to support myself, I needed a summer job. In my middle year at art school, I left it too late to get a good job. All my classmates (who were less talented than I) found great jobs with high pay – driving Post Office vans, filling in as PAs in the financial district, or working up north as park rangers.

The only job I could find was working for a real estate company going door-to-door, trying to get the owners to give me instructions to sell their property. For this I was to be paid a commission relative to the value of the property.

I spent the first two days suffering every form of rejection known to mankind: I was chased by the snapping guard dog, saluted by drugged-out housewives, threatened by irate night shift workers I had woken from slumber, and greeted by the stony silence of the locked door. On top of that, the elements were very unkind. It was the hottest heat wave in living memory, and I developed blisters.

I went back to the owner of the agency and told him I couldn't do this anymore. I was prepared to do anything but. I would carry out the trash, mow the grass, and paint the shutters – anything but go door to door. Unfortunately, his was the only job available. And I needed a job desperately, or I wouldn't be able to finish art school.

I timidly asked him how many doors I would have to knock on until I got a 'Yes'. I already had forty-seven rejection slips. He looked at the map on the wall, scratched his chin, and said 'About a hundred'. A hundred! I couldn't imagine that.

Still desperate for a job, I asked him how much commission I would get for that. Again he studied the chart, pulled out some sales figures and said 'About $4000' (£2000).

So I decided that the only way this would work for me was to reframe the problem in my mind: 'You mean $4000 divided by a hundred means $40 for every "No"?'

I raced around the neighbourhood. I knocked on door after door. You want to sell your house? No? Great! And I would earn another $40. I could hardly wait for someone to say 'No', because I knew I was one closer to my payoff. Sure enough, after one hundred and seventeen, I had my first instruction. The next was eighty-seven, and it really did average around a hundred 'No's' to one 'Yes'. I had the best summer job I ever had.

However you do it, you have to be able to depersonalize rejection. Try to make it fun.

Which is why Raindance has teamed up with Focal Press to offer something positive to writers struggling with rejection. Whenever you get a rejection letter, send me a copy, c/o Focal Press. I will instantly send you a letter of acceptance to the Raindance Gallery of Rejection. And you know what I'm going to do, don't you?

When you are famous and have a hit film, I will advertise the fact that, that when you were unknown, you read this book and wrote me a letter in your moment of deepest despair. And I have the proof right here in the Gallery of Rejection. I will market the fact that you read this book!

I will send you a personalized letter of acceptance to the Gallery of Rejection so you will have at least one 'Yes' in your file.

Happy screenwriting,

Elliot Grove
London September 2008

Glossary

Ad lib
Extemporaneous lines or phrases used by actors appropriate to a given situation. Often used in group scenes such as parties.

Adaptation
The reworking of a story in a medium different from its creation.

Aerial Shot
A shot taken from the point of view of an airplane or helicopter.

Aleatory filming
Filming techniques based on chance and probability.

Antagonist
The opponent to the protagonist (hero).

Anticlimax
An emotional letdown in the buildup to the climax of the story.

Backstory
That which happens to the main characters before the movie begins. Omission of backstory can make a story flat and difficult for an audience to relate to a main character. See also Exposition.

Beat
A plot point within the overall story structure. The analogy of screen writing to music is often made, with individual scenes broken down into beats, organized overall into acts or movements.

b.g. (Background)
Any action or prop which is secondary to the main action.

Big Gloom
The moment where the main character is the furthest from their goal, and often considers abandoning their vision.

Black stuff
Industry term for descriptive passages.

Business
Technique of writing props into scenes for actors to work with, making dialogue dominated scenes more active and physical.

Character arc
Curved line tracing the changes and development of character over the course of the screenplay.

Cinéma vérité
A filmmaking technique designed for a scene to be filmed with as little intrusion of the camera as possible.

Close-up (C.U.)
A camera shot which emphasizes some part of the actor or an object.

Complication
An unexpected situation which threatens to thwart the hero's objectives. Used to add texture to a story.

Crosscut
The technique of alternating between two scenes in different locations which have a bearing on each other.

Cutaway
A shot away form the main action. Used by filmmakers to cut between awkward shots, or to highlight specific details.

CUT TO
A scene ending which varies use, but is often employed when cutting back and forth between two locations during a chase.

Deus ex machina
A resolution to a plot problem which is too convenient for the author, and unbelievable to the audience.

DISSOLVE TO
A scene ending which indicates that the final shot should gradually fade into the next scene.

Dolly
A camera cue used by directors indicating that the camera is to move in, out, or with the actors during scene.

Epilogue
A brief unit of action following the conclusion of the story.

Exposition

The process whereby events that happened prior to the beginning of the movie are explained to the audience so they can understand the motivation of the main characters. Exposition is an area most often ignored by new screenwriters. They usually rely on hackneyed and overworked devices such as the general, the pointed, and the flip chart.

EXT. (Exterior)

Used in scene headings to indicate that a scene will be shot outside.

Extreme close-up (E.C.U.)

A camera cue which is generally used to emphasize a particular detail.

EXTREME LONG SHOT

Camera cue in direction used to describe a shot taken by a long distance from the subject.

FADE IN

The first two words of a screenplay.

FADE OUT

Scene ending which is used in television at the end of an act, or at the very end of a feature film.

f.g. (Foreground)

Objects or action which is closet to camera.

Flashback

Established Hollywood wisdom is against the use of this device, but there are many successful examples of film narratives structured around flashbacks including Citizen Kane. The two types of flashbacks to avoid are the flipping calendar and harp music. Try to be imaginative with your use of this device. Flashback does not refer to time-line experiments where the A to B of a narrative story is chopped and changed, as in The Usual Suspects.

Foreshadowing

A dramatic tool where an event is hinted at early on such as Silence of the Lambs: 'You don't want Hanibal Lecter inside your head.'

FREEZE FRAME

Camera direction indicating that the picture stops dead and becomes a still photograph. Sometimes used to end scripts.

Genre

A story that follows certain rules pertinent to a specific type of story – horror, science fiction, comedy, love, detective, mystery, crime, etc. Specializing in genre is essential to success as a writer.

Ghost

The thing or event from the past which the main character in your story fears. The ghost should be so powerful that it cripples your hero at the outset of the story – but then is overcome. Different genres treat the ghost in different ways – necessary to the particular genre, which creates specific problems the writer must deal with. See also, Nightmare, Troubleshooting.

High concept

A phrase connected with scripts which have a premise or storyline which is easily reduced to a simple appealing one line. Aliens was summed up as 'Jaws in Space.'

Inciting scene

The necessary scene at the beginning of the script which serves as a catalyst for the main action of the story.

INSERT

A shot within a scene which calls our attention to a specific piece of information such as a book, a watch or a calendar.

INT. (Interior)

A scene heading which indicates that a scene will be shot inside.

L.S. (Long Shot)

A camera cue indicating a shot taken from a distance.

MATCH CUT

A transition from one scene to another matching the same, or a similar subject within the frame.

MED. SHOT (Medium Shot)

A camera angle often used to describe a shot of character from waist up.

Mirroring

The mimicking of a main character's actions or emotions in order to heighten drama.

MISE-EN-CADRE

Direction or staging within the camera frame.

MISE-EN-SCENE

The staging or positioning of the actors on the stage.

Montage

A rapid succession of shots. Also used as a scene heading, interchangeable with the Series of Shots heading.

Nightmare
The ultimate low that a hero must face if they fail to achieve their goal.
See also Ghost.

On the nose
A phrase which describes dialogue which too plainly reveals the
character, and more importantly, the author's intentions. Often, dialogue
will simply repeat what action has immediately preceded it.

Option
Agreement where a writer rents the rights to a script to a producer
or production company for a specific period of time.

O.S. (Off-screen)
Dialogue or sounds heard while the camera is on another subject. Typed
'(O.S.)' next to the character cue, and 'o.s.' in scene description.

Over the top
A phrase used in a broad way to describe a scene or action in a script
which goes too far in one direction and stretches believability.

Pan
A side-to-side camera movement.

Payoff
The necessary result of a complication for which the audience has
a been prepared.

P.O.V. (Point of view)
A camera positioned from the point of view of a particular character.

Premise
The basic idea for a story, often taking the form of a question or
a problem.

Producer's notes
A short form of story analysis, without synopsis, where development
executives make comments about a script, particularly in terms
of commercial viability.

Protagonist
The main character (hero) in the screenplay.

Resolution
The part of the end of a script that ties up all of the story's loose ends.

Reveal
When new information is revealed to the audience.

Rising action
Notion of dramatic rhythm in which events in a story build upon one another with increasing momentum.

Scene cards
Method used by some writers to outline their script by describing each scene on an index card, then arranging and rearranging them to work out the story structure.

Script development
The process where an idea is turned into a script, with funding from a studio or government funding agency. Development financing is often the most difficult to obtain for new writers.

Second-act curtain
In Three-act structure, the movement of the greatest conflict.

SERIES OF SHOTS
A series of short shots, typically used to show the passing of time.

Set-up
Term describing both the function of the first act in posing of the problem which the story will try to resolve, and in more general way, the process of laying the groundwork for dramatic or comic situation which will later be complicated, and then resolved or paid off.

Shooting schedule
Production schedule for shooting a film with the scenes from a script grouped together and ordered with production considerations in mind.

Shooting script
The final version of the screenplay incorporating the notes of the director, director of photography, designers, and producers.

SFX (Sound tracks)
Special effects which require some kind of technical production.

Spine
The essential events in a story.

Stacking
A writing technique where different storylines are played on top of each other to heighten drama and suspense.

Step outline
A method used by some writers to outline their story by numbering the major scenes and the order in which they occur. Not to be confused with a Treatment which is stylized version of the story used in seeking financing.

Story analyst
Also called a reader – both a full-time guild and part-time independent position in the industry, whose responsibility it is to cover feature film and television scripts being considered by a company for production. Generally included in the coverage is a one-line story description, a synopsis of the plotline, and the reader's comments, including the words 'Pass' or 'Consider' at the end.

Subplot
Sometimes called the B story, the subplot is used in various ways, weaving in and out of the main action. Often it is in the subplot that the major characters are developed more fully.

SUPER (Superimpose)
The photographic effect of showing one image over another. Typically, titles are superimposed over the opening scene.

Switch
A dramatic device where the writer plays on an audience's expectation and takes the story, or scene in a completely new direction.

Synopsis
Summary of a story told in the present tense. When the synopsis is a single line, it is referred to as log line.

Theme
What the screenplay is really about. Not to be confused with a topic. Anti-pollution is a topic, revenge is a theme. The more universal the theme is, the wider the appeal of the story.

Three-act structure
In the Hollywood storytelling tradition, the basic organizing principle of the sequence of fiction events including the set-up, the complication, and the resolution. The three-act story structure was considered the ultimate story paradigm until the early nineties. This paradigm is rooted in Greek history. In Hollywood, Syd Field's books and Robert McKee's teaching made the three-act story structure the industry standard until Chris Vogler's The Writer's Journey and John Truby's 22-Step Story Structure paradigms exploded the theory. It is now considered an obsolete story paradigm in Hollywood. See also 22-Step Story Structure and Vogler, Chris.

Three-camera format
Specific script style used for TV shows produced in a video studio.

Titles
Printed information to be read by the audience, either as separate graphics or superimposed over images. When an individual is mentioned in the titles, it is called a credit.

Treatment

Summary of a story told in the present tense. A treatment is often used as a tool to sell a writing project before it is written.

Tripling

Basic writing principle of creating action which occurs in three distinct beats over movements.

Twenty-two step story structure

A script structure paradigm created by LA-based John Truby and considered the most advanced of the story structure paradigm. Further details from www.truby.com

Vogler, Chris

Author of The Writer's Journey, the most influential screenwriting book of the 1990s, based on the teaching of Joseph Campbell.

V.O. (Voice over)

A character's voice heard over a scene, as in narration, a tape recorded voice, or a voice heard over the phone.

Visit to death

A plot point near the end of the movie where the hero is defeated and can foresee their own death.

Writers' credits

Writer 1 and Writer 2 – both writers worked separately on the project. Writer 1 & Writer 2 – both writers worked together on the project. In cases of dispute on a screenplay that has been rewritten, The Writers' Guild of America will award a sole writer credit based on which writer's script maintains fifty-one percent of the dialogue.

ZOOM

A camera cue indicated by the inward or outward movement of the camera to the subject. Distinguished from the dolly shot in that with the zoom shot the camera itself doesn't move, the effect is achieved solely by the manipulation of the zoom lens.

Index

Action, 82
Actors, 108, 112
Agents, 36, 52, 85
Allen, Woody, 79
Aristotle, 26
Audience, 10, 31
Aukin, David, 4

Battle, 48
BECTU, 146
Bender, Lawrence, 213
Bible, the, 2, 3, 65
Bible stories, 12, 65
Bier, Suzanne, 44
Black stuff. See Description
Blueprint, 6, 16–17, 87, 127–137
Books fairs, 223
British Independent Film Awards, 227
Brooks, Paul, 212
Buzz, 39
Bier, Suzanne, 44
Byrne, Gabriel, 122

Camera directions, 229
Cannes, 123, 175–178, 222–223
Casting, 52
Character, 51–84
    creation, 52
    cues, 236
    development, 59
    tools, 59–63
    essays, 130
    motivation, 62
    on the brink, 62
    research, 130
    rewriting, 138
    stereotypes, 58
Characterization, 47
Churchill, Winston, 249
Cinema, 1. See Movies
Community, 75
Confidence, lack of 23, 97. See also
    Procrastination
Conflict, 71–72
Contacts. See Power File, the
Copyright, 6, 131, 145–155
    Certificate of registration 146
    non-disclosure agreements 151

ownership, 146
protecting ideas, 145
rights acquisition, 153
screen rights, 171
submission releases, 150–151
ten thousand monkeys, 145, 149
waiver letters, 150
Conman, Roger, 179, 208
Creativity, 218–219
    left brain, right brain 186, 218
Credits. See Screen credits
Curtis, Richard, 156

Deal, the, 201–216
    option deal, 201–202, 212
    outright purchase, 201, 211
    step deal, 205, 213. See also Marketing;
    Self-promotion
Description, 92–98
    formatting of, 231–238
Dialogue, 101–126
    beat. See Rhythm
    diagnostics, 111
    dialect, 106
    directing from the typewriter, 107–108
    endpoint, 103
    fifteen tricks and traps of, 105–110
    format, 229, 238
    key words, 105
    moral dialogue, 104–105
    on the nose, 109
    page three, 110
    parentheticals, 107, 237
    punctuation, 109
    reality, 109
    rewriting, 138
    speech rhythms, 108
    starting and ending, 109
    story dialogue, 102–103
    table reading, 111
    tracks, 102
        mixing, 105
    twists, 103
    underlining, 107–108
Directors Guild of America, 176
Directors Guild of Great Britain, 176
Discipline, 24, 245, 246
DIY filmmaking, 169

Eastwood, Clint, 176
Economy, 8, 94–95
Editing, 98 See also Rewriting
Empathy, 31, 58. See also Audience
Entertainment lawyers, 203
Equity, 176
European Media Development Agency, 158

Field, Syd, 25–27, 139, 245
Film Council, the, 158, 159
Film festivals, 222
    Cannes Film Festival. See also Cannes
    Edinburgh Film Festival, 4
    Aarhus Film Festival, 119
Film industry, the, 6–7, 222–228
Film markets, 177, 178, 222
Film organizations, 142. See also Raindance
Film rates, 209, 210
Films. See Movies
Final draft, 132
Finance, 158
Finder's fees, 215
First draft, 207
Formatting, 229–241
    binding, 231
    capitalization, 236
    covers, 231
    first page, 114, 232
    font, 229
    length, 230
    margin width, 239
    numbering scenes, 230
    paragraph techniques, 235
    title page, 232
Ford, Harrison, 208, 227
Four line rule, the, 90, 95
Fraser, Mad Frankie, 171

Genre, 35, 217
Golding, William, 120
Grammar, 231
Greek myth, 2, 13
Grove, Elliot, 108, 109, 148, 203, 204, 249

Hague, Michael, 25, 139
Hamlet, 13
Hemingway, Ernest, 245
Hero, 19–20, 27–29, 37, 78
    Achiles heel of, 64
    basic action of, 36
    battle, 48
    Big Gloom, 38, 41, 49, 248
    ghost, 20, 35, 53, 60, 241
    goal of, 45, 59, 242
    (inner) problem of, 46, 60
    (inner) need, 59, 242
    introduction of, 27
    moral argument, 21
    motivation of, 46, 60
    nightmare, 35, 54
    plan, 34, 47
    relationships, 63, 65
    (self) revelation, 49, 60
    types of, 29, 30, 76–78
    values of, 54, 63

weaknesses of, 22, 60, 242
Hierarchy, 71, 72, 82
Hodge, John, 4
Hodge, Fred, 227
Hollywood, 9, 10, 159, 217, 223
Hot scripts, 3

Ideas, 128–130, 222
    common currency of, 149. See also
    Copyright, 10,000 Monkeys
    downloading, 245, 246
    polishing, 245, 246
    true life stories, 171
Identification. See Empathy
IFP, 142, 169
Insecurity, 174, 188
Internet, 184
IPTV. See Raindance.tv

Jarmusch, Jim, 44
Jean, Vadim, 212
Jensen, Andrew Thomas, 44
Jordan, Neil, 208

King, Don, 187

Language:
    verbs, 94, 97
    vocabulary, 94
    words, 8, 106. See also Dialogue

Lawyers See Entertainment lawyers
Leonardo Da Vinci, 137, 219
Letter writing, 147, 148, 151–153, 175, 198
    eight-line letter, the 195
    elements of, 196, 197
    process, 199
Litigation, 139, 148,
Logline 180

MacDonald, Andrew, 4
MacLuan, Marshal, 11
Marketability, 213, 214
Marketing, 137–144
    pedigree, 142
    plan, 137
    receptionist theory, 142
    shingling, 158
    stars, 143
Martell, William C, 95, 98
Metaphors, 74, 74, 81. See also Symbol
McKee, Robert, 25, 42, 101
Misfortune, 12, 149
Movies:
    21 Grams, 44
    Airplane, 180
    Alien, 19, 192
    Analyze This, 180
    As Good as it Gets, 28, 34, 102, 105
    Assassination of Jesse James, 34, 41
    Bambi, 13
    Basic Instinct, 20
    Bee Movie, 192
    Being John Malkovich, 58, 76
    Being There, 79